Linguistic Theory
and
Computer Applications

Linguistic Theory
and
Computer Applications

Edited by

P. Whitelock
M. M. Wood
H. L. Somers
R. Johnson
and
P. Bennett

Centre for Computational Linguistics
UMIST, Manchester, UK

1987

ACADEMIC PRESS

Harcourt Brace Jovanovich, Publishers
London   San Diego   New York   Berkeley
Boston   Sydney   Tokyo   Toronto

ACADEMIC PRESS LIMITED
24–28 Oval Road, London NW1 7DX

United States Edition published by
ACADEMIC PRESS INC.
San Diego, CA 92101

British Library Cataloguing in Publication Data
Linguistic theory and computer applications.
1. linguistics – Data processing
I. Whitelock, P.
410′.28′5   P98

ISBN 0-12-747220-7

Printed in Great Britain by
St Edmundsbury Press Limited, Bury St Edmunds, Suffolk

Participants

Doug ARNOLD, Language & Linguistics, University of Essex, UK
Eric ATWELL, Computer Studies, University of Leeds, UK
Paul BENNETT, CCL, UMIST, Manchester, UK
Ted BRISCOE, Linguistics, University of Lancaster, UK
Bran BOGURAEV, Computer Laboratory, University of Cambridge, UK
Bruce CAMERON, GEC Research Ltd., Wembley, Middlesex, UK
David CATTON, Artificial Intelligence Ltd., Watford, Herts, UK
Brian CHANDLER, ICL & CCL, UMIST, Manchester, UK
Anne DE ROECK, Computer Science, University of Essex, UK
Roger EVANS, Cognitive Studies, University of Sussex, UK
Gerald GAZDAR, Cognitive Studies, University of Sussex, UK
Jerry HARPER, Educational Research Centre, St Patricks College, Dublin, Northern Ireland
Graham HOOK, ICL, London, UK
Lieven JASPAERT, Katholieke Universiteit Leuven, Belgium
Rod JOHNSON, CCL, UMIST, Manchester, UK
Val JONES, Computing Science, University of Stirling, Scotland
Ronald M. KAPLAN, Xerox PARC, Palo Alto, California, USA
George KISS, Psychology, University of Warwick, UK
Jackie KNIGHT, Logica UK Ltd., Cambridge, UK
Jan LANDSBERGEN, Philips, Eindhoven, The Netherlands
Hamid LESAN, STL Ltd., Harlow, Essex, UK
Mitchel P. MARCUS, AT & T Bell Laboratories, Murray Hill, New Jersey, UK
John McNAUGHT, CCL, UMIST, Manchester, UK
Bob MOORE, SRI International & Computer Lab., University of Cambridge, UK
Nick OSTLER, Scicon Ltd., London, UK

Steve PULMAN, Computer Laboratory, University of Cambridge, UK
Graeme RITCHIE, Artificial Intelligence, University of Edinburgh, Scotland
Louisa SADLER, Anglo-American Studies, University of East Anglia, UK
Anca SCHIP, ICL, London, UK
Richard SHARMAN, IBM UK Ltd., Winchester, UK
Stuart M. SHIEBER, SRI International, Palo Alto, California, USA
Harold SOMERS, CCL, UMIST, Manchester, UK
Karen SPARCK JONES, Computer Laboratory, University of Cambridge, UK
Henry THOMPSON, Artificial Intelligence, University of Edinburgh, Scotland
Pete WHITELOCK, CCL, UMIST, Manchester, UK
Mary McGee WOOD, CCL, UMIST, Manchester, UK

Preface

On 4–6 September 1985 a workshop on 'Linguistic Theory and Computer Applications' was held at the Centre for Computational Linguistics of the University of Manchester Institute of Science and Technology. Our aim was to bring together a number of the leading international researchers in computational linguistics, to exchange ideas on fundamental issues in the relation of linguistics to computation and their intersection. Both the small number of participants and the generous scheduling were designed to encourage open discussion. The entire workshop was recorded, and full transcripts of the recordings were later circulated to all the original participants. Those transcripts, minimally edited, are here made publicly available.

We are grateful to many people who in different ways made the workshop possible and memorable. The financial support came from the Alvey Directorate, within its Natural Language Theme, led by Karen Sparck Jones, and from the Translation and Publishing division of International Computers Limited (ICL), under Graham Hook. Further hospitality and support came from Prof. J. C. Sager and the Department of Languages and Linguistics at UMIST.

Credit is due to all the participants – primarily, but not exclusively, those directly represented here – for the openness, liveliness, and very high standard of discussion. We would like to mention in particular Henry Thompson, who led a discussion session on 'Implementation' which owing to regrettable technical problems at the time we are unable to include here.

The labour of making the first transcripts from the recordings was heroically and admirably carried out by Liz Diggle. Further copy-editing has been done by all the contributing authors and editors.

Finally, we would like to thank Rosemary Altoft of Academic Press for her interest, assistance, and patience (at times sorely tried) throughout our preparation of the manuscript.

Midsummer's Eve, 1987   PJW, MMW, HLS, RLJ, PAB
                                        Manchester

Contents

Separating Linguistic Analyses from Linguistic Theories

Stuart M. Shieber

1. Introduction

This workshop concerns the relationship of linguistic theory and computer applications. I will therefore address the general point of what the role of linguistic theories and their associated formalisms and analyses should be in the engineering discipline of designing and building natural language processing (NLP) applications [1]. For the remainder of this talk, I will use 'NLP' to refer to such applications, and not to the important, but separate, issues of computational or mathematical approaches to linguistics.

I will assume the possibly controversial viewpoint that NLP efforts can benefit from using insights expressed in linguistic analyses of particular languages. For instance, in writing systems to interpret English sentences that include the comparative construction, a system-builder or grammar-writer might find it valuable to make use of one or another of the previous linguistic analyses of this construction to be found in the literature. Given that this is so, the question arises as to what sort of commitment to

---

1. This research has been made possible by a gift from the System Development Foundation. The author is indebted to John Bear, Fernando Pereira and Ray Perrault for their comments on earlier drafts of this paper.
   An extended version of this paper will appear in the **Proceedings of the Workshop on Word Order and Parsing in Unification Grammars** to be published by D. Reidel Publishing Company, Dordrecht, Holland.

linguistic theories and formalisms this forces us to, that is, how dependent particular analyses are on the particular formulations found in the linguistic literature.

To distinguish more clearly the problem that concerns me, let me draw an analogy with computer programming. Consider the following rewording of the previous paragraph:

> I will assume the probably uncontroversial viewpoint that computer programming can benefit from using algorithms from computer science. For instance, in writing a system to sort records in a database, a system-builder or programmer might find it valuable to make use of one or another of the previous sorting algorithms to be found in the literature. Given that this is so, the question arises as to what sort of commitment to particular programming languages this forces us to, that is, how dependent particular algorithms are on the particular formulations of them found in the computer science literature.

This latter question is easy to answer. Algorithms from computer science are not at all tied to the particular formulations in which they are described. Despite the fact that quicksort was first described in Algol, it can still be used by programmers writing in Pascal. Indeed, many algorithms were originally described only informally, e.g. Earley's (1970) algorithm. Nonetheless, any effective procedure has an implementation in some programming language, that is, if we believe Church. And since programming languages are all interreducible, it follows that they have implementations in all programming languages. Thus, in the case of programming, the use of algorithms from computer science does not in theory tie us to any particular language for expressing algorithms.

Similarly, the question as to whether a particular linguistic analysis requires allegiance to a given language for expressing analyses, i.e. grammar formalism, can be at least partially elucidated by exhibiting reductions from one linguistic formalism to another. As a side effect, such reductions help to pin down exactly which differences among linguistic theories that use the formalisms are purely (though not merely) **notational**, and, on the other hand, which ones are **notional** [2].

   The analogy can be taken one step further. Not all
programming languages are equally useful for all
applications. For instance, Pascal is better suited for
writing a quicksort than, say, FORTRAN, simply because
Pascal allows recursion whereas FORTRAN does not. The
intuitive perception that Pascal is in this sense more
notationally expressive is reinforced by the fact that
reducing a FORTRAN program to a Pascal program is generally
simpler than reduction in the opposite direction,
specifically because of the recursion device. Thus, the
details of the reductions can show quite graphically just
how close the various formalisms are to one another. The
simpler the reductions, the closer the formalisms. In other
words, reductions among formalisms can not only tell what
can be done in the various formalisms, but how easy they are
to do.

   This brings us back to the original point. Are
linguistic analyses separable from their formulations within
particular linguistic theories and formalisms? Here the
answer is much less straightforward. It rests first of all
on **what** the distinctions are between the concepts of
analysis, formalism and theory, concepts whose meanings are
not always agreed upon, let alone made precise in the
linguistics literature. Second, it requires serious
research to be done on exactly **how** formalisms and theories
can be interreduced. Finally, even if such a separation
could be shown, by exhibiting certain complete or partial
reductions among linguistic formalisms, it remains to be
shown **why** this would aid NLP efforts.

   This talk will be divided, therefore, into three parts
corresponding roughly to the three questions: what, why, and
how? First, I will briefly discuss the notions of theory,
formalism, and analysis as they are used in linguistics and
other fields in an effort to clarify the terminology.
Second, I will provide some methodological motivation for
the attempt to separate analyses from their formal and
theoretical underpinnings. Third, I will describe some work

---

2. The use of the terms 'notional' and 'notational' for
this purpose is due to Martin Kay.

in progress in the area of characterizing the relations among certain formalisms within theories of syntax. I will concentrate on syntax because it is the subfield of linguistics most familiar to me. In particular, I will stress the LFG (Bresnan, ed 1982), GPSG (Gazdar et al 1985) and GB (Chomsky 1982) theories because these three theories seem to be the major 'contenders' for use by people interested in utilizing syntactic theories for NLP computer applications.

2. What: Some Terminology

Before discussing the separation of linguistic analyses from formalisms and theories I need to make clear what I (and linguists themselves) mean by these terms 'formalism', 'theory', and 'analysis' - especially because they are not always well-differentiated in the linguistics literature and because they are used in linguistics in relatively nonstandard ways vis-a-vis other disciplines.

In many scientific fields, the scientist is interested in building a 'theory' of some observable phenomena (say, the laws governing the motion of objects). He may use a special notation or 'formalism' - the calculus, for instance - to write down one of several possible theories of motion. These theories in turn yield 'analyses' of certain specific observable phenomena, for instance, the motion of a ball

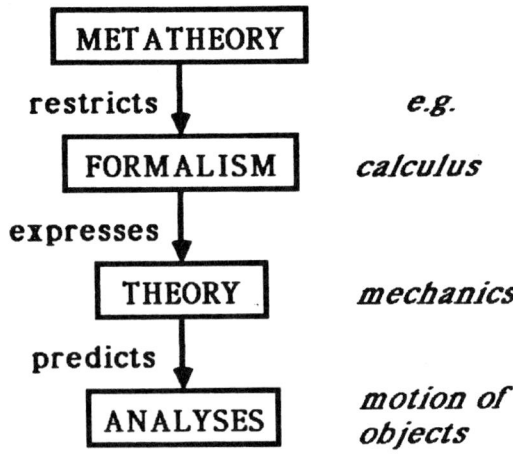

Figure 1

thrown into the air or of people jumping in elevators can be analyzed by a theory of kinematics. The notations for describing theories are typically designed to be as general as possible, thereby allowing a broad spectrum of theories to be stated and facilitating comparison among them. The picture is roughly like Figure 1.

The mode of operation is slightly different in linguistics. As before, attempts to characterize observable data are generally thought of as 'analyses' (e.g. the analysis of a particular English sentence). But a description of an entire language (what would be referred to in nonlinguistic terminology as a theory of the language) falls usually under the label 'analysis' as well (e.g. an analysis of English syntax). These analyses predict the observable phenomena, e.g. the LFG analysis of English predicts the grammaticality and ambiguity properties of English sentences. The term 'theory' is primarily reserved for a characterization of general properties of or relationships among analyses - what would in other fields be considered a 'metatheory'. For instance, the study of possible geometries is not a theory of space, but a theory of theories of space of which Euclidean geometry and Riemannian geometry are but two. There are metatheories in other fields as well, but in linguistics, unlike other fields, the metatheory is the real object of study. To summarize, the analogous picture looks like Figure 2.

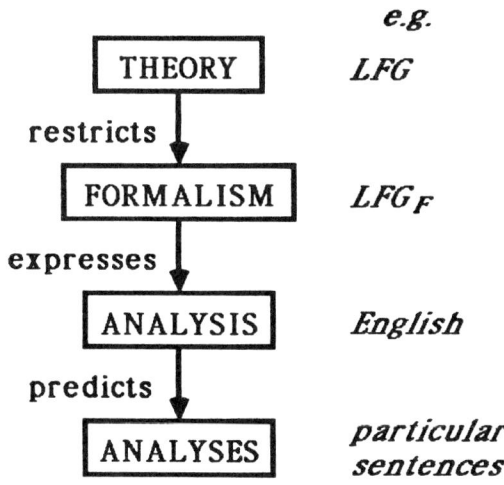

Figure 2

The differences are, of course, only in the words used; the ideas are the same. But terminological differences like these can be confusing. For example, in other fields, theories are **expressed in** formalisms and theories are expressed **alongside** formalisms. Since in each case the primary object of study is referred to as a theory, this distinction is important. The relationship between formalisms and the object of study in the two cases is quite different. In one case it is a tool, in the other a theoretical device.

In the rest of this paper we will follow linguistic practice in using the words 'theory', 'formalism', and 'analysis' rather than 'metatheory', 'formalism', and 'theory'. It is, however, important to keep in mind that these terms refer to different things, especially as regards 'formalism' and 'theory'. To make this distinction explicit, we will henceforth use the acronym of the theory (say, 'LFG') to stand for the theory itself, and the acronym subscripted with an F (as 'LFG$_\text{F}$') for the formalism associated with the theory. Note also that the notion of analysis is used ambiguously in linguistics jargon. In general, I will use the term 'analysis' as vague (not ambiguous) between the two interpretations.

3. Why: Methodological Motivation

We now digress to discuss why we should want to separate linguistic analyses from linguistic theories in the first place. Of course, there is the obvious intellectual advantage of thereby gaining a firmer understanding as to which differences among theories are nonformal as opposed to emergent from the respective formalisms (i.e. which theoretical concepts from one formalism are difficult or impossible to state in another), but I am concerned here with the application of linguistic theory to NLP. In such an application, why not just incorporate an entire theory of linguistics, with its associated formalisms and analyses, into an NLP system?

The reason is that the fields of linguistic theory and NLP have inconsistent goals that are reflected in practice. In deciding whether to incorporate a linguistic theory wholesale into an NLP system, we need to have an understanding of what the respective goals of linguistic

theory and NLP are;   then, insofar as the goals of
linguistic theory are consistent with and aid those of NLP,
devices from the former can beneficially be incorporated
into an NLP system.   Where the goals are contradictory, the
associated techniques should be avoided.   In this
digression, I want to identify these goals and show how they
differ.

3.1 Goals of Linguistic Theories and Formalisms

3.1.1 Goals of Linguistic Theory

Traditionally, linguistic theory has, for reasons
usually motivated by the problem of language acquisition,
been interested specifically in universal properties of
language.   Chomsky summarizes the goals thus:

> Let us recall the basic character of the problem we
> face.   The theory of UG must meet two obvious
> conditions.   On the one hand, it must be compatible
> with the diversity of existing (indeed, possible)
> grammars.   At the same time, UG must be sufficiently
> constrained and restrictive in the options it permits
> to account for the fact that each of these grammars
> develops in the mind on the basis of quite limited
> evidence. (Chomsky 1982:3)

That is, a theory of linguistics should **characterize
all and only the possible natural languages.**   I have chosen
a quite recent quotation to this effect, but, of course, the
idea has pervaded the practice of linguistics since the
appearance of **Syntactic Structures** (Chomsky 1957).

Secondarily, of course, other requirements are usually
imposed on the task, three examples of which we discuss
here.   First, it is desired that the characterization be
generative in the sense of being explicit or rigorous.
Chomsky defines the term thus:

> By a generative grammar I mean simply a system of
> rules that in some explicit and well-defined way
> assigns structural descriptions to sentences.
> (Chomsky 1965:8)

Second, Occam's razor tends to cut in favor of theories

that admit relatively simple, elegant analyses. Although such a comparison is perforce based on aesthetic or subjective standards, it is hard to imagine any other criteria that could serve for comparison of theories with the same expressive power [3]. Certainly, simplicity as a criterion for choosing theories is a common standard in other fields of research.

In fact, we see this criterion of 'linguistic felicity' used at least implicitly in linguistics. Gazdar notes the importance of simplicity in choosing between base-generated and transformational approaches:

> If to do things exclusively by direct phrase structure generation was to lead inevitably to aesthetic disaster (re simplicity, economy, generality, empirical motivation, etc.) whilst competing transformational analyses were paragons of elegance and enlightenment, then one might reasonably feel inclined to reject the former in favour of the latter. (Gazdar 1982:134).

Finally, current practice seems to place a value on the characterization's being declarative (or order-independent, or order-free). Kaplan and Bresnan write:

> The constraint of **order-free composition** is motivated by the fact that complete representations of local grammatical relations are effortlessly, fluently, and reliably constructed for arbitrary segments of sentences. (Bresnan & Kaplan 1982:xlv)

Regardless of the soundness of this reasoning, the goal of declarativeness is shared by at least LFG, GPSG, and GB. These theories all define sentential grammaticality in terms of simultaneous well-formedness constraints rather than procedures for recognition.

To summarize, then, the goals of linguistics are, first and foremost, **completeness** (characterizing all possible natural languages), and **restrictiveness** (characterizing only

---

3. By expressive power, I mean to include not only formal expressive limitations but theoretical, nonformal limitations as well, whatever they might be.

the possible natural languages), and, secondarily, such goals as **rigour, simplicity, elegance,** and **declarativeness.**

3.1.2   Goals of Linguistic Formalisms

These are the goals of linguistic theory, but what of the goals of the associated formalisms? This question is especially important in light of the fact that NLP systems are inherently formal. Those aspects of theory that are not formally explicable cannot be used directly in such systems. The formal aspects of linguistic theories become paramount for NLP applications.

Furthermore, the answer to this question is complicated by the fact that the relationship between theory and formalism differs from theory to theory. One common notion is that the theory and the formalism are one and the same, that is, that the formalism itself should embody all the constraints on universal grammar. This view is explicitly propounded by the originators of GPSG:

> A grammatical framework can and should be constructed as a formal language for specifying grammars of a particular kind. The syntax, and, more importantly, the semantics of that formal language constitute the substance of the theory or theories embodied in the framework. (Gazdar et al 1985:2)

The same view is also at least intimated by Bresnan and Kaplan:

> The lexical theory of grammar provides a formally explicit and coherent theory of how surface structures are related to representations of meaningful grammatical relations. (Bresnan 1982a:4)

On the other hand, a view of grammar could be propounded in which the formalism is but one part of the theory. Constraints supplied by formal limitations would indeed constitute universal claims, but so would other constraints, that, while not formal in character, are nonetheless essential to the theory. This, I take it, is Bresnan's view, as expressed in the following excerpt:

Having no formal theory at all will lead to vague and inconsistent formulations at both the theoretical and descriptive levels. Despite its importance, however, a formal theory of grammar is only one step in the construction of a substantive linguistic theory of universal grammar. The present work adds to the theory of LFG a set of substantive postulates for a universal theory of control and complementation. (Bresnan 1982b:282)

Thus, Bresnan distinguishes formal and substantive constraints in a theory [4], whereas Kaplan (personal communication) and Gazdar et al would require all constraints to be formally embodied. But, in either case, at least part of the burden of restrictiveness is placed on the formalism itself, that is, more restrictive formalisms are favored over less restrictive ones. If this were not so, then arguments against LFG, say, on the basis of the overexpressiveness of LFG (cf. Berwick & Weinberg 1984) would have no force. Thus the same criteria of restrictiveness, completeness, simplicity, rigour, and declarativeness that linguists apply to their theories apply to the formalisms as well. In fact, the latter two seem to require some sort of formal system to be applicable at all.

3.2   The Goals of NLP Systems and Formalisms

What, then, of the goals of natural language processing efforts in computer applications? Simply put, such efforts aim to **computationally characterize one or a small number of languages**. As mentioned earlier, the grammar formalism, in this case at least, is of paramount importance, since unformalized theory finds little place in computer application. For this reason, we will be concentrating on the desired characteristics of formalisms used in NLP systems.

---

4.   Chomsky also distinguishes notions of 'formal' and 'substantive' though they are slightly different in scope from Bresnan's usage. Though I find the choice of the term 'substantive' unfortunate - formal constraints seem to me to be as substantive as any - I will continue to use Bresnan's terminology.

Obviously, formalisms intended for NLP should be designed to facilitate such a computational characterization. They must therefore be at least expressive enough to characterize the subset of natural languages of interest to the application; we might call this criterion 'weak completeness'. On the other hand, they are constrained by limitations of computational effectiveness, not only in the technical sense used in the term 'effective procedure' but in the informal sense of 'usable under current technology.'

On a secondary level, of course, other characteristics are important. For instance, to aid in articulating the grammars of natural language and changing them as new consequences of a grammatical analysis are discovered, they should be as flexible and expressive as possible. To make implementation and verification of correctness easier, they should be kept simple, with a firm mathematical foundation. In short, they should obey all the rubrics of a good programming language as commonly constructed in current computer science. Programming-language designers are increasingly putting forward concepts of rigorous mathematical foundation, declarativeness, simplicity, expressivity [5] and flexibility. These criteria seem to be so well accepted in computer language design that it seems almost ludicrous to cite references attesting to their importance, let alone call attention to them at all. Nonetheless, I will do both, mentioning, for example,the work on explicit programming-language semantics by Scott (1982) and many others, the Turing Award lectures by Dijkstra (1972), Backus (1977), and so forth. In fact, these same criteria apply equally well, and for identical reasons, to computer languages for encoding linguistic information, namely, to grammar formalisms.

To summarize, then, the characteristics of grammar formalisms promoted by the goals of NLP are, first of all,

---

5. Clearly, since virtually all programming languages are equivalent in formal expressive power, what we (and others) have in mind here is the notational expressivity, that is the sense of expressivity according to which Pascal is a more expressive language than that typically assumed in Turing machines.

weak completeness and **computational effectiveness.**
Secondarily, they are the goals of computer language design
in general: **expressivity, simplicity, declarativeness,
rigour,** etc.

3.3 Comparing the Goals

As is apparent from the foregoing discussion, there is
a great deal of overlap between the goals of linguistic
theory and NLP. For instance, both require formalisms that
are rigorous and preferably declarative, and that allow
simple and elegant formulation of grammars. The main
differences occur in their primary goals. Linguistic theory
design is characterized by a dialectic counterposing
completeness and restrictiveness. For NLP, restrictiveness
is not only not a primary goal, it is a characteristic to be
avoided wherever possible. In NLP, the dialectic is between
generality, on the one hand, and the constraints of
computational effectiveness and practical felicity, on the
other.

Thus, insofar as possible, those aspects of linguistic
formalisms that support rigour, declarativeness, and
linguistic felicity should be incorporated into NLP.
However, those aspects of the formalisms that are geared
towards restrictiveness should be eschewed, unless, of
course, they provide auxiliary benefit by improving
computational efficiency or simplifying analyses. Finally,
aspects of the formalisms designed to aid the goal of
completeness may or may not be pertinent to NLP, depending
on the weakness of the particular application's completeness
requirement.

Some examples of this sort of reasoning are in order.
Certain particular formal constraints in the linguistic
theories may be detrimental in a formalism for NLP if their
inclusion decreases the expressivity of the formalism
without serving to simplify analyses. For instance, the
functional locality principle of LFG falls into this class.
By requiring that "designators in lexical and grammatical
schemata may specify no more than two function-applications"
(Kaplan & Bresnan 1982:278), the generality of the formalism
is reduced in such a way that grammars become more, not
less, complex. I am not arguing against this formal
restriction as a grammatical universal, but only as a device

in NLP systems.

On the other hand, the head feature convention (HFC) of GPSG might be usefully added to an NLP formalism on the grounds that it makes the job of grammar-writing simpler. It is no coincidence that typical implementations of LFG do not include functional locality, whereas those of GPSG do include the HFC. Ideally, however, we would want an even more general formalism - one in which the head feature convention or similar devices could be stated as a formal construct.

4. How: Separating Analyses From Formalisms

Thus, we see that the goals of NLP and LT, though sharing many factors, are different in certain key places, especially as regards the notion of restrictiveness. Since the constraints and restrictions in LT play such an important role, this brings us back to the question of how separable the analyses in the theories are from their theoretical and formal commitments. Is there a way of expressing such analyses in a formal language that is more consonant with the goals of NLP, less restrictive, simpler, more flexible, etc.? Again, reviewing the previous argument, the displaying of notational reductions from one formalism to another gives us a tool for deciding such questions.

In this section we will discuss some research being carried out by a group at CSLI, in which I have been participating, to find such reductions and their properties. The project is an attempt to extract and compare the main ideas in the various formalisms, theories, and analyses. Because time is limited, I will be able only to sketch the ideas here, but this should be sufficient to give the general picture.

To facilitate this enterprise, we chose to make use of certain formalisms that are not part of any linguistic theory - namely the Functional Unification Grammar (FUG) formalism of Martin Kay (1983), and the PATR-II formalism from SRI International (Shieber 1984). These formalisms were designed from the outset to be tools satisfying the goals of NLP rather than of linguistic theory. They are quite simple and expressive, and thus serve ideally as both targets and sources of reductions. I will assume a certain familiarity with all of the formalisms mentioned so far.

4.1   Summary of Reductions

Figure 3 summarizes the reductions that are at least currently proposed:

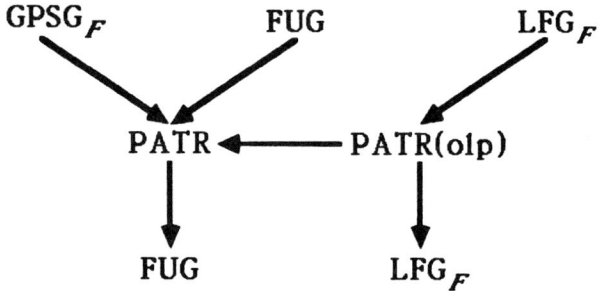

olp - off-line parsable

Figure 3

Rather than discussing all of the reductions, I will limit myself to a few examples in more depth.

4.2   PATR-II and FUG

I start with reductions between PATR-II and FUG, and vice versa, because these are the simplest of the reductions, yet they provide a good example of the role reductions can play in clarifying the difference among formalisms and theories.

PATR-II grammars use rules that simultaneously constrain string concatenation and directed-graph unifications. They can be viewed as FUG grammars with the following properties:

- They are in disjunctive normal form.

- No embedded 'cset' features are allowed.

- No embedded 'pattern' features are allowed.

- All values of the 'pattern' features are of the following simple form: a sequence of its cset elements.

This observation can be used as the basis of a simple notational reduction from PATR-II to FUG. The reduction thus engendered is **expressiveness-losing** in the sense that it does not make full use of the FUG notation. It is this loss of expressivity that is taken advantage of in the ability to implement (relatively) efficient parsers for PATR-II. It is also **linear** in the sense that the FUG grammar is related linearly in size to the PATR-II grammar. Finally, the reduction is itself declarative in the sense that it can be stated independently of a procedure for building an FUG rule for a PATR-II rule.

In the reverse direction, any FUG can be converted to a PATR-II grammar by converting it to disjunctive normal form and somehow dealing with the special ANY values that FUG allows as existential constraints. The question of ANY values, along with constraint equations in general, will be dealt with later. Suffice it to say that PATR-II is expressive enough to model them indirectly through a reduction that is not particularly perspicuous or attractive. This is thus a clue that ANY values truly constitute a notional difference between the formalisms. The conversion to disjunctive normal form, it should be noted, is not a linear transformation; in fact, it is exponential. Thus, the difficulty in reducing FUG to PATR-II relative to the converse reduction lends support to the intuitive conclusion that PATR-II is a notational subset of FUG. Note that this conclusion holds even in the face of the formal equivalence of the two formalisms (since they are both Turing equivalent).

4.3   GPSG$_F$ and PATR-II [6]

The most complex of the formalisms - in terms of its notational complexity and the complexity of grammar

---

6. A more thorough discussion of this reduction is presented by Shieber (1986).

interpretation - is $GPSG_F$ [7]. Nonetheless, it can be viewed substantially as a constrained version of PATR-II with a complex notation using metarules, feature principles, and so forth. The claim is substantiated by the fact that GPSG grammars can be reduced to PATR-II through a process of compilation. We give a sketch of this nondeterministic process here. Note that the compilation process uses an operation add_c, which adds a unification into a PATR-II rule 'conservatively'. That is, if adding the unification would cause the rule to fail, the unification is not added. Instead a set of unifications are added (conservatively), one for each child feature. Thus given that features **a**, **b** and **c** are head features, and if a rule already specifies (1) then the operation (2) would in fact add the two unifications (3a) and (3b), since the addition of the given unification itself would cause rule failure. Thus the earlier constraint of values for the **a** feature is given precedence over the constraint to be added.

(1) $\langle C_0$ head a$\rangle \neq \langle C_1$ head a$\rangle$

(2) $add_c(\langle C_0$ head a$\rangle = \langle C_1$ head a$\rangle)$

(3a) $\langle C_0$ head b$\rangle = \langle C_1$ head b$\rangle$
(3b) $\langle C_0$ head c$\rangle = \langle C_1$ head c$\rangle$

For each ID rule of GPSG (basic or derived by metarule) $C_0 \dashrightarrow C_1, \ldots, C_n$:

CAP If C_i controls C_j (determined by $Type(C_i)$ and $Type(C_j)$), then

$$add_c(\langle C_i \text{ con}\rangle = \langle C_j \text{ con}\rangle)$$

where

$$con = \begin{cases} \text{slash if slash} \in dom(C_i) \\ \textbf{agr otherwise} \end{cases}$$

---

7.   We refer here to the version of GPSG found in the recently published book by Gazdar et al (1985).

FFP If the rule does not mention foot feature **f** then

$$add_c(\langle C_i\ f\rangle = \langle C_j\ f\rangle)$$

for one or more i such that $0 < i \leq n$.

DEF For all features **f** with a default value, say, **d**, and for all i such that $0 < i \leq n$, if

$$f \notin dom(C_i)$$

then

$$add_c(\langle C_i\ f\rangle = d)$$

HFC For C_i the head of C_0 and for each head feature f,

$$add_c(\langle C_i\ f\rangle = \langle C_0\ f\rangle)$$

The sequence of operations is critical. Because the **add$_c$** operation is nonmonotonic, the order in which the additions occur determines which unifications have precedence, earlier additions having precedence over later ones.

This precedence ordering was based on evidence from the GPSG book. For instance, the CAP is given precedence over the FFP by virtue of following excerpt:

> We must modify the definition of control in such a way that it ignores perturbations of semantic type occasioned by the presence of instantiated FOOT features. (Gazdar et al 1985:87)

Such a modification is achieved in the case of our compilation by having the CAP apply before foot features are instantiated by the FFP. Similarly, in another passage from the same work, the FFP and CAP are both seen to take precedence over the HFC:

> Intuitively, the **free** feature specifications on a category [the ones the HFC is to apply to] is the set of feature specifications which can legitimately appear

on extensions of that category: feature specifications which conflict with what is already part of the category, either directly, or in virtues of the FCRs, FFP, or CAP, are not **free** on that category. (Gazdar et al 1985:95)

Highly suggestive is the fact that current efforts by at least certain GPSG practitioners are placing the GPSG type of analysis directly in a PATR-like formalism. This formalism, Pollard's (1984) head-driven phrase structure grammar (HPSG) variant of GPSG, which uses a run-time algorithm of this sort, also happens to order the principles in just this way.

Admittedly, we are playing a little fast and loose in our claims. Because of limited time, we have not discussed the status of lexical versus phrasal defaults, feature cooccurrence restrictions, or ID/LP format. The general idea, however, should be clear: GPSG grammars can be substantially converted to equivalent PATR-II grammars through a simple (albeit procedural) mapping. In fact, we would claim that defining the semantics of a GPSG grammar in this way yields a much simpler formulation, the need for which is evident to anyone who has studied Gazdar et al (1985).

But even if certain parts of the $GPSG_F$ formalism are found not to be reducible (or easily reducible) to PATR-II, this in itself would be an interesting fact. It would show that exactly that portion of the formalism was truly essential for stating certain analyses (either stating them **at all** or stating them **simply**, respectively), i.e., that analyses using this formal device do so necessarily. In fact, feature cooccurrence restrictions (FCRs) in $GPSG_F$ grammars seem to constitute such a device. Interpretations of FCRs must be done at 'run-time', so to speak, or else the formalism must incorporate a notion of negation in one guise or another. Thus, an analysis of this sort can be seen as motivating negation in grammar formalisms for NLP.

4.4 LFG_F and PATR-II

The LFG_F formalism is a unification-based formalism quite similar to PATR-II in its overall design, though with certain extra devices and at least two additional well-defined formal constraints. It is not surprising, therefore, that most of the PATR-II formalism can be directly reduced to LFG. The only problems arise in overcoming the constraints of 'off-line parsability' (Pereira & Warren 1983) and 'functional locality'. The former is provably impossible, in that the constraint diminishes the generative capacity of LFG to a level below that of PATR-II. The use of extra features, however, makes functional locality relatively straightforward. Thus, off-line-parsable PATR-II grammars can be simply translated into LFG.

The reverse reduction, i.e. reducing LFG grammars to PATR-II, is more difficult because extended devices such as semantic forms, constraint equations, and functional completeness need to be modelled. We will discuss these three devices briefly. Semantic forms are easily modelled with the standard PATR-II logical form encoding. Constraint equations have been shown by Kelly Roach to be reducible to ANY values. Perhaps more surprisingly, Mark Johnson has demonstrated that both ANY values and constraint equations in general can be modelled in a purely monotonic system such as PATR-II. Functional completeness can be modelled with ANY and, therefore, in PATR-II as well.

Similar arguments show that virtually all, if not all, aspects of LFG are directly embeddable within the PATR-II formalism. But the fact that the encoding of constraint equations and ANY is difficult, though both are easily interreducible, points to another important notion in grammar formalisms that is missing in PATR-II - the notion of nonmonotonic modes of combining information. Once again, the technique of reducing grammar formalisms has resulted in an observation about what is notionally important in the formalisms.

5. Summary and Consequences

These arguments are not proofs of the equivalence of formalisms. Rather, they are informal demonstrations that the formalisms commonly employed in linguistics today are relatively similar. To the extent that this is so, analyses from one formalism can be stated within another. For instance, the type of analysis of subcategorization applied

in many PATR-II grammars and used exclusively by HPSG,
involving lexical encoding of complements in terms of lists
of complements rather than sets of grammatical functions,
could be embedded with the LFG$_F$ formalism or FUG.
Similarly, LFG-style analyses based on the lexical encoding
of subcategorization with grammatical functions are easily
embeddable in FUG or PATR-II augmented with ANY values (but
less easily without ANY).

Once this view of the mutual independence of analysis
and formalism takes hold, we can start looking for the key
ideas which are shared across analyses, across formalisms,
and across theories. It is these ideas, not the particular
formal devices, that are critical to embed in an NLP system
intended to make use of the analyses.

Looking then at LFG, GPSG and even GB, we see at least
the following underlying commonalities:

- Expressions are constructed directly from subexpressions.
  The notions of 'constituent' and 'constituent structure'
  are important.

- Expressions are of different types, and the grouping of
  expressions is sensitive to these types. This gives rise
  to the notion of 'category' or functional structure or
  feature structure.

- Types can be more or less specific. This leads to the
  notion of 'sub-type' or partial information, and is often
  captured in the guise of feature/value structures or
  functions that can be more or less partial with respect to
  one another.

- Partial information (types) can be combined by certain
  algebraic operations. Primary among these operations is
  unification, but other operations can be envisioned and,
  indeed, have been proposed (e.g. disjunction, negation,
  priority union, default operations).

- More particularly, the combinatorics of expression
  grouping is encoded lexically through explicit
  representation of the complements of a lexical item.

Analyses from LFG, GPSG and GB all share these basic
properties. This commonality shows a remarkable convergence

of syntactic theories echoed in the similarity of their associated formalisms. Certainly, NLP systems should take advantage of this convergence, especially since they are thereby enabled to use analyses from any and all of the theories.

6. Conclusion: Preventing Misconceptions

In an attempt to forestall certain questions that will inevitably arise concerning the points made in this talk, I would like to mention certain misconceptions to be avoided.

First of all, linguists might complain that I am ascribing too much significance to the notion of formalism in linguistic theory. On the contrary, by precisely delimiting the role formalisms play in furthering the goals of linguistic theory, as, for instance, by the technique of notational reductions, I feel this work has demonstrated that differences among the various formalisms are considerably less than is commonly thought. In this sense, the research seems to put formalisms in their proper place, as particular notations for very general ideas that transcend the formalisms themselves.

Second, I would like to make it clear that I am not recommending PATR-II (or FUG for that matter) as a formalism in which to write LFG grammars or GPSG grammars. PATR-II is an egregious notation for LFG. That is why LFG exists in the first place. In fact, the pure PATR-II formalism was never intended to serve as a formalism in which a grammar-writer actually composes any kind of grammar at all. I quote an authority on this topic:

> Clearly, the bare PATR-II formalism ... is sorely inadequate for any major attempt at building natural-language grammars ... However, given a simple underlying formalism, we can build more efficient, specialized languages on top of it, much as MacLisp might be built on top of pure Lisp. And just as MacLisp need not be implemented (and is not implemented) directly in pure Lisp, specialized formalisms built conceptually on top of pure PATR-II need not be so implemented. (Shieber 1984:364)

Thus PATR-II is playing the same role here as kernel

languages in computer science. Cardelli and Wegner have
summarized the idea nicely:

> Although we have used a unified language throughout
> the paper, we have not presented a language design. In
> language design there are many important issues to be
> solved concerning readability, ease of use, etc. which
> we have not directly attacked. We propose [the unified
> language] as a framework to classify and compare
> existing languages. We do not propose it as a
> programming language, as it may be clumsy in many
> areas, but it could be the basis of one. (Cardelli &
> Wegner 1985:41)

The claim here is that very general languages like
PATR-II or FUG can serve as the bases of particular computer
languages for encoding linguistic information and which can
employ analyses from different syntactic theories.
Furthermore, the differing goals of linguistic theory and
natural language processing make such an enterprise
eminently desirable. Finally, research in this area can
help to elucidate theoretical questions from linguistics
concerning the true nature of constraints in theories, to
determine whether they inhere in the formalism or require
substantive restrictions.

That concludes the formal part of my presentation. I
will now take questions, Ron.

Ron KAPLAN [having arrived 45 minutes late]: Well, I do have
one question: What did you say for the first 45 minutes? But
I have a comment, based on my extrapolation backwards from
the last 15 minutes. You're talking about notational
reduction, I assume, and arguing that in a certain sense
these various theories are notational equivalents -

SHIEBER: No. That was in the first 45 minutes, you see, you
missed it. The formalisms have certain notational properties
relative to each other. They may or may not be notational
variants. I don't want to say that, for instance, LFG and
PATR-II are notational variants; I don't think they are,
because of certain particular devices in them. But the
theories on this kind of grounds are completely
incomparable. I'm not making any claim about the theories,
I'm talking about the formalisms within the theories.

KAPLAN: I want to make a point about the mathematical concepts, the notions that underlie the formalisms, and suggest that, even if the formalisms come out the same, the operations like unification come out to be the proper implementations of these formal notions, that different mathematical conceptions might suggest different directions of extension that might differ from one theory to the other. For example, within LFG we have the notion of structural correspondence, and trying to make very clear and crisp mathematical distinctions between the description language and the formal objects that are being described. When you do that, you see that you can vary the description language along certain dimensions, or you can vary the mathematical structure of the objects being described along certain dimensions, and come out with different effects.

So, given that none of these theories is adequate and complete in its present form, there can be interesting differences among them, based on the mathematical notions that they bring to the front. I think that's important. That might not be relevant to the point you're making in your talk, but that's what the last 15 minutes suggested.

SHIEBER: No - that's why, to take an extreme case, even things that **are** notational variants, which I don't want to claim all these things are, I wouldn't want to call **mere** notational variants. Because even notational variants, as you say, bring different ideas to the front, and cry out for different kinds of extensions. This is an argument, as far as I can tell, to allow all kinds of different ways of expressing these things, playing around with different foundational ideas, so that lots of ideas are generated about the ways of extending things. It's especially useful for natural language processing, because one thing that I claim in the early part of this paper is that expressivity and generality is something to be striven for, in the case of natural language processing, whereas it is not necessarily a goal of linguistic theory. So I agree with the general point.

Karen SPARCK JONES: I feel extremely nervous about asking on this, because perhaps the point is so obvious - I wasn't quite clear why you were saying that linguistic theory is characterized by a dialectic striving to be restrictive, whereas in NLP restrictiveness is not only not a primary goal but is a characteristic to be avoided wherever possible. I wonder if you could make that absolutely clear. As you say NLP is only going for weak constraints, I wasn't quite clear why restrictiveness was a thing you positively backed away from.

SHIEBER: First of all, the reason it's not necessarily a goal is because typically the argument for restrictiveness is based on some criterion like language acquisition, or something like that. And unless you're interested in building some program that acquires language, in which case you really would want a restrictive theory, presumably, that argument doesn't necessarily go over to the problem of building formalisms for natural language processing applications. But then there's the question of why is it actually a goal to be non-restrictive, and the argument there is, if it doesn't hurt you to allow very general expressive formalisms, why not allow them, since in general you're not necessarily looking for a right theory of language, what you're looking for is the ability to express linguistic information about a particular language, and there the more rope you give yourself - to hang yourself with ...

SPARCK JONES: But you might say that then completeness and restriction are being used in slightly different senses from what they are in the theory.

KAPLAN: Isn't there something going on here which has to do with the historical state of the science? Suppose that we have a restrictive linguistic theory that was actually the true linguistic theory.

SPARCK JONES: In terms of what Stu [Shieber] said, restrictive means characterizing only -

KAPLAN: Only and correctly, not just some linguist's hypothesis based on three facts in five languages. That's half a fact per language!

SHIEBER: At that point, I might be willing to say, yes, at that point, just take that linguistic theory and import it wholesale - once that happens. Now - the burden is now on you to ...

KAPLAN: We have to give ourselves the benefit of the doubt here.

SHIEBER: No, that's the point - you give yourself the benefit of the doubt in the sense of leaving your options open until you've got the God-given truth.

KAPLAN: That's right, you don't want to do premature restriction in the absence of truth. But if you know what the truth is, then you can ask the question whether or not you should try to confine your formalism to be just according to that kind of restrictions.

SHIEBER: Maybe there's the unwritten assumption here that, as far as I can tell, linguistics hasn't come across the truth yet.

KAPLAN: This I'm sure is true. It took a long time to get perfect vacuums, we've just got to keep working on it.

SHIEBER: Absolutely. I want to make the point that I think restrictiveness is a perfectly reasonable goal for linguistic theory, I'm not arguing against it. I'm merely arguing against it for formalisms directed toward the task of engineering natural language processing applications.

KAPLAN: But suppose that we knew what this theory is, and we had a formalism, a formal natural language processing theory, that was bigger than that restrictive theory, that enclosed it. Now the question is, is there any advantage in building natural language processing systems that take advantage of the fact that we now know that there's some restriction that could be further imposed without giving up any accuracy. And there could be. There may or may not be. But it's an open issue. It could be that you could make it more efficient, for example. by knowing that certain things never happen. You said all this?

SHIEBER: I think I made the point that if these restrictions do gain you some auxiliary benefit that works in favour of the goals of natural language processing, for example allows something to be computationally characterized that couldn't be before, or that you want for some efficiency reason, then you might want to bring that kind of idea across.

SPARCK JONES: It seems to me that the distinction you're making is between saying, don't go for restrictiveness in a premature and unmotivated way, but that's slightly different from saying, be positively anti-restrictive.

SHIEBER: It's a ceteris paribus thing, certain restrictions might buy you something and certain ones don't. The reason you take some restriction into the application, I'm saying, isn't because it's a restriction, it's because it does something else for you, there's some other goal that it's in service of.

KAPLAN: Other things being equal, presumably you would choose the more restrictive theory just because -

SHIEBER: No, no, that's what I'm saying. Other things being equal, you choose the less restrictive theory, until such time as you know that the more restrictive theory is God's own truth.

KAPLAN: What I'm saying is always conditioned on the assumption that it **is** God's truth.

Mitch MARCUS: That's always the wrong assumption. It's a common one in linguistics, but it's the wrong one.

SHIEBER: Let's have that discussion, the one that's based on the assumption of the truth of - and now name your favourite linguistic theory - in 50 years or 100 years or whenever it is that God has appeared to us and told us that's what it is.

KAPLAN: You want to wait until then for that discussion?

SHIEBER: Yes. In the meantime what I'm saying is, while people are actually building applications, they shouldn't be taking linguistic theories and the formalisms associated with them wholesale because, for the time being at least, there's a difference in the goals of the two enterprises.

KAPLAN: There's a real danger in substantive constraints, I totally agree. Substance is a real danger in this game.

MARCUS: Two comments. The first is just a question about what seemed to be a flaw in your argument. It was to be taken as evidence that all of these theories that you've stated were to be inter-reducible, and yet it was eminently clear from what you said that the FUG formalism allowed one to say things that would be reducible to PATR-II nearly only in the sense of Turing-equivalence -

SHIEBER: No, this is significantly different, I mentioned that in the paper. This is one of the misconceptions that I get, which I should have forestalled but didn't. I'm not trying to show that one of these things is a notational variant of the other. I don't think that a notational reduction shows that, unless it's such a trivial one that it's like "replace all the v's with a's", or something like that. What these notational reductions show is, where does that go wrong? And for FUG, for instance, it really pinpoints what are big differences between the two formalisms; and it shows in which direction that difference lies, which is the subset of which. There's always that intuition, but this really gives it some substantive grounding.

MARCUS: The statement that you had made is, because they're relatively similar, it's straightforward to restate the generalisms in one another, and yet -

SHIEBER: I said that for one direction, I think. Only the PATR-II to FUG direction.

MARCUS: Fine. My second comment is that I want to quibble in a practical sense with this notion that generality is a good thing, the truth of the theories utterly aside, for the same reasons that the generality in our computer languages turns out to be a terrible thing for building large software systems. It seems to me that the basic idea that you've argued for is just great if what you want to do is sit down and one person build a grammar, but that if you're talking about building a somewhat complete system for a language, or you're trying to build a series of systems for different languages, for mechanical translation systems, for instance, to go across them, there are several real problems.

Let me list what they are briefly. You have a team of people working - this is the software methodology problem - they need to have a framework that forces them to come up with roughly the same things so that you can put them together. You'd really like your analyses to be comparable. If you've got analyses of different languages, you'd like them not to have been done in such a way that when two teams of people are finished writing grammars, then we haven't gotten very far.

A related argument is the incremental nature of things.

You can always hack the last ten or fifteen percent, on a good day, but until you get down to the lees, you'd better have the general framework robust.

SHIEBER: There's two responses to that. First of all, I think I'm making a little smaller point, which is the ceteris paribus point. The sleazy out to this thing is to say, one of the goals of NLP is modularity, and maintenance of systems, and so on, and in that sense certain restrictions, though not others, might serve one or the other. But I think that's the sleazy way out. The better response is that - what you're arguing is that if I apply this same rhetoric to programming languages I would end up with programming in the untyped lambda-calculus, or some abomination like that -

Henry THOMPSON: Ada.

SHIEBER: Ada, or something like that, right.

THOMPSON: - Untyped Ada! No, I think there's a crucial difference between Ada and the untyped lambda-calculus, and it's a confusion that Mitch [Marcus] is making too, between simplicity and generality.

SHIEBER: What I would like to propose is not going in a direction analogous to untyped systems, where it's a free-for-all, but to something where you can state the various more limited things in this one general system. In other words, going for some degree of modularity in the goal of generality.

MARCUS: It seems to me that there's a classic out. The view that was held from very early on in natural language processing, that we could write grammars that were nearly context-free - the ATN formalism (Woods 1970) is a good example - allowed people to provide a very restricted formalism, such as the recursive transition network formalism, for forcing people to state that part which seemed to fit nicely into it, and then threw in a couple of different levels of augmentation that allowed you to bring the kitchen sink in where you needed it. It seems to me that that might be an alternative paradigm, to build systems that have certain things built into them, but allow you to bring in any number of pulls up to arbitrary Lisp code when you've got to get a problem solved that you know you can't do within it.

SHIEBER: Yes, I'm sympathetic to that idea, but I would stop
far short of arbitrary Lisp code. I maybe have a chip on my
shoulder about declarativeness, but that's a separate issue.
A charitable view - or possibly an uncharitable view - of
PATR-II is that that's what it is, it's a context-free
grammar, but then you let in all these constraints on the
side, with which you can model almost anything, that let you
do arbitrary things, to the extent that you can model Turing
machines in this; so I'm sympathetic with that view.

Nick OSTLER: I thought your paper was surprising in that it
didn't do justice to what really are the difficulties of
doing NLP. Your representatives of NLP were these very
general things like FUG and PATR-II, which you then
proceeded to show were reducible to each other and had some
relations at least to the theoretical formalisms. But in NLP
you actually want to do a lot of things which linguistic
theory isn't interested in doing at all, like the internal
structure of numerals in defense documents, or paragraph
structure, or things like that, which have no place and will
never have any place in linguistic theory, but probably have
some place in our general cognitive ability - we can pick
these things up and we can become proof-readers of defense
documents if we wish to. So when you said, as people were
saying here, when we've got God's truth about linguistic
theory then we can incorporate it in our natural language
processing systems, well maybe we can, maybe it will do good
to us, but it will not give us a complete natural language
processing system in any sense.

SHIEBER: This is a nice example of the problem with writing
a paper on a word processor. Because there was a paragraph
on that point which I now realize I didn't read, so it must
have disappeared somewhere in the process of editing the
document. Remarkable. But no, absolutely. The point being
that there are certain things that linguistic theory just
abstracts away from from the beginning, especially those
theories that start the introductory pages of the book
saying, we're abstracting away from performance and we're
only talking about competence, so we'll ignore half, if not
three quarters of what happens when people talk. Absolutely
- most of what goes on in natural language processing, first
of all isn't syntax, of course, and then is in areas of it
that linguistic theory doesn't touch. Extreme examples are

things like parsing ill-formed input, and that kind of thing, which linguistic theory specifically abstracts from.

OSTLER: You'd never expect to get a formalism which would elegantly deal with everything which could ever come up. I think this leads to the same sort of point that Mitch was making, that you need always to have scope for bringing in the kitchen sink.

SHIEBER: I think this is another argument for wanting generality in natural language processing, where it isn't wanted in linguistic theory. Generality may not be the right word there.

OSTLER: What do you see as the relationship of building these great big things like FUG and PATR-II to the actual practical enterprise of NLP then? Because from what I can see they're just watered down versions of practical notations.

KAPLAN: I think your characterization is not quite right. FUG was originally designed to be a linguistic theory, that's what Martin [Kay] intended. He just didn't use all of the rhetoric that we've come to expect of linguistic theoreticians. And likewise, LFG was originally designed to be a computationally based theory.

SHIEBER: But it's a computationally based theory of linguistics, not a computationally based tool for doing NLP. That's what I'm saying, those are two different things.

KAPLAN: Well, we tried to do them both. That's how we came up with LFG. We also wanted to do psychology at the same time. It's misleading also to be surprised that there are fundamental concepts in common between PATR-II and FUG and LFG, and maybe some other things. In fact, in the case of LFG and FUG, they evolved in the same room at the same time, and Martin and I had a disagreement about the role of constituent structure, and how explicit the formalism should be about that. But it's basically the same idea. And I think some of those ideas also then went across the creek over to SRI, and infected some of the work that you guys were doing. So it's not a surprise that these things are inter-reducible but have minority relations.

SHIEBER: I don't know. Take the example of the role of

constituent structure, I think one of the things that this shows, or one of the interpretations of it, is that maybe this disagreement wasn't as big a disagreement as you thought it was.

KAPLAN: It wasn't, no - it was a political disagreement, and we were very conscious of this. The formalisms we knew to be essentially equivalent, and the issue was, what's the best way of connecting up with linguists, getting linguists to understand what it was that we were doing? I thought that you should give linguists trees, that's what they're used to looking at, and Martin thought no, that's an excrescence, we'll make them implicit, because what you really want is to emphasize the output structures, the underlying representations.

SHIEBER: So there's formal factors, substantive factors, and now there's political factors -

KAPLAN: Oh yes, sociological factors.

SPARCK JONES: Different judgements of what linguists are capable of, clearly.

KAPLAN: What would sell, what would sell. And given that at least some people think that we landed on the theory side, we seem to have made that judgement correctly at least in terms of what linguists were prepared to accept. It looks like a linguistic theory!

I don't think that at this level Martin's theory is significantly different than LFG. At the level of the underlying mathematical conception, which maybe I'll talk about tomorrow, there are some concepts that we emphasize in LFG, and that we can make use of, that are only implicit in FUG.

SHIEBER: I didn't really want to emphasize the political or for that matter philological aspects of the formalisms.

KAPLAN: I think you have to judge these things in their historical context.

SHIEBER: I would rather judge them relative to the goals that whatever discipline it is wants to use them for. And towards the goal of linguistic theory, restrictiveness is important, and for NLP it seems to me that it's less important. So things like, for instance, the example in the paper of functional locality in LFG, seem to be the kind of thing that you wouldn't want in an NLP application.

KAPLAN: You might not even want it in a linguistic theory.

SHIEBER: You might not. I didn't want to go that far, I was going to talk to **you** about that.

KAPLAN: One late night.

SHIEBER: Yes. I was going to talk to you about that just between you and me. But, for the rest of these people, no, you certainly wouldn't want it, it seems to me, in an NLP application. And that is an example of where LFG, least in the literature, has gone one direction which shows that it's heading towards the linguistic theory end, as opposed to the direction in which its going towards the NLP end.

[To Ostler] I don't think I ever answered your question adequately though. So maybe I won't.

OSTLER: Well, there's something at the end, which is, what are these things like PATR-II and FUG doing in NLP? I'm getting some sort of answer, maybe you can give me a yes/no to that, which is, that it's a way of building a bridge to people who are building real formalisms in linguistic theory. So you couldn't actually expect it to be the real representative of natural language processing. You might take a natural language processing system that does something and see what formalism it uses, in order to make the sort of comparisons which maybe I'd expected at the beginning of the paper.

SHIEBER: As it's actually used, PATR-II is a very small part of certain particular systems that are being built at SRI. It's just the part that goes, roughly, between morphological analysis and building some kind of predicate argument structure. Most of the work is done after that. The other point about PATR-II is that it of course is much younger than most of the other systems that are used in NLP applications, so it doesn't have anywhere near the work that's been done on it that others have. But the idea was exactly what you said, which is to have a formalism which, although it isn't part of a linguistic theory, at least has enough commonality that it can make use of analyses from, say, LFG or GPSG, or GB, for that matter, if those seem reasonable. Or with which you could build languages on top of it.

OSTLER: That's sort of sold the pass, in a way, so that you give these apologies and say, well, you can't actually use PATR-II to write anything, you've got to jazz it up with syntactic theories and that sort of thing, so that it's not being developed as an adequate formalism for NLP.

SHIEBER: No, the pure PATR-II formalism isn't. The system that we have that is called the PATR-II Experimental System has a lot more stuff in there, but hopefully it's done in a general way so that - what you do in that system is you build on the top of the formalism. The user builds, not Ron Kaplan building LFG$_F$, or Gazdar building GPSG-whatever, but just any user can build his own way of constructing an intended usage for the formalism.

OSTLER: At which point Mitch's point begins to come into play, namely, have you in fact restricted people enough, with this account, or will you still go in completely different directions?

SHIEBER: If you want to have vast numbers of people using it simultaneously, you need somebody in charge to say, well, on top of it I'm going to build this one, and that's what everybody uses. But at least you've done it in such a way that if you decide down the road that that's wrong, you don't have to re-write the code, you just re-write what you've built on top. Maybe I hadn't made that clear.

THOMPSON: This is quite brief: it seems to me that what both Mitch and Nick [Ostler] have been dancing around reveals a tension between two of the goals that you're trying to impose on your notion of the fundamental formalisms. One goal is, being a basic NLP mechanism, and the other goal is, providing a semantics for linguistic formalisms. And it seems to me that the constraints that follow from which of those two versions of the goal you take are different. Most of your paper was directed at satisfying the goal of providing a uniform semantics, a vehicle for expressing the semantics of differing notations; and the ancillary top-level goals that you set, of allowing comparisons to proceed in an orderly manner, discovering where differences are

significant, and where the differences are not significant,
satisfying certain perceived lacks in various publications,
all of those are versions of the goal which says, we need
some kind of language with which to specify the semantics of
linguistic formalisms. And that's a very different goal, it
seems to me, which is only partly related to the goal of
being a foundation for natural language processing. And I
think that Nick and Mitch's criticisms are validly directed
at PATR-II qua the latter object but much less relevant to
the criticism of PATR-II as a candidate for the former
object. That distinction is very important to make.

SHIEBER: I think my own criticism that I read out is
exactly directed to that point. It says that you wouldn't
want to use the pure PATR-II formalism, the very simple
thing that has all these reductions going on -

THOMPSON: A good parallel is that you wouldn't want to use
predicate calculus as a programming language, but predicate
calculus is a very good language for expressing the
semantics of various formal systems. But before you use it
you need to decorate it.

SHIEBER: The only point I'd like to make about decorating it
is, preferably you'd want people to have a way of decorating
it so that you can re-decorate when necessary, as opposed to
just throwing it out and starting all over. That's the idea
of not committing yourself prematurely. And that's the idea
that's been pursued, whether successfully or not, in the
PATR project. The actual system that's used adds to this a
whole bunch of devices to allow a grammar-writer to decorate
the formalism in his or her own way, as opposed to just
saying, well, we'll add this, we'll add that, we'll add the
other thing and that's what you can use.

References

Backus, J. 1977. Can Programming be Liberated from the von
    Neumann Style? **Communications of the ACM** 21, 613-641.

Berwick, R.C. & Weinberg, A.S. 1984. **The Grammatical Basis
    of Linguistic Performance: Language Use and Acquisition.**
    Cambridge, Mass.: MIT Press.

Bresnan, J., ed. 1982. **The Mental Representation of Grammatical Relations.** Cambridge, Mass.: MIT Press.

Bresnan, J. 1982a. The Passive in Lexical Theory. In Bresnan, ed., 3-86.

Bresnan, J. 1982b. Control and Complementation. In Bresnan, ed., 282-390.

Bresnan, J. & Kaplan, R.M. 1982. Introduction: Grammars as Mental Representations of Language. In Bresnan, ed., xvii-lii.

Cardelli, L. & Wegner, P. 1985. Understanding Types, Data Abstraction and Polymorphism. Ms.

Chomsky, N. 1957. **Syntactic Structures.** The Hague: Mouton.

Chomsky, N. 1965. **Aspects of the Theory of Syntax.** Cambridge, Mass.: MIT Press.

Chomsky, N. 1982. **Lectures on Government and Binding.** Dordrecht: Foris.

Dijkstra, E.W. 1972. The Humble Programmer. **Communications of the ACM** 15, 859-866.

Earley, J. 1970. An Efficient Context-free Parsing Algorithm. **Communications of the ACM** 13, 94-102.

Gazdar, G. 1982. Phrase Structure Grammar. In Jacobson, P. & Pullum, G.K., eds., **The Nature of Syntactic Representation.** Dordrecht: D. Reidel, 131-186.

Gazdar, G., Klein, E., Pullum, G. & Sag, I. 1985. **Generalized Phrase Structure Grammar.** Oxford: Basil Blackwell.

Kaplan, R.M. & Bresnan, J. 1982. Lexical-Functional Grammar: A Formal System for Grammatical Representation. In Bresnan, ed., 173-281.

Kay, M. 1983. Unification Grammar. Technical Report, Xerox Palo Alto Research Center, Palo Alto, CA.

Pereira, F.C.N. & Warren, D.H.D. 1983. Parsing as Deduction. **21st Annual Meeting of the Association for Computational Linguistics** (Cambridge, Mass.), Proceedings, 137-144.

Pollard, C.J. 1984. **Generalized Phrase Structure Grammars, Head Grammars, and Natural Languages.** PhD dissertation, Stanford University.

Scott, D. 1982. Domains for Denotational Semantics. **ICALP 82,** Heidelberg: Springer-Verlag.

Shieber, S.M. 1984. The Design of a Computer Language for Linguistic Information. **COLING 84: 10th International Conference on Computational Linguistics / 22nd Annual Meeting of the Association for Computational Linguistics** (Stanford, CA), Proceedings, 362-366.

Shieber, S.M. 1986. A Simple Reconstruction of GPSG. **COLING 86: 11th International Conference on Computational Linguistics** (Bonn, West Germany), Proceedings, 211-215.

Shieber, S.M., Uszkoreit, H., Pereira, F.C.N, Robinson, J.J. & Tyson, M. 1983. The Formalism and Implementation of PATR-II. In **Research on Interactive Acquisition and Use of Knowledge** (SRI Project 1984 Final Report), Menlo Park, CA: SRI International, 39-79.

Woods, W.A. 1970. Transition Network Grammars for Natural Language Analysis. **Communications of the ACM** 13, 591-606.

Linguistic Applications of
Default Inheritance Mechanisms

Gerald Gazdar

I'm glad I came after Stuart [Shieber], because he says so much more eloquently some things that I might otherwise have stumbled through. I will therefore not make my metatheoretical preamble quite as long as it might otherwise be. What I'm going to do is begin with a few remarks about relations between disciplines, in particular the relation between linguistics and computational linguistics. Then I'm going to look at a particular topic, the topic of defaults and more especially default inheritance, to illustrate the rather slight metatheoretical point that I'll begin with. Then depending on time at the very end I might, or might not, talk about a particular approach to default inheritance that I've been thinking about, but I may not get to that. So there are basically three chunks, the third of which is optional, the first of which is fairly brief I trust.

It seems to me that during the '70s, at least in this country and I suspect elsewhere, certainly in the States,

---

An antecedent of the talk was given at the Syntax Research Center, University of California, Santa Cruz in May 1985. I am grateful to the locals on that occasion for their comments and to Kelly Booth, Alex Borgida, David Israel, Rich Thomason and Meg Withgott for relevant conversations. The activity from which this paper emerges was supported by a grant (C00242003) from the ESRC (UK) and was greatly facilitated by the tenure of a Fellowship at the Center for Advanced Study in the Behavioural Sciences through 1984-85 and by visitor status at the Center for the Study of Language and Information at Stanford over the same period.

LINGUISTIC THEORY AND COMPUTER APPLICATIONS
ISBN 0-12-747220-7

touched as it was by the Sloan Foundation, there was a
notion of interdisciplinarity which was rather a naive one.
This was that you just bunged together disciplines (within
some sort of domain, like philosophy, linguistics,
psychology) and that this was a good thing and that they
would have things to say to each other. The idea was that
you somehow forced people (with the aid of large cheques) to
sit in the same room and eventually these people would end
up in reciprocal intellectual relationships. I think with
the wisdom of hindsight that was silly in many ways. There's
no reason why the relations between disciplines, perfectly
sensible disciplines with their own right to exist, should
always be reciprocal. So to take an extreme case,
mathematics: most sensible disciplines relate to
mathematics, in that they pinch stuff from it. Social
sciences help themselves to large chunks of statistics;
linguistics and computer science invariably help themselves
to other chunks of maths; and so on with physics and
chemistry. Ofcourse there's some feedback, in that some
areas of maths are developed because of applications and
they then turn out to be intrinsically interesting and so
on. But basically the drain of knowledge is from maths into
these other disciplines. But nobody thinks the worse of
physics, say, because it uses a lot of maths.

When we come closer to home and look at linguistics and
psychology, for example, there doesn't seem to be any very
obvious reason why linguistics should get anything from
psychology. Now this would have been a heretical thing to
have said 10 or even 5 years ago and I don't really want to
pursue it here. Whereas the converse, for example, in some
sense has to be true, since language is such an important
aspect of being human. Psychologists are concerned with
what being human is about - there's necessarily going to
have to be a psychology of language. What is language? Well
you ask a linguist what language is, at least you ought to
be able to.

I want to actually focus now on linguistics and
computational linguistics. Having begun in this rather
cynical fashion, you may expect me to say something that I'm
actually not going to say. It seems to me that a
conventional view of the relation between linguistics and
computational linguistics would go something like this.
Linguists are doing the science of language and they develop
grammar formalisms/theories of language, modulo all the

things that Stuart [Shieber] said. They do analyses of language, descriptions of language. Computational linguistics is a branch of engineering and they borrow these descriptions and these grammar formalisms and implement them - they hack away. The transfer of knowledge is entirely from linguistics to computational linguistics; there's no particular point in any feedback the other way round.

I suspect there are large numbers of theoretical linguists, at least, who would regard this as the proper picture of the relationship between linguistics and computational linguistics. Now put the way I've just put it, probably not many computational linguists would subscribe to it, though they might have to think for a while to rebut it. And if I put it in a less pejorative fashion, then maybe I could have got some of you to subscribe to it. But I think it's all wrong, and I think it's all wrong because of a misconception about the way linguistics really is, caused by one of the most effective aspects of linguistics, namely its public relations. Its public relations has it that this is what linguists do, they devise grammatical theories = grammatical formalisms, and they describe languages by grammars and so on. But really they don't do those things, for the most part, as people really know when they think it through. Look at what the majority of theoretical syntacticians are doing at the moment in the US, the numerical majority, not the schools of syntax represented in this room. They're not working on formal theories of language, they're not developing grammatical formalisms for natural language, they're not doing grammatical description of fragments of natural language, they're not writing grammars. None of those things are being done.

Syntax, the core tradition of theoretical linguistics, has been oriented round 'cute' facts for a very long time. Where you score points as an American syntax graduate student, is by first finding 'cute' facts, and then developing a 'cute' analysis of them. The constraints on a 'cute' analysis are very slight. You're not required to write it in a particular formalism. Of course, you may well be required to have some sort of framework allegiance, but that doesn't particularly constrain what apparatus you can use. Indeed the whole nature of your 'cute' fact paper may be to argue for some previously unknown bit of apparatus. If one has this (what I take to be the) conventional perception of the relation between linguistics and computational linguistics, then computational linguists are going to find themselves waiting and getting irritated and reading linguistics literature and scratching their heads and saying 'Gee where is this stuff, maybe I'm reading the wrong journal but they told me that LI [**Linguistic Inquiry**] was the journal to look in, where's this grammar?'.

On the contrary it seems to me that, certainly now, the situation is that grammatical formalisms are being developed not by linguists but by computational linguists, or by linguists in collaboration with computational linguists. And for a very good reason. If you're doing computational linguistics you'd better have linguistic formalism. If there's some moral of the last 20 years of computational linguistics it's that you don't just want to mess up your grammar and your phonology in the code. You want to pull it out, for good software methodology type reasons. You need some sort of formalism and so you've got to develop one. What Stuart [Shieber] referred to as theoretical grammar formalisms - he mentioned three, one of them I don't believe exists - of the two that I do believe exist, I think it's no coincidence that of one of them, LFG, one of the two progenitors - sitting right here [Ron Kaplan] - certainly comes from the computational linguistics side of things. Likewise in GPSG: although historically, and continuingly to some extent, the four authors of the GPSG book (Gazdar et al 1985) are linguists by training, it's again no accident that that book is as formal as it is and that two of those authors have for three or four years now been consultants on a major computational linguistics project run by Hewlett Packard. I doubt somehow that that book would have been the way it is - it would·have been much more cute fact oriented - had it not been for that fact.

So the rather slight metatheoretical, sociological, moral I want to draw from this is that actually computational linguistics should see itself, since linguistics is not doing the job, as having a theoretical branch, what we might call theoretical computational linguistics, by analogy with theoretical computer science. Now one's familiar with the notion of theoretical computer science. People who do theoretical computer science are mathematicians, who have no particular need to touch computers, though they may do so. Likewise it seems to me we can have a discipline, or sub-discipline, of computational linguistics which we might choose to call 'theoretical computational linguistics' which has much the same character. At the present time, of course, people doing theoretical computational linguistics are also doing practical, engineering type, computational linguistics, and that's quite reasonable, but some time in the future you might see the sort of specialization of activity that I believe you see in computer science. I think this would be healthy for linguistics, though linguistics may not like it.

One of the reasons is that linguists are not trained to develop formalisms, to think about formalisms having semantics, to know about a range of alternative formalisms, formal languages and the like. Whereas people with some computational training are oriented to thinking in that way. The consequence of this is that there are a lot of formal techniques available in the computational linguistics literature, which it seems to me make good, or potentially good, sense from the perspective of theoretical linguistics. Theoretical linguistics has been extremely conservative about the form of mechanisms it's used. It's been promiscuous and profligate, but it's also been conservative. A lot of it's been tied to thinking about strings and operations that map strings to strings because historically that's where generative grammar came from. But of course formal language theory has moved way beyond the early days of grammars thought of in terms of strings. Most linguists don't know that, and are unfamiliar with, for example, tree grammars and the like.

I want to illustrate this point by talking about defaults. The illustrative side of this is largely to do with default inheritance. But I'll begin by just saying a few words about default mechanisms in general. These have shown up in linguistics. (1) shows something from Chomsky & Halle (1968).

(1) Default values of phonological features

```
[u high]  -->  [+ high]
[u nasal] -->  [- nasal]
[u low]   -->  [- low]
[u ant]   -->  [+ ant]
[u cor]   -->  [+ cor]
[u cont]  -->  [+ cont]
```

The **u** notation says that the unmarked value for the high feature is '+high' and so on down the list. Now these are one type of Chomsky & Halle markedness conventions. What they are telling you is the default values, the unmarked values, of these phonological features. There are one or two asides that I could perhaps make - notice this arrow, a familiar bit of notation, but of course really quite different in its semantics from, say, the rewrite arrow. Although you could presumably construe all that in a rewriting system, but it hardly seems to be an appropriate way to think about it.

Now these notions of markedness, like the rest of phonology feature theory, have found their way into syntax. You quite often see in the syntax literature (all syntax literature, I don't just mean GPSG) remarks of the form 'the default value of the feature PRO is minus', or 'PRO defaults to minus', or whatever. What you don't see is actually a theory about what that might mean or any kind of maths to go with such claims. However in doing the GPSG book (Gazdar et al 1985) we were forced, or at least we felt ourselves forced, to confront this issue, because we made extensive use of features in that book. Perhaps it would be more accurate to say we made explicit our extensive use of features in that book. In doing so we constantly wanted to have default values of features to save endless redundant specifications of things that were obviously going to have such and such a value. And we had to develop a theory of defaults. Now this actually turned out to be very difficult to do, and I will say a word or two about why.

It's not too difficult to develop a theory of defaults if you restrict yourself to defaults that look roughly like FSDs 1, 2, 3 and 4, in (2).

(2) Feature specification defaults

```
FSD 1:  [-INV]
FSD 2:  ~[CONJ]
FSD 3:  ~[NULL]
FSD 4:  ~[NOM]
FSD 5:  [PFORM]        ⊃ [BAR 0]
FSD 6:  [+ADV]         ⊃ [BAR 0]
FSD 7:  [BAR 0]        ⊃ ~[PAS]
FSD 8:  [NFORM]        ⊃ [NFORM NORM]
FSD 9:  [INF,+SUBJ]    ⊃ [COMP for]
```

FSD10: [+N,-V,BAR 2] ≡ [ACC]
FSD11: [+V,BAR 0]   ⊃ [AGR NP[NFORM NORM]]

The first one says something like the default value for the feature INV (for inverted sentences) is the value 'minus'. The second one says the default state for the CONJ feature is for there to be no specification at all for the feature. The details of this don't matter. Even with this relatively simple kind of default there is one problem you get into, which is if you believe that grammatical formalisms should be declarative then that of course commits you to not having any ordering; yet a very natural way of thinking about defaults is to say 'you do everything else and then you just paste the default values on at the end'. But if you've got a declarative formalism you can't really say that, at least not just as I said it. You have to come up with some declarative version.

However, the real difficulty we got into was the fact that when you actually articulate a large feature system, the defaults you want are in general not straightforward ones like FSDs 1, 2, 3 and 4 in (2). You want to say things about the default state of particular configurations of features. So you want to say 'when this feature's got this kind of value then this other feature defaults to something or other'. So it's not just simple cases of a single feature defaulting to some value or another. You've got configurations or combinations of features that have, as it were, default states. Getting a theory of this together drove us, or me, mad, for a while. It was a painful process. Of course, once one's done it one can look back and think 'well, that wasn't so hard', but actually getting away from thinking about the single case to thinking about these multiple cases was very difficult. What you actually have to move to is a view where defaults are not crudely properties of particular features but they're properties of categories. So categories try and satisfy the Boolean things in (2). I don't want to go through the GPSG theory of defaults, I just want to give you a sense of why defaults are a non-trivial issue.

Just to elaborate that point slightly further. Take something like the default [CASE ACC], which probably anybody would want for a treatment of English. You want to say the default case in English is accusative, assuming that there is an accusative/nominative case distinction in the

English pronoun system. You're likely to want to say that
whatever your grammatical framework is, assuming you have
something to say about case. Look what's going to happen.
If we take a phrase structure grammar, then in the case of
the tensed sentence rule (3), we just want to stipulate that
the subject is nominative.

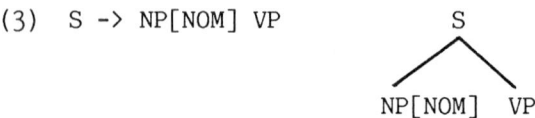

(3) S -> NP[NOM] VP

Our theory of defaults is going to have to leave this
nominative, not overwrite accusative on it. That shouldn't
be too difficult, or at least if you can't do that you can't
do anything. (4) is the verb phrase rule.

(4) VP -> V NP

We don't want to say anything about this object NP, it ought
to default to accusative. This is precisely why we want a
default. We want to get from that rule to a bit of structure
like that. Likewise in the case of (5).

(5) PP -> P NP

What's going to happen though in cases like (6)? We
don't want this thing to default to accusative, because if
it does, then we'll never get this construction in sentence
subject position.

(6) NP -> NP PP

This is, of course, just a bizarre claim about English -
this construction occurs in subject position just as easily
as it occurs in any other position. Likewise in the case of

coordinate NP's (7) - again the details don't matter, I
don't believe that's the right constituent structure.

(7) NP -> NP and NP   NP[ACC]

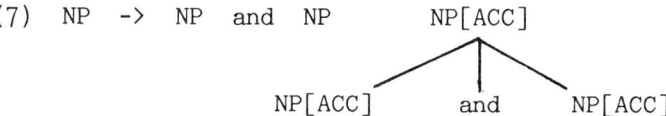

                       NP[ACC]   and   NP[ACC]

We certainly don't want this thing defaulting to accusative.
So in our theory of defaults, at least in the GPSG version
of it, we have to have some notion of things co-varying.
We've actually got three cases here - case (3), where the
default is just straightforwardly violated or contradicted;
cases (4) and (5), with the default operating as we want;
and cases (6) and (7), in which we've got a situation where
bits of the structure co-vary and we don't want the default
to apply.

     Working out a theory that has those properties is
tricky. Here's the kind of problem you get into. I said that
when things co-vary you don't the default to apply. But
here's a case where you do want it to apply. You want to
say that the default state of a passive feature is its minus
value - things are not passive unless you say they are. The
verb-phrase rule (4) gives us a transitive verb and an NP.
The VP and the V will co-vary in respect of a feature like
passive, so it seems that they should be free of the default
and we should be allowed to make them passive. If we're
allowed to, then we're going to get junk like (8).

     (8) * Kim is eaten the chicken.

Those hurdles are jumped in the book. I mention them here
only to convey the fact that there is a genuine difficult
problem.

     Now, having talked about ordinary defaults in what I
hope are fairly familiar kinds of cases, I want to talk
about default inheritance. Unlike the notion of marked
feature values, unmarked feature values, syntactic features
defaulting to accusative and so on, this is a much less
familiar notion within linguistics proper, although it's a
very familiar notion in the AI literature. Indeed one AI
professor said to me about a week ago that more than half of
AI was predicated on default inheritance. I don't know
enough about the AI literature to know whether that's a true

appreciation of the situation. But it is certainly the case
that inheritance, and default inheritance, are important in
AI. So what do I mean by this, for those of you who are not
absolutely au fait with the AI literature? (9) will be
familiar to many, though it's nothing to do with
linguistics.

(9)   Network of properties

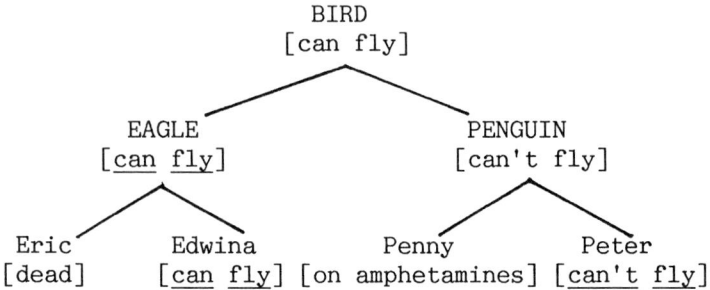

Fact 1. If you're dead, you can't fly
Fact 2. If you take amphetamines, you can fly

We have this network here rooted in BIRD. BIRDs have a
property, namely they can fly. EAGLE and PENGUIN are both
types of BIRD. PENGUIN has a property, namely it can't fly.
However, nothing's said about whether EAGLE can fly or not.
The things that are underlined are not really there.
However, since nothing's said about it, then it will just
inherit from being a BIRD the property 'can fly'. Now down
at the bottom here we've got Eric who's an EAGLE, only
Eric's dead and we know a fact about the world, which is if
you're dead you can't fly. So even though these are not
superficially inconsistent, given other things that we know
about the world, on a particular account of this which
somebody might implement, hopefully Eric wouldn't inherit
the 'can fly' property. On the other hand, nothing's said
about Edwina, so she can fly, and we have the kind of
opposite case under PENGUIN. This is the sort of thing you
will see if you dip into the AI knowledge representation
literature. These things are known as 'ISA links'. Eric isa
EAGLE, EAGLE isa BIRD. Actually, as people have pointed out,
in that literature, there's a fudge going on, because
there's two types of isa relation - EAGLE is a **subset** of a
class of BIRD, whereas Eric is a **member** of the class of

EAGLE. But that is not our concern at the moment.

What kind of applicability might that sort of default inheritance have within linguistics? My sense is that it actually has a good deal of applicability in ways that are interesting far beyond implementation issues. And as my first exemplar, I'll look at a treatment of Dutch verb morphology due to de Smedt (1984).

(10)

$$
\begin{array}{l}
\text{VERB} \\[4pt]
\left[
\begin{array}{l}
\text{past tense stem = present tense stem} \\
\text{past tense suffix = +te or +de/voice} \\
\text{past participle prefix = ge+} \\
\text{past participle stem = past tense stem} \\
\text{past participle suffix = +t or +d/voice}
\end{array}
\right]
\end{array}
$$

```
                    VERB
       ┌─────────────────────────────────────┐
       │ past tense stem = present tense stem │
       │ past tense suffix = +te or +de/voice │
       │ past participle prefix = ge+         │
       │ past participle stem = past tense stem│
       │ past participle suffix = +t or +d/voice│
       └─────────────────────────────────────┘
            ╱         ╲
        werk          MIXED VERB
       (work)   [past participle suffix = +en or +n/syll]
                     ╱         ╲
                  bak          STRONG VERB
                (bake)    [past tense suffix = 0]
                              ╱         ╲
                          zwem            ...
                         (swim)
                 [past tense stem = zwom]
```

(10) is a net of essentially the kind we've just been looking at. The top node says VERB, which of course means Dutch verb. Dutch verbs have a bunch of properties - their past tense stem is equal to their present tense stem, their past tense suffix equals +t or +d and so on. Then there's a sub-class, MIXED VERBS, and also just simple members of the class VERB, like werk. This is just a verb - nothing else is said about it, so it's going to inherit all those properties. By looking at those properties and applying the rules implicit in those equations, you can infer what the past participle, past tense and so on of werk is. In turn, the sub-class MIXED VERB has a property associated with it, that the past participle suffix is en. Of course, this contradicts the information associated with VERB and so

overrides the default. The past participle of <u>bak</u> will be <u>gebakken</u>. On the same basis, we can work out the past participle of <u>zwem</u> is <u>gezwommen</u>.

Now I think that this is linguistically interesting. One of the reasons for this, apart from the fact that it provides a non-redundant and therefore generalization-capturing representation of the Dutch inflexions, is that it accounts automatically for the phenomenon known to linguists as 'blocking' - the existence of an irregular form in general stops the simultaneous production of a regular form. If you look at linguistic treatments of morphology, they acknowledge the existence of blocking, but normally it has to be stipulated. I'm not familiar enough with the literature to assert that it always has to be stipulated. But in general, the effect of blocking is stipulated as an extra constraint, which says that these regular rules may not apply when there is some more particular rule. There's a whole terminology - 'proper inclusion precedence' and so on - which goes with that. Well, in the de Smedt case it's quite automatic - there's no mystery about why the past participle of <u>zwem</u> isn't whatever it would be if you followed the rules at the top there. It can't be, because of the way these equations get inherited down the tree. So the regular derivations are not an issue with this kind of knowledge representation.

I think this is an interesting consequence. It's not one, incidentally, that de Smedt pulls out of this, at least I don't think he does, which is a bit of a pity. De Smedt is primarily concerned with the implementation that he presents.

Essentially the same idea is used in Flickinger, Pollard & Wasow (1985), henceforth FPW, which is also about the lexicon. In that paper, they are not primarily concerned with inflexional morphology, but rather with subcategorization frames. They propose a treatment of lexical organization which inherits subcategorization frames in just this fashion. They also incidentally do inflexional morphology the same way de Smedt does.

Both these two things I've referred to are implemented in object-oriented programming languages, and I'll make another remark about that in a moment. Just let me give you another couple of empirical cases in the morphology area, where this sort of default inheritance could provide a theory of things that have been suggested in the linguistics literature.

Looking at Marantz (1984), he proposes that features on affixes override those on the root, but that features on the root get through if there's no conflict. So again here, you have a claim about the way features on affixes and roots combine. I'm not concerned with the veracity of the claim, but you have a claim that can be naturally treated with a default inheritance mechanism. The kind of example he gives is that the passive affix is [-transitive], but it goes on [+transitive] roots. You don't want the thing that's formed to be [+transitive], you want [-transitive] to be inherited from the affix.

There's a paper by Halvorsen & Withgott (1984) on tone in Norwegian. Apparently in the Norwegian tone system, inflexional markers, for example the definite marker, can give a particular tone to an unaccented word. So you have a stem that's not accented, and you put on a definite marker, and then the whole resulting word has some tone, which it has inherited from the definite marker. The tone is not just on the definite marker, it's a global property of the word. However, this doesn't happen when the word already has a tone of its own. If you have a stem that has an inherent tone, and you bung a definite marker on it, then the tone of the stem wins through. So this is actually the opposite case to the Marantz case. In Marantz's case, the affix was winning; in the Norwegian tone case the stem wins.

Turning from morphology and the lexicon to syntax - in the book version of GPSG, though not in earlier (published and unpublished) versions, the Head Feature Convention (HFC), which Stuart [Shieber] alluded to in passing, is treated as a default inheritance mechanism of a rather particular kind. The idea of the HFC is extremely simple, (and this is implicit in an awful lot of (non-GPSG) linguistics work). It's simply that phrases and their heads share various syntactic properties. One way of formalizing that is to have features pass from lexical heads to phrasal nodes, carrying information up or down, or merely requiring identity of certain sorts of information. Previous formulations just required identity of relevant classes of features. What the book version does is not require absolute identity, but rather says 'pass up whatever features you

can, but if passing something up would lead to an
inconsistency on the mother node, then forget it, don't
bother'. Likewise, 'pass things down if you can, but if
you're going to get an inconsistency then forget it'. So
this is bidirectional default inheritance of features.
There's an attempt by both mother and daughter, to put it
anthropomorphically, to pass information to each other, and
only the information that's consistent with what they
already think gets carried across. How does this pan out?

What will happen in (11) is that everything associated
with the mother category will get passed down into that H
position, because there's no reason for it not to. So if the
mother category is a finite S, then that H category will be
a finite S as well.

(11)   S -> H, ADV

Likewise in (12), again nothing's going to stop that head
having all the properties of its mother. So the property of
being a VP, the property of being a bare infinitive (BSE),
just get equated.

(12)   VP[BSE] -> H, ADV

Now look at (13)

(13)   VP -> H[BAR 0] ...

Here we have a VP with a lexical head, i.e. BAR 0, a lexical
category immediately dominating a word. What happens if we
have a bare infinitive mother category? There's nothing to
stop this BSE feature going down, but this VP has some BAR
level, e.g. 2. This is a feature that we passed down in the
previous case, but we can't pass it down here, because it
would be inconsistent with the head being a V[BAR 0]. Given
the way the mechanism works in the GPSG book, that's no
problem. This is a default inheritance mechanism - since the
bar level is already specified, the mother's bar level does
not get handed down - to do so would give rise to
inconsistency.

Now the nice feature of that is that you can then treat
bar level as the sort of information that **is** propagated by
the HFC. Previous treatments have not permitted that. Why is

that a nice thing to do? You get a rather curious consequence, namely that recursion is the default situation with rules like this. So rules that introduce an adverb, like (11-12), by default get recursion.

Now of course that's in flat contradiction to what people like Jackendoff (1977) have said. But then constructions like this were a severe embarassment to Jackendoff, so this turns Jackendoff on his head. Instead of saying that these are the bizarre, 'out-in-left-field' constructions, this says that these are the primary ones. So that's one kind of nice consequence, at least it's nice if you think that's the right way to go.

The other nice consequence of treating information about whether something is a phrase or lexical as a head feature, is that you then get its propagation automatically in coordination. The point here is that when you coordinate two noun phrases, what you get is a noun phrase; when you coordinate two verb phrases, what you get is a verb phrase; when you coordinate two sentences, what you get is a sentence. It is normally, possibly always, the case, that the bar level of the two or more daughter conjuncts is the same as that of the mother. If the properties of the daughter conjuncts are theirs simply in virtue of coordination being a multi-headed construction, then if the phrasal status of something is the sort of thing that is manipulated by the HFC, then that just falls out for free. That's another consequence.

I'm actually doing something I didn't intend to do at the moment: I'm trying to motivate this analysis. But its main purpose here is illustrative of the use of a default mechanism within syntax. That analysis may be wrong, but it at least has some arguments going for it, and it is a default inheritance mechanism and it's being used in a superficially very different kind of domain to the lexical domains I was just sketching.

Now I want to give a final case that is even further afield from what you might think these mechanisms would apply to. This is the theory of implicature and presupposition, that Scott Soames and I developed independently in the '70s (Gazdar 1979, Soames 1979). I don't want to say anything about the merits of this theory. Indeed it's known to be inadequate in various respects.

However, it can be seen, with the wisdom of hindsight, as a default inheritance theory.

As you're all probably aware, many words and construction types in natural language give rise to certain potential presuppositions. A verb like <u>stop</u> gives rise to the presupposition that something was going on, something that subsequently stopped. A verb like <u>regret</u>, as in (14), presupposes that I missed the workshop. Of course I haven't, so that would be an anomalous thing to say.

(14)   I regret having missed the workshop.

Now these presuppositions get inherited. When you put a verb like <u>regret</u> deep inside some large and complicated sentence, the presupposition associated with <u>regret</u> may or may not be inherited by the whole sentence. This happens, not in any kind of random way, but in some completely systematic and apparently predictable way. There was a literature in the 1970s on how this worked. The same problem arises with implicatures (this bit of terminology coming from Grice 1975). When you say (15),

(15) Some of the post-graduates were at the party.

you're typically heard as implying that not all of them were. If we embed that in some large and complicated sentence, does that still imply that not all of the post-graduates were at the party? Well, sometimes it does, and sometimes it doesn't. The Gazdar and Soames account of these phenomena was a theory about when it does and when it doesn't. The way it worked is shown in (16).

(16)   Gazdar-Soames Pragmatic Theory

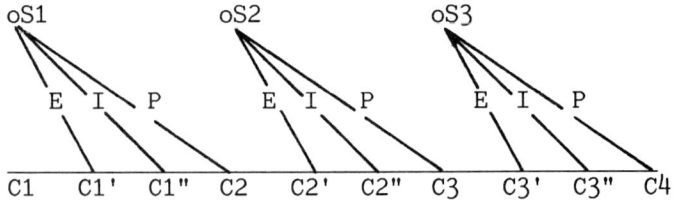

The line represents the passage of time - well it's really

pseudo-time, bits of it are time, and other bits aren't. We're in some context C1 which we can take to be mutually accepted beliefs, or whatever your theory of context is, and we utter sentence S1. That moves us to a new context C1', in which all the entailments E of S1 are added to context C1.

This is a very idealized world in which there are no disagreements. Everything that is said is believed by everybody and so on. Our first step is to move to context C1' augmented with all the entailments. The next step (and this is what I mean by pseudo-time, since this is just a formal ordering, not a genuine temporal ordering) is to augment context C1' with all the implicatures I that you can assemble on sentence S1. And by 'assemble', I just literally mean pulling them all out and adding them together, not doing anything fancier than that. You add all those that are consistent with C1' in order to form C1". Then finally, (although of course there's no notion of process here, it's just static definition) you add all the presuppositions P of S1 (again assembled just by lumping them all together) which are consistent with the context C1", which you've got by augmenting it with the implicatures. So then you arrive at C2 which is the context in which the next sentence S2 is uttered. Then you go through the routine again.

So it's a theory about how entailments, implicatures and presuppositions augment contexts, in a very idealized model - one speaker giving a monologue of utterly uncontroversial material. My point here is not to defend this or to elaborate it or anything, just to show it to you as an instance that can be seen in retrospect as a kind of default inheritance mechanism. And indeed there's a paper by Mercer & Reiter (1982) that does construe the presuppositional part of this theory in terms of a default logic. They make a point which I think is worth pulling out here. They comment on my work and say that what I did was basically ad hoc. They don't mean ad hoc in the linguist's sense, namely that there was no linguistic motivation for it. Their comment was addressed to the formal side of the theory. I developed a bit of formal apparatus that said what this diagram says. But the formal apparatus came out of nowhere. I just spent two years of my doctoral research time staring into space until I developed this thing. It doesn't relate to any other formal apparatus, it doesn't have any other use except this. So from the point of view of a logician it's ad hoc.

What's interesting about the Mercer & Reiter paper is that they show that you can reconstrue all this in terms of their default logic, which can also be used to reconstrue the networks you've been looking at. There's another paper coauthored by Reiter, this time with Etherington (Etherington & Reiter 1983), in which they discuss using Reiter's default logic to reconstruct the eagle/penguin/bird net I exhibited earlier (9).

So I think there is an advantage to be gained - namely avoiding the logician's sense of ad hoc - by taking this kind of perspective on various things that you might want to do with default inheritance mechanisms in linguistics - standing back and saying 'maybe we can have a general theory of such and such a kind'. But of course it's possible that we may not. It may be that the sort of default inheritance theory we need for this case is actually going to turn out to be formally different, interestingly formally logically different, from the sort you would need in the lexical case. It wouldn't be a priori surprising, because this is such a very different domain. However, at least standing back and seeing that they're similar allows us to ask the question, which we can't if one of them's buried in the pragmatics literature and the other is somewhere else.

Well, I'm coming to the end and I'm not going to do my section three. However, I would like to say one or two things to take some of the positive edge off this. I think this is an illustration where linguists who are interested in these matters, but not at all interested in computational linguistics or engineering, could usefully look at the AI literature, for example, particularly the recent AI literature, on networks - stuff like Etherington & Reiter (1983), work by Touretsky (1984) and Brachman (1985) and so on. There's also more exotic, but closely related, work on default logic - by Mercer and Reiter (1982), Bob Moore (1985) (who's here), McDermott & Doyle (1980), and so on, which ties up with this.

When you do go and look at that literature, as I've been doing recently, you realize somewhat to your distress, in this case my distress, that actually this stuff is not anywhere near as fully worked out as one would like. What one would really like to do is go to that literature, pick out ready made formal theories of this stuff and import it into linguistics. But you can't really do that. It appears to have been the case, and there are people here probably in a position to correct me if I'm wrong, that until at least 1980 people who were using the network notations were really deeply confused in various fundamental ways about what they were doing and what the status of it was. As far as I can tell, much of the recent literature has been attempting to sort out the confusion and to make sense of what had been done.

Now there's a bit of a moral here. It's a moral that's not one that needs to be drawn for people with a computational background, but I think does for linguists. Just because somebody's got an implementation of something doesn't mean that they've got a theory of it. Unfortunately the cases I've given you, de Smedt and FPW, are in their present state simply implementations. They used a couple of different object-oriented programming languages to implement lexicons that did the sort of thing that I said they did. But as far as I know there's no abstract declarative theory of what those lexicons are. That's what one needs if one's going to do theoretical linguistics. One probably needs it if one's going to do what they're doing as well.

So the issue of the implicit semantics of default inheritance networks seems to be the absolutely crucial one. One route to go is the Etherington & Reiter route, using default logics. That doesn't actually seem to me an attractive route, at least not for these cases of lexicon and morphology; my sense is - and I don't have any arguments here, this is really just concluding back-of-the-head remarks - that there's much more power there than one wants and one can get away with a much simpler semantics for such devices, such formalisms - for those applications. Maybe you need the other for the general knowledge representation issues that are addressed in AI. But for the particular linguistic applications I've talked about, (though not the last one, which I suspect gets you into the full horror of default logic) my hunch is that something much simpler and more straightforward will do. Had I allowed myself time for the third section I would have talked about a possible route into that. But I didn't.

Karen SPARCK JONES: What is the moral for natural language

processing? You carefully said at the beginning that shoving things together doesn't [necessarily] mean that there's any real fertilization - in particular, you can use some of the formal apparatus and concepts of one field, for your own purpose, without implying that this generates a new synthesis. Now you're saying 'let's make the assumption that AI has got all this stuff about default inheritance nicely tidied up'.

GAZDAR: I wasn't.

SPARCK JONES: Let's imagine that. Then you might say 'this will serve our purposes - this is very nice for us as theoretical linguists'. And we say, 'how nice it is for us to be useful'. But what do we get back from it? Maybe you don't think anything.

GAZDAR: No, I don't think you do, at least not immediately. The problem with what I called 'the conventional view of the relation' is that it attributes to linguistics what linguistics really hasn't got to offer. It pretends to have them to offer, but really doesn't. The moral is that one shouldn't waste too much time looking for things that aren't there. Another moral is that it behoves computational linguists to do theoretical computational linguistics and applied computational linguistics in parallel. They're going to have to do that, since linguists aren't doing theoretical computational linguistics for them, for the most part. In this particular instance, here's a case of something developed over in computer science/AI, which is an illustration of the kind of thing that linguists should be thinking about - a novel formal technique that has wide applicability.

SPARCK JONES: So it's entirely a contingent matter, that we might or might not get something back, but we should have no expectations about it.

GAZDAR: Yes.

Ron KAPLAN: I want to defend linguists a little bit. But first I want to say that I agree with your assessment that linguists don't do formalisms, rather that is something that comes from computer science and computational linguistics. One of the reasons that Chomsky has been so successful all these years is that he's the one guy in that whole area who has significantly changed the formalism. All the others are merely rearranging things.

GAZDAR: But he doesn't really any more.If you look through the stuff he's written in the last ten years, you'll barely find an alpha. Counting alphas is a crude metric, but it'll do.

KAPLAN: Generally, your assessment of the vast majority of present day linguists and their motivations and activities is probably correct. They're not writing grammars, many of them are not going out and getting the crucial facts and so forth. But if that is true of the majority it's not true of all. There is something that linguists who really do linguistics do bring to the table - they have a vast understanding of the facts of language. I used to think I could do linguistics, for example; I was doing ATN grammars in the early days. Then I met some real linguists and started to work with them. There's such a vast difference in their talent for perceiving and organizing facts, even pre-theoretically. I think there really is a difference in the skills of people from these two disciplines. I can fiddle around with formalisms in a way that, say, Joan Bresnan can't. But she has a grasp of the data - and what matters are her intuitions about the data, where the generalizations are likely to lie - that goes way beyond anything I can ever conceive of. I think a linguist who really does linguistics well can bring back to NLP or CL a real sense of what the descriptive problem is - what kind of data bear on the problem, where to go look for the data, how to look for the data.

GAZDAR: I was concerned to highlight a disparity between the PR and the actuality. I don't think that linguists are worthless people who do nothing at all.

To make your point, which I forgot to make. The closest analogy I can think of would be the surgeon's knowledge of the human body. I take it that there are all kinds of things that surgeons know about people's insides - say, that fat people have their spleens displaced to the right, that kind of thing. There are lots of things that you don't find out by reading medical text books, but you do by talking to surgeons. It seems to me that what many linguists are good at is that; you can find out an awful lot by talking to them that you don't by reading their papers.

KAPLAN: Or even by going out and pretending to do linguistics yourself, if you're not that well-trained or competent, as several of us are not.

I wanted to make one further point about this interdisciplinary foolishness. Again much of what you say is correct. But there is a legitimate new discipline where the particular talents, skills and interests of linguists, computational linguists, and psycholinguists can relate to each other. That's where we take, as **the** intellectual problem we're concerned with, the question of how it is people understand, learn and produce sentences in their languages. You can go about that in various ways. One particular way is to make the assumption that there's some common core of knowledge for all those behaviours, and that store of knowledge is what linguists should be characterizing. The question then remains, how does that relate to computational intepretations and psychological models. But there is an enterprise that does integrate all the disciplines. Small subsets of people have taken that seriously. Some of that emerged from the Sloan [Foundation] effort. So it's slightly misleading if you say there was just a random mixture of people. There really is a serious interdisciplinary area there. But perhaps it doesn't fall within any of the original disciplines.

Bob MOORE: Do you know of any examples from linguistics that suggest a need for interacting defaults? - because that's one of the big technical problems of the formal work that's been done on defaults.

GAZDAR: I think at least the FPW **implementation** fits multiple inheritance. A question not addressed at all in that paper is what happens when you get clashes between information from the multiple sources of inheritance. I know of nothing else in linguistics that has anything to say on the matter at all. It's something I've been thinking about.

KAPLAN: I have a technical question. These unification based theories, they're descriptive theories which have propositions in them in the form of equations or whatever. Even though they're propositional, they're not full first order predicate calculus, because they're really quantification free - all the quantifiers are universal. I wonder, when you go to these default logics, is there a special case of default logics without the quantification, that is what is needed for linguistic cases?

Henry THOMPSON: It goes exactly the other way. I think there is quantification in the system Gerald outlined, in the worst case.

KAPLAN: You get interactions of existentials and universals?

THOMPSON: I think that's there. There's a comment in Stu [Shieber]'s paper (this volume) - unfortunately he's out of the room at the moment - about the potential existence of negation in the logic that underlies the HFC in the default system Gerald was talking about. My sense is that it is that complicated, but I don't know exactly how complicated, because I don't know what the questions are. I'm sympathetic to a lot of what Gerald says, but I have to be a little bit more negative than he is.

The inheritance mechanisms of the 'ERIC isa EAGLE' variety bear a lot of relevance to the morphological examples. I'm not at all convinced that that goes very far towards a theoretical foundation for feature defaults and inheritance mechanisms, which are the other example that Gerald used. There's an obvious distinction in that there is a directionality in the simple cases that isn't present, or anywhere near as obvious, in the syntactic case. There is also a distinction in that the hierarchies in all the other cases are tight hierarchies with a 'member' link at the bottom. That's really not the generalization you want at all for the tree structures you see in the syntactic case. For these reasons, and some others, I think the formal foundation of the feature mechanism that Gerald talked about in the syntactic case is going to turn out very different, and rather more complicated, than the formal mechanisms for the inheritance networks, whether there's multiple inheritance or not.

GAZDAR: I think that what you call the lack of directionality, which I call bidirectionality, may get you into graphs with cycles in, which are much more complicated objects than graphs without cycles in, but they're all in the same space.

KAPLAN: It's not clear they get you into circular graphs. There's a way of thinking about the structures as being described. The structures you come up with are not cyclical.

It's only in your description of them that you have what
looks like a cycle.

THOMPSON: The problem that you have to take on board is that
the dimensionality of the pictures appears to be the same in
the two cases - the basic mechanism (not underlined) and the
inherited properties (underlined) in (9). The
dimensionality of the morphological and syntactic cases
appears to be the same. But that's misleading. In the
syntactic case you can't actually fold the multiple
dimensions down into the page in that way. The relation you
end up needing is between sets of trees, not between
individuals as you have in the morphological case. The truth
of the matter is that the defaults of syntactic features
are, as you said, properties of whole categories (in fact
whole trees, but certainly sub-trees). The relationships are
between trees, whereas the relationships in the
morphological case and the 'ERIC isa EAGLE' case are
relationships between sets, or individuals, and that's a lot
simpler.

MOORE: In the syntactic case, if there's any quantification,
isn't it normally bounded quantification? - you're dealing
with some restricted set of values of features - so in
principle you could expand that out into a purely
propositional case. You'll be happy to know that the
propositional case for all the default logics I'm familiar
with is at least decidable. Whereas the general first-order
case is normally worse than undecidable - in some cases the
sets of 'theorems' are not even recursively enumerable.

THOMPSON: That means we're OK for English and we're worried
about Swedish. What you just said makes one concerned about
the finiteness of the category vocabulary.

KAPLAN: No, but for any particular language, or for any
particular grammar of a particular language, the grammar has
all the features in it that could possibly be mentioned -
finitely specified.

THOMPSON: Not if there are recursive categories.

KAPLAN: So you're not talking about GPSG anymore.

THOMPSON: Sure I am. As it says very carefully in the book
(Gazdar et al 1985), we are able to avoid recursive

categories because we are focusing on English. But there is at least suggestive evidence that in other languages, we are not going to be able to avoid recursive categories. You [Gazdar] may want to take that back or I may be misrepresenting you.

GAZDAR: Your point, that if you allow recursive categories, then there isn't just a finite set of possible expansions, is right. But that still might keep you in some restricted space.

KAPLAN: That basically puts you in the LFG-type space, and there are a lot of things that are decidable in that space. I've been looking at an operation in the description language of LFG to represent defaults and interpretation of fragments, which I call 'priority union'. I don't really understand its mathematical properties. It's a thing I'll talk about in my session tomorrow.

THOMPSON: It's clear that there are a number of people splashing around in the same area.

KAPLAN: Splashing each other.

Mitch MARCUS: Are the cases where you want to use this default reasoning going to interact in a way that's going to blow you out of a finite space?

THOMPSON: I hope not. In the contexts that I'm worrying about, category-valued features and defaults tend to be relatively disjoint phenomena.

GAZDAR: That's my sense as well.

THOMPSON: That's a contingent fact of the grammars that one tends to write, rather than a necessary property of the theory at the moment.

GAZDAR: Since the theory doesn't cover them.

THOMPSON: Even if you restrict yourself to non-recursive categories, it seems to be the case that the kind of defaulting mechanisms that you need tend to steer clear of constructing default categories to be the values of category-valued features.

MARCUS: Fine. Another question. In terms of the AI discussions on default reasoning, there are different kinds of situations that one wants to deal with, but they're fairly impoverished. One is the monotonic reasoning case, Bob [Moore (1985)]'s autoepistemic restriction is another interesting case, that seems weaker. I wonder if there's a kind of hierarchy of these things emerging in any interesting sense.

GAZDAR: My sense is that there is, but Bob would be the one to have anything intelligent to say about that.

MOORE: A lot of the uses that have been made of default inheritance in AI are in some sense incomparable, because they're fundamentally different from a pragmatic, in a formal sense, point of view. I've particularly tried to argue in my paper on the subject (Moore, 1985) that default reasoning as the term is used in AI is default conjectural reasoning. Whereas the defaults here are more in the form of default specification. So there's no sense of getting additional information. The defaults in the syntactic and phonological cases are not cancellable, whereas in the pragmatic case, in some instances, they are.

GAZDAR: In the syntactic case, they are.

MOORE: Not in the same sense. This is very difficult to explain.

KAPLAN: Let me try with this. Do you know any cases where you could dispense with default mechanisms by redundantly elaborating grammatical and lexical specifications?

GAZDAR: In the cases I'm most familiar with you could always do that, but you would end up with a horrendous grammar.

KAPLAN: But if it's a substitution for a finite specification then you would expect it to be well-behaved mathematically.

GAZDAR: Yes, and I think in the lexical cases it'll be the same, at least in the cases that have been talked about. What you do with the lexicon that has some recursion in it, or plain iteration, I haven't thought through. One can't assume that lexicons are finite, or rather that the set of words is finite.

KAPLAN: [To Moore] Does that get at the issue?

MOORE: That gets at the issue I was going to deal with next.
I won't try to expand on that pragmatic distinction. As far
as the formal properties are concerned, one would like to
look for special cases. Reiter and his colleagues have
identified a special case of what they call 'normal
defaults', where if all defaults are of the form, 'if p is
possible then p', things are computationally tractable. But
one of the cases you were discussing amounted to 'if it's
possible that p iff q then p iff q'. That might be the same
case, I'm not sure whether p has to be atomic. So some of
the defaults you had in the syntactic case were certainly
more complicated than would suggest any simple restriction
of propositional default logic.

THOMPSON: A difficult question is the interaction of
defaults and well-formedness constraints, which is a
characteristic of GPSG. It's a characteristic of the EAGLE
network, but that aspect of semantic nets seems to me
underdeveloped. It's a question of where 'dead eagles can't
fly' is represented - it's not in the network, it's
somewhere else. There's a way of reconstructing that with
multiple inheritance, which says that there are dead things,
and they inter alia don't fly, and Eric is one of those as
well as an eagle. Then the question becomes one of
resolution in the case of conflicting inheritance.

MARCUS: I'm just thinking of the consequences of defining a
set of dead things. You quickly find yourself in a situation
where you take all implications and create categories for
the things of which the left hand side is true. There are
lots of things that dead animals don't do - they don't play
the piano either.

One other comment, which is not about default
inheritance per se, more about defaults in general. If one
is trying to do a competence theory, where everything is
simply specified, you end up with one kind of story about
defaults which is the restricted kind you're talking about.
If one thinks about the processing case, either for
engineering purposes or as a psychological model, one might
want to bring the entire non-monotonic apparatus to bear, to
allow one to do default reasoning about things that are
incrementally true. In my work I've tried to avoid that, but
it's an interesting possibility - to consider things true by

default until you discover evidence further on in the
sentence that they're false. In some sense it's the
difference between the original ATN approach which was
chronological backtracking, versus the kind of dependency-
directed backtracking that people in AI are working on. To
my knowledge this has not been applied to natural language
understanding. If you set up some state in an ATN, and it
turns out to be wrong, you back up entirely and push on
again. Whereas the rest of the AI literature has moved away
from that to dependency-directed backtracking and even more
subtle kinds of things. From my point of view, it's an
interesting engineering question. What kind of parsers might
result if we try to apply dependency-directed techniques,
the kind of things that Johan de Kleer is doing? Has anybody
done this, Ron?

KAPLAN: I'm sure this kind of thing has been done.

MARCUS: If people here don't know about it, I guess it
hasn't.

KAPLAN: I'm not sure it was interesting.

Mary McGee WOOD: One linguistic theory which is based almost
entirely on this kind of thing is Dick Hudson's (1984) Word
Grammar, which isn't very well known. Since that book was
published he's explicitly started using the isa relation
from AI. He has a network that says 'verb isa word',
'transitive verb isa verb', etc. One interesting consequence
you can get if you push that far enough, which is coming out
in some stuff I've done (Wood 1985), is that you end up
abolishing the lexical component. I'm throwing this out as a
marker for tomorrow really. Once you see the whole thing as
a flexible default network, with priority to the particular,
then you lose any very good justification for putting a
sharpcut-off point across that network and saying, these
things are general enough to be syntax and these thingsare
specific enough to be lexicon. If you're implementing, you
can create a virtual lexicon and virtual syntax by putting a
cut-off point at whatever level suits your application. So
this kind of mechanism, if you use it thoroughly enough, can
have some pretty far-reaching implications for the form of
your grammar.

Graeme RITCHIE: Have you got the ordering sorted out? When
you gave about a dozen default rules, the non-inheritance

ones, you mentioned in passing there was a problem with integration and the notion of ordering if you had a declarative approach.

GAZDAR: There's a solution to that in the book (Gazdar et al 1985). There's an apparatus which does not give rise to the bad cases and which is not particularly ad hoc in its own terms. But it's pretty indigestible stuff. It all hangs on the notion of 'privilege'. It takes me about half an hour to reconstruct what I meant by it whenever I look at it. But it isn't particularly unnatural - it's not hard to reconstruct because it uses weird notions and ad hoc tricks. It's just hard to reconstruct - probably because it's a bad way of doing it. As far as the authors of the book know, it's a solution of sorts.

RITCHIE: It solves all known problems?

GAZDAR: We had a bunch of paradoxes, some of which I showed you, that we were addressing throughout that work. And all the ones we knew about were taken care of by what we developed. There aren't any residual ones that we know of. There may be others - I think it likely that there are, because it feels kind of fragile to me.

References

Brachman, R. 1985. 'I lied about the trees', (or Defaults and Definitions in Knowledge Representation). **AI Magazine**, 6.3.

Chomsky, N. & Halle, M. 1968. **The Sound Pattern of English**. New York: Harper and Row.

Etherington, D.W. & Reiter, R. 1983. On Inheritance Hierarchies with Exceptions. **3rd National Conference on Artificial Intelligence (AAAI)**, (Washington, DC), Proceedings. W. Kaufmann, 104-108.

Flickinger, D., Pollard, C.J. & Wasow, T. 1985. Structure Sharing in Lexical Representation. **23rd Annual Meeting of the Association for Computational Linguistics** (Chicago), Proceedings, 262-267.

Gazdar, G. 1979. **Pragmatics: Implicature, Presupposition and Logical Form.** New York: Academic Press.

Gazdar, G., Klein, E., Pullum, G. & Sag, I. 1985. **Generalized Phrase Structure Grammar.** Oxford: Basil Blackwell.

Grice, H.P. 1975. Logic and Conversation. In Cole, P. & Morgan, J., eds. **Syntax and Semantics 3: Speech Acts.** New York: Academic Press, 41-58.

Halvorsen, P-K. & Withgott, M. 1984. Morphological Constraints on Scandinavian Tone Accent. Technical Report CSLI-84-11, Centre for the Study of Language and Information, Stanford, CA.

Hudson, R.A. 1984. **Word Grammar,** Oxford: Basil Blackwell.

Jackendoff, R. 1977. **X Syntax: A Study of Phrase Structure.** Cambridge, Mass.: MIT Press.

Marantz, A.P. 1984. **On the Nature of Grammatical Relations.** Cambridge, Mass.: MIT Press.

McDermott, D.V. & Doyle, J. 1980. Non-monotonic Logics. **Artificial Intelligence** 13, 401-72.

Mercer, R.E. & Reiter, R. 1982. The Representation of Presuppositions using Defaults. **4th National Conference of the Canadian Society for Computational Studies in Intelligence** (Saskatoon), Proceedings, 103-107.

Moore, R. C. 1985. Semantical Considerations on Non-monotonic Logic. **Artificial Intelligence** 25.1:75-94.

Reiter, R. 1978. On Reasoning by Default. **Theoretical Issues in Natural Language Processing (TINLAP),** 210-218.

de Smedt, K. 1984. Using Object-Oriented Knowledge-Representation Techniques in Morphology and Syntax Programming. O'Shea, T., ed. **ECAI-84: Proceedings of the Sixth European Conference on Artificial Intelligence** (Pisa). Amsterdam: Elsevier, 181-184.

Soames, S. 1979. A Projection Problem for Speaker Presupposition. **Linguistic Inquiry** 10, 623-666.

Touretsky, D.F. 1984. **The Mathematics of Inheritance Systems.** PhD dissertation, Computer Science, Carnegie-Mellon University. Published by Morgan Kaufmann, Los Altos, 1986.

Wood, M. McG. 1985. Language Without the Lexicon: A Computational Model. CCL/UMIST Report 85/2.

Deterministic Parsing and Description Theory

Mitchell P. Marcus

I'd like to tell you this evening about some of the practical, engineering implications of the theory of deterministic parsing that I've worked on in the past (Marcus 1980). The primary focus of my own research has been to pursue computational linguistics as a form of theoretical linguistics - not for engineering purposes but as an account of language. What I'd like to do here, though, is to look at some of the principles behind deterministic parsing and argue that they make for good engineering; this is just the kind of thing that I was arguing for more generally this afternoon. I believe that the same principles that one argues for on scientific grounds may be independently motivated by quite different engineering concerns.

As an aside, I think that it's often useful to be simultaneously interested in both the theoretical and the practical aspects of the same problem. I should also say quite explicitly that solving practical problems is usually just as hard as solving theoretical ones, and that finding the principles of construction of practical systems, what might be called engineering science, is a fairly interesting thing to do. I also ought to note, though, that it's extremely important not to confuse or conflate scientific and engineering concerns, particularly when one is discussing exactly what the implications are of one for the other. I think that it's usually catastrophic when one confuses engineering with theory or vice versa.

First, I'd like to tell you about one real application of deterministic parsing done by Don Hindle, and some quite surprising results that Hindle has achieved in a deterministic parser called Fidditch. The second thing I'll talk about is some new work that Don Hindle and I are now doing together, which we call Description Theory, and sketch that theory somewhat. Partially, this is just to fill you in on some of what we're up to, but the real point is to suggest that Description Theory may provide a solution to what I take to be a particularly thorny engineering problem, namely the problem of limiting the interaction between syntax and semantics in practical systems. From a theoretical point of view, Occam's razor suggests that a theory of natural language processing should separate syntax and semantics as much as possible, parallel to the thesis of the autonomy of syntax in conventional competence linguistics. And this is just what we're trying to do. We're not sure it will work, of course, but it seems to us that we have to find out what the limits of this kind of approach are. But there are other compelling reasons, I think, to try to do just the same thing from an engineering point of view.

The aspects of the theory that I intend to talk about come out of a somewhat nonstandard view of the cognitive processing of language. Hindle and I view language analysis as flowing unidirectionally through a series of processors, if you will. Analysis is performed as information flows through the system, with the constraint, crucially, that each aspect of the system is to say all and only what it can say accurately about the current utterance, passing the predications that it makes on to the next component incrementally. Each component will be sensitive to a subset of the predicates passed through it, and may well make new predications on the basis of these. It may well ignore many other predicates, but it will pass them through to the next component in the pipeline. It may even take some of the predicates passed to it and treat them as if they had a different semantics than that intended by the asserting component; in fact, I'm going to show you one predicate central to Description Theory that we believe gets reinterpreted in just this way. So we view the language processor as a pipeline of processors, each of which monotonically adds to a growing stream of predications. We also want to suggest that each component can be fundamentally characterized by the kinds of predicates that, first of all, it's allowed to add, and, secondly, that it interprets.

While Don Hindle and I have been led to this point of view because of theoretical concerns, I'd like to suggest this evening that there are fairly obvious engineering reasons to adopt a similar architecture for practically motivated systems as well. As Simon points out in **The Sciences of the Artificial** (1981), things get hairy at the interface between components, and if all the boxes in a system have to talk to each other, then you get n^2 interfaces and things quickly get out of hand. So my intention this evening is to focus on engineering implications of a range of work on deterministic parsing theory, as well as other implications that may follow from the modified framework that Don and I call Description Theory.

Let me start off with a brief sketch of what I call the 'determinism hypothesis' (Marcus 1980), the working assumption that the syntax of a natural language can be parsed by a purely left-to-right 'deterministic' mechanism. 'Deterministic' is in quotes here - the intended meaning is that such a parser works without simulating some kind of non-deterministic mechanism through either parallelism or backup, that such a system indelibly constructs just the structure that it needs as it parses and then goes on. I've argued for this for the syntactic component - I'm really not sure that it holds for, say, semantics, and there are certainly aspects of cognition and general problem solving that are invoked during comprehension for which it doesn't hold.

From an empirical point of view, this determinism hypothesis seems highly counter-intuitive, because of sentences like (1) and (2):

(1) Have the students take the exam!
(2) Have the students taken the exam?

When a parser sees the beginning of these sentences, it can't know whether <u>have</u> is an auxiliary or a main verb, so it doesn't know whether the sentence will turn out to be an imperative or a yes-no question. Because of this, of course, it doesn't know whether to begin a subordinate clause after <u>have</u> or not, as it must if the sentence is an imperative. The initial insight behind deterministic parsing is to note that if the parser can see three chunks of structure ahead of where it's fully determined the

syntactic structure (where constituents like noun phrases,
verb phrases and the like all count as chunks), it can see
enough of the following context to decide reliably what to
do next, by and large. In the case of sentences (1) and
(2), the single word have is the first chunk, the noun
phrase the students is the second chunk, and either take or
taken is the third chunk. In one case, the third chunk
provides enough context to diagnose between the two
structures that are possible. If the third chunk is take,
then the parser knows that the overall structure must be an
imperative, as in (1).   If the third chunk is taken, you
might think that it must be a yes-no question as in (2); but
in fact, as people have noted, there are sentences like (3):

(3) Have the students taken to the principal!

In this case, with taken, the correct structure cannot be
determined within three items, and I have a whole
psychological story about what happens in this case. The
claim is that people by and large only say sentences which
the parser can analyze in this size of window, and if they
utter a sentence like (3), then the hearer initially
misanalyzes the sentence - is led down the 'garden path', we
say - and needs to do special error correction, after
becoming aware of the misanalysis. From an engineering
point of view, if this deterministic approach turns out to
be a useful technique (and part of what I want to argue here
is that solid evidence now exists that this approach is a
useful technique) then this becomes an extremely efficient
way to parse because such a parser gives linear time
behaviour, as opposed to the n^2 behaviour (or worse) of most
parsing algorithms.

The way such a mechanism works is roughly the
following. The grammar consists of a set of context-free
phrase structure rules, augmented by a set of local
transformations, if you will, associated with each position
on the left-hand side of each rule. Each of these
transformations is actually just a pattern-action
production, where the pattern matches against the one, two
or three chunks that I just talked about, and the actions
are taken from a very limited set of actions (a reasonable
number is three or four). Here are some of the local
transformations associated with parsing the subject of a
sentence in a small example grammar:

(4)   S -> NP VP PP

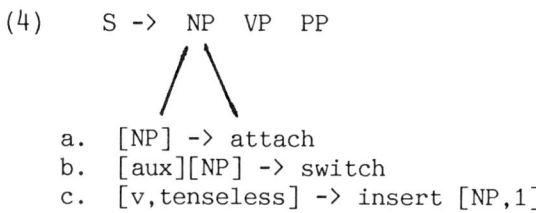

    a. [NP] -> attach
    b. [aux][NP] -> switch
    c. [v,tenseless] -> insert [NP,1]

The fact that these rules are associated with the NP position of the S rule means that they will only be used when the parser is looking for the subject of a sentence. Rule (4a) just adds a noun phrase to the structure when one occurs as the first chunk. Rule (4b) says that if the first chunk the parser is examining is an auxiliary verb, and the second chunk is a noun phrase, then switch the first chunk and the second chunk (thinking of each chunk as occupying some kind of hook). This rule is intended to handle what linguists call "aux inversion", which happens at the beginning of questions. Rule (4c) is for handling imperatives. It says that if the first chunk the parser encounters is a tenseless verb, then the parser should insert an empty noun phrase into the first hook, which shifts whatever is there onto the second hook, and so on. The fourth operation that we think the parser needs to use is to be able to insert one of a language-particular set of specified lexical items like of to undo the deletion in phrases like all the books, and the like.

Let's look at how these rules will begin the analysis of an input like (5):

(5)   Is John ...

We'll assume that the parser somehow recognized it should parse an S, and so began scanning the phrase structure rule (4). First the auxiliary Is comes into the buffer and occupies the first hook, and then John gets analyzed as an NP and occupies the second hook as the result of simple extensions of what I've just told you about. But now rule (4b) applies, since Is is an auxiliary and John is an NP. The rule flips Is and John, leaving John in the first place of the buffer, and Is in the second. But now rule (4a) applies, since John occupies the first hook, and this NP is attached to the S node, resulting in this partial structure (6):

(6)   S

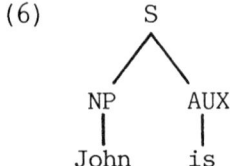

The parser will then try to match another set of rules
associated with the verb phrase node in just the same way.

Given the topic of this workshop, I don't intend to
argue this evening that this theory can be defended in terms
of theoretical linguistics; what I'd like to do here is
simply to present some evidence that shows that this model
actually works pretty well in practice. One needs to
demonstrate a couple of things to show that this model is
computationally adequate for the task of parsing natural
language. The first is to build a large grammar for such a
mechanism that handles a wide range of linguistic phenomena
fairly reliably, and show that it can build plausible
linguistic structures deterministically. The second, as
many people have been fast to note, is to demonstrate that
some extension of this deterministic approach can solve the
problem of lexical ambiguity. The argument goes (and it's a
perfectly good one) that much of the problem of apparent
non-determinism in natural language is due to this rampant
lexical ambiguity that language seems to embrace; as Herb
Clark has pointed out, in English any noun can be verbed.
There would appear to be a real question as to whether a
purely deterministic model can handle this kind of pervasive
low-level ambiguity.

Both of these have been successfully demonstrated, at
least to my satisfaction, within a parser called Fidditch
that Don Hindle built a few years ago (Hindle 1983), whose
architecture is a variant of my Parsifal parser (Marcus
1980). Actually, Fidditch differs from Parsifal in a number
of interesting ways, most of which were motivated by the
desire to cover a wide range of English. Don built this
parser because he and Tony Kroch wanted to do a statistical
analysis of a large corpus of transcribed sociolinguistic
interviews. They had about 15,000 sentences and fragments,
and the coverage of Fidditch for this corpus is pretty good.
I would guesstimate that it handles 70-85% of the fragments
correctly. I've pushed Don unsuccessfully to try to come up
with some specific number, and suggested this figure. Don's

response was that he hadn't checked enough structure to see
what the accuracy was overall, but that he thought my
estimate was high. (I should note that very few of the
parsers we hear about are designed to handle a wide range of
unrestricted text, and that the ability of these parsers to
analyze this kind of material is very limited.)

Let me give you a sense of Fidditch's coverage by
telling you how I typically demonstrate what this parser can
and can't do. I usually grab a book from my shelf; usually
I'll pull out my copy of **Situations and Attitudes** (Barwise &
Perry 1983), which seems to be the book that everybody's
pulling out these days. (This is a mention of situation
semantics rather than a use of it, by the way.) I open it to
some page at random, put my finger down on the page and type
in the first three sentences that I see. Typically,
Fidditch will get one of the three sentences fully correct,
and it will make two or three mistakes total in analyzing
the other two, with the bulk of its analysis of each of
these sentences by and large correct. (Since it's a
deterministic parser, it only produces one analysis per
sentence, of course.) I'm fairly convinced that most of its
errors are due to the fact that it runs with a lexicon of
only 2000 items, including some large number of closed class
items. Another, related, big source of error is that it
doesn't know the complement structure for most verbs, so it
often makes mistakes due to incorrect guesses about
complements. My guess is that if it had a large lexicon and
some knowledge of what kinds of complements which verbs
take, then it would probably be able to get two out of my
three random test sentences correct, with maybe one residual
error on the third.

How does Fidditch get along with such a small lexicon?
It handles words that it doesn't know simply by assuming
that any word not in its lexicon must be either a noun or a
verb, and then letting its lexical ambiguity rules figure
out which of these two is the case. This implies, of
course, that it handles lexical ambiguity pretty well, and
in fact it seems to. About half of its grammar (which
contains about 700 rules) is to cover lexical ambiguity. So
lexical ambiguity, surprisingly perhaps, turns out not to be
a terrible problem for deterministic parsing after all,
although neither I nor Don, I'm fairly certain, would want
to claim that this is a solved problem yet. And the success
of Fidditch on unconstrained transcribed speech demonstrates

that parsing deterministically with a moderate size grammar appears to be no more difficult that parsing with non-deterministic schemes.

Fidditch's behaviour when it runs into trouble is a good illustration of one special property of deterministic parsers that may well be of special importance for doing a wide range of practical problems: because a deterministic parser is always working on a single analysis, rather than lots of analyses in parallel, say, it always has some fragment constructed if it can't continue its analysis for some reason. If the parser loses, it just stops, hands off whatever it has built, and then starts analyzing whatever input remains. It can be locally confused but usually the confusions are brief and then it goes on. There are certainly lots of applications where this property is of real value. Machine translation is one. If an MT system loses while parsing some part of a sentence, it's important that the machine can recognize that it failed, and it's also important that it can go on and then parse the rest. Essentially what you want is an analysis that says 'here are the pieces of the sentence that I'm sure of and you can translate these, and here are some fragments whose structure I'm not too sure of'. And Fidditch does pretty well with that. It's worth mentioning in passing, by the way, that Fidditch **never** attaches prepositional phrases or relative clauses; given just syntax, a deterministic system can't do modifier attachment with any certainty.

One last comment about Fidditch's speed: it parses at around 10 words per second on a VAX*/750, so it's not slow. It's written in compiled Franz Lisp. The grammar's running interpreted, the interpreter itself is compiled and it uses a bunch of subtle tricks to do the rule matching.

Now I'd like to turn to another kind of parsing of fragments - this time where the fragments exist in the parser's input itself. I want to show you that a simple set of rules added to Fidditch can handle the range of real fragments that occur in naturally spoken discourse. It turns out that a simple deterministic process can decide what material to edit out of the input stream when the

---

* VAX is a trademark of Digital Equipment Corporation

parser comes across one of the phonetic 'self-correction markers' that get produced involuntarily when a speaker suddenly changes his or her mind about what they're going to say. Fidditch can take an input of transcribed speech, with the speech divided into fragments, chock full of self-corrected material and these self-correction markers, and turn out analyses of the underlying full sentences - all deterministically. While it makes mistakes in the analysis of these inputs, it makes far fewer than on the kind of text I discussed above; in large measure because it turns out that the syntactic complexity of spoken language is lower than that of written text, not surprisingly. But Fidditch can determine deterministically exactly what material to edit out in the case of a self-correction with about a two percent error rate. The details of what I'm about to talk about, by the way, are discussed in Hindle (1983).

I think this work on self-correction is important to know about if you're interested in speech recognition in the long term, in building machines that can ultimately understand fluently spoken language, not just carefully pronounced test cases. Many people interested in speech recognition are trying to work with simple grammars, and want to use those simple grammars to constrain the job of the underlying word recognizer. But the fact is that this kind of self-correction happens enormously frequently in speech. A large percentage of the sentences that people utter actually don't go to completion, as you'll see.

The material that Fidditch analyzed came from some sociolinguistic fieldwork at the University of Pennsylvania. A couple of sociolinguists went over to another school in Philadelphia and got some freshmen talking, recorded what they said, and then transcribed the speech. They ended up with things like (7):

(7) **A transcript sample**

    A: (I don't know how he stopped in time.) (I thought he was gonna hit us.) (and he, stopped) (and I was like-- I just got-- I got almost fainted.) (I just sat down.)

    I: (really)

    S: (I was there like-- right in front of school.)

(I was just crossing the street.)

Each of the strings in parentheses is an intonational
sentence, so the periods are more or less gratuitous and
Fidditch ignores them. The commas get treated as minor
phrase boundaries, and these dashes indicate a speech-
editing signal.

There's one important side point to make, given this
kind of input, about the grammar of the spoken language.
It's not important for short-term applications of the
natural language understanding technology, but I believe
it's of crucial importance for long-term applications
involving speech understanding. The point I want to make is
that the grammar of the spoken language is really quite a
bit different from the grammar of the written language. In
fact this is something that Don Hindle has argued (Hindle
1983) following the work of Labov (1978:203), that in fact
there is exceedingly little ungrammaticality in the spoken
language. It's just that the grammar of spoken language is
different. So here (8) are some regular spoken
constructions in American English, at least as spoken in
Philadelphia. While you can't use any of these
constructions in writing, they really are quite standard in
speech.

(8) Regular spoken constructions

   a. What I did I came back and I went to Princeton
      University where I had matriculated originally.
   b. That's the only thing he does is fight.
   c. I imagine there's a lot of them must have had
      some good reasons not to go there.
   d. Oh aaa take the three bus. Will take you to
      Erie and Torresdale, just walk home. It's not
      far from there.

So, for example (8c) shows that in speech the relative
marker can be dropped even in subject relatives, and (8d)
shows that there are lots of contexts in which we can
fluently drop subjects. These are all absolutely standard
constructions in the spoken language. The grammar that
Fidditch uses reflects just this grammar, and not the
grammar of the written language, since it was built to
analyze spoken, not written, language. One key implication
of this is that parsers for spoken language really don't

have to include combinatorially expensive special meta-
mechanisms for handling ungrammaticality if the grammar
writer understands what's going on.

Before I talk about how Fidditch handles self-
corrections, I should show you what the output looks like;
whenever someone tells you they have a parser that parses a
certain input, you need to ask them what it builds. (9b) is
the output it builds for (9a):

(9) Parser output

    a. I-- the-- the guys that I'm-- was telling you
       about were

    b.

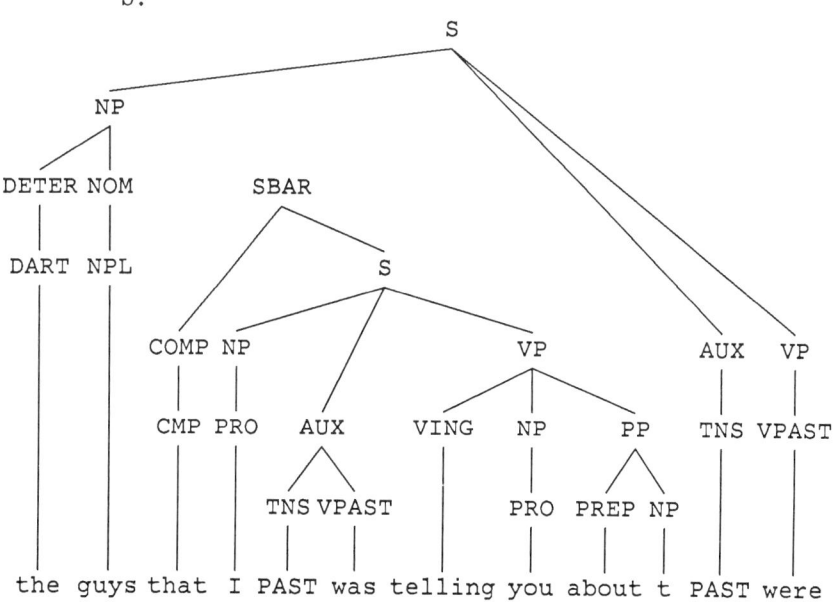

    c. The guys that I was telling you about were.

    d. the guys that t[race] I was telling you about
       t[race]

The underlying sentence here, after self-correction, is
(9c), which is an elliptical answer to a question like "Who

was doing that?". Actually, the parser builds the internal structure of the fragments that it knows were self-corrected out, but it doesn't show those structures in the output mode that I'm showing you here. You might notice that the parser accurately puts back the Wh-moved trace which is the object of the preposition about; the point here is not the version of trace theory which this parser uses, but merely that it builds a fairly rich syntactic structure and that it correctly identifies the gap in this case.

So how does it work? First, it crucially uses the phonetic editing signal transcribed here as a double dash; it looks for a self-correction whenever it notices an editing signal in its transcribed input. (It's important, of course, that this speech was transcribed by someone who didn't know what the editing signals they were asked to detect were to be used for.) Hindle's mechanism uses four rules which are all variants of what you might view as one simple meta-rule, loosely speaking: that whenever the parser sees the same kind of thing on either side of the editing signal, it edits out the first copy. So, whenever the parser sees two copies of either the same surface phonetic string or of the same lexical category, one on either side of an editing signal, or whenever it sees two constituents, either complete or incomplete, of the same category on either side of an editing signal, then it just deletes the first copy. (That there are separate rules for complete and incomplete constituent types is an artefact of the state of the theory at the time that Hindle implemented Fidditch, but unfortunately, it's still a problem we have now.) To these four versions of one underlying rule, one other rule needs to be added: a rule that restarts the parsing of a top level sentence whenever one of a special set of words like oh and well occurs immediately after an editing signal. In all these cases, by the way, the material which is edited out can't be simply discarded, because it turns out that people can use pronouns to refer to phrases in edited fragments. It's useful to view the resulting structure as a three-dimensional syntactic structure with the fragments stacked up, as it were, 'under' the correct analysis.

Here are some naturally occurring examples of cases where the two simplest of these rules apply, just to give you the flavour of the rule set. Deletion of copies of identical phonetic material occurs in sentences like (10):

(10) Surface copy editor

   a. Well if they'd-- if they'd had a knife I wou--
      I wouldn't have been here today.

   b. I just know that-- that it was a lot of-- of
      childish and-- and immature kind of name
      calling.

In (10a), If they'd-- if they'd triggers the deletion of
identical phonetic material, as does I wou-- I wouldn't: in
both cases we delete the first copy. Examples of restarts
triggered by words like oh and well following an editing
signal are utterances like (11):

(11) Restarts

   a. That's the way if-- well everybody was so
      stoned anyway.

   b. But when I was young I went in-- oh I was
      nineteen years old.

How well does it work? Extremely well, I think. Hindle
recently tested this set of rules on 1500 sentences like
those we saw a minute ago (Table 1).

Table 1: Self correction rule application

total sentences	1512	
total without edit signal	1108	(72%)
Editing rule	Applications	
expunction of edit signals only	128	(24%)
surface copy	161	(29%)
category copy	47	(9%)
stack copy	148	(27%)
restart	32	(8%)
failures	17	(3%)
remaining unclear and ungrammatical	11	(2%)

Of course, one has to check each one of the parser's analyses by hand; you need to look at the structure and see if the word string without the material that the parser edits out makes sense. So out of 1500 sentences 1108 were without any editing signal, but of the remaining 404 sentences Hindle's rules handled 97% of the sentences with editing signals in them correctly. This includes cases where there was nothing to be deleted at all. In these cases, the parser stopped at the editing signal, discovered that there weren't two copies of the same material on either side of the signal, and kept on going. I should make it clear, by the way, that these figures indicate success in deciding what material should be edited out, and not necessarily for successfully analyzing the remaining material. Failures of this rule set to flag the correct material amount to 3%, and 2% of the sentences remain unclear or ungrammatical, meaning that the original sentences are unacceptable in the spoken (as well as written) language. By the way, this figure is consistent with Labov's figure (1978:203), where a manual check showed that only about 2% of sentences in the spoken language are truly ungrammatical.

To give you a sense of what these true ungrammaticalities look like, here are some samples from the 1500 sentence corpus (12):

   (12) True ungrammaticalities

      a. I've seen it happen is two girls fight.

      b. Today if you beat a guy wants to blow your head off for something.

      c. And aa a lot of the kids that are from our neighbourhood-- there's one section that the kids aren't too-- think they would usually-- the-- the ones that were the-- the drop outs and the stoneheads.

This work shows that a simple extension of the theory of deterministic parsing may well prove to be crucial when we try to do spoken language understanding on fairly fluent natural speech. As a whole, I believe that Hindle's work has demonstrated that deterministic parsing really is tractable enough to withstand industrial-strength application.

An important fact about this work is that Hindle is a good linguist. One problem with my deterministic parsing model is that it doesn't give you much freedom. If you don't find an appropriate analysis of some linguistic phenomenon, you can't get a grammar to work at all. The experience of the few linguists who have tried to build grammars for this kind of parser is that to get an analysis that will stand up depends upon finding rules that are natural for this framework. It's tricky. But if you have some training in linguistics, and if you try to capture the relevant structural generalizations, then your grammars will tend to work.

Just to summarize, I've really wanted to make two rather different points in what I've had to say so far. First, it looks like this deterministic theory will bear all the weight that one might want to put on it for practical short-term applications, and, second, it actually looks like this model has a shot at doing a fairly remarkable range of things in terms of analyzing the fragments of spoken language. It's hard to see how to get a conventional non-deterministic machine to deal with this kind of fragmentary input - and one thing that's crucial is that you get lots of it.

Let me push along to a discussion of 'Description Theory' (Marcus et al 1983), and in particular to a phrase structure analyzer within this framework. Description Theory takes as central the notion that each component doing linguistic processing should say all and only what it can say with certainty and then just stop. As a result, what the phrase structure analyzer builds is strangely impoverished; it will say all that it can with certainty given only phrase structure information, and that isn't very much, as it turns out. The output representation has to be correct, as far as it goes, and the phrase structure analyzer can't even use information about verb complement structure, which we suppose comes from another component which handles predicate/argument structure. How impoverished this representation is may not be entirely clear from the examples I'll discuss, but I'll try to point it out as I go along.

The crucial idea here is that the analyzer is going to build a single description which turns out to be true of an entire family of syntactic structures. The philosophy underlying D-theory is that a sentence is a physical entity, an acoustic entity, in much the same sense that this chair in front of me is a physical entity. And a parse of a sentence has to be viewed as a description of that sentence in the same way that my visual faculty parses the scene including this chair. So after I recognize the chair [a moulded fiberglass chair, in this case] as an entity, as part of recognizing that it's a chair, presumably, I break it up into having two arms, a back and a seat, even though of course the distinction between the arms and the back is just virtual. I derive a functional description of this thing, a functional description of an object which in some real sense isn't there in the world at all per se. Similarly, one parses a sonic utterance up into words, even though the words aren't physically distinct, and then the phrase structure analyzer in your head describes that putative word string at this somewhat higher level of functional detail. The key point is that syntactic structures aren't entities in my head; what I have in my head is a description of a syntactic structure which is imputed to be out there in the world.

One consequence of this view is that the primary predicate that Description Theory uses to describe syntactic structure is not the customary 'directly dominates' but merely 'dominates' (13):

(13) D (vp1, np1) :   vp1
                            .
                            .
                           np1

Roughly speaking, the motivation for this is that the parser has to build up a description of what's going on incrementally. The parser can be sure, we claim, that one node dominates another, but it may turn out, given more information, that the first node dominates the second only indirectly, through some other node. One other unusual consequence of this view is that np1 and vp1 in this description aren't to be taken as nodes but rather as **names for nodes**; the nodes themselves are taken to be out there in the world, much like the putative back and arms of this chair. The reason that this is important is that names and descriptions in terms of those names have a rather nice property. If you have two descriptions, each in terms of a different name, you can't tell whether the names are

coreferent or not, if the descriptions are compatible. So
if I know the facts in (14), there's no way that I can tell
whether x = y or not. Given just these facts, the
descriptions are compatible, so there's no way to tell
whether x and y are names that stand for the same individual
or not; without more information, one just can't tell.

(14)   Male (x)   Male (y)
       Black-hair (x)   Bearded (y)
       First-name (x,"Aki")   Last-name (y, "Tanaka")
       Age (x, >30)

But if I add (15), then I know for certain that $x \neq y$,
because now I know that the descriptions are **incompatible**,
because x is over 30, and y is clearly not.

(15)   Age (y, <20)

Description Theory, as you'll see, takes crucial advantage
of this funny property of names and descriptions.

     What I intend to do in the rest of my talk is first to
briefly show how D-theory has important implications for the
analysis of conjunctions and other coordinate structures.
Then I'll discuss the parsing of simple Japanese sentences,
and then turn to an interesting ambiguity in Japanese
involving the particle no. In Japanese, this particle marks
genitives, appositives, and flags headless relatives, as
well as several other usages which I won't go into. The
problem this creates for a parser is that it's often
completely unclear which one of these usages it has
encountered; it looks as if the parser has to guess in these
cases, or else immediately bring lots of world knowledge to
bear. We want to argue that a D-theory analyzer will build
a description which is, as it were, ambiguous between all of
these usages. Finally, I'll turn back to conjunction in
English, sketching an approach to gapping in a little more
detail. By the way, what we have to date is still a highly
underspecified description of a theory of conjunction; all
I'm going to show is that the descriptions we get are
ambiguous in the right kinds of ways. We clearly need a
semantic theory to go with this phrase structure account,
and we don't have one yet.

     Consider the problem that sentences like (16) present
for a deterministic parser:

(16)   They sell red x's, y's and z's from Erie.

Depending upon what the x's, y's and z's are, you're
going to think that either the x's, y's and z's are all red
and from Erie, or that the x's are red and the z's are from
Erie, while the y's are just plain y's. And in either case,
given an appropriately strong biasing context, you'll never
notice that there was another possibility. Of course, this
is a serious problem for earlier versions of deterministic
parsing, because the structures in the two cases are vastly
different. In the case where only the x's are red, and so
on, the structure of the VP after sell will look like (17),
with three conjoined NPs, while if the x's, y's and z's are
all from Erie, you've got one noun phrase with three
conjoined nouns.

(17)

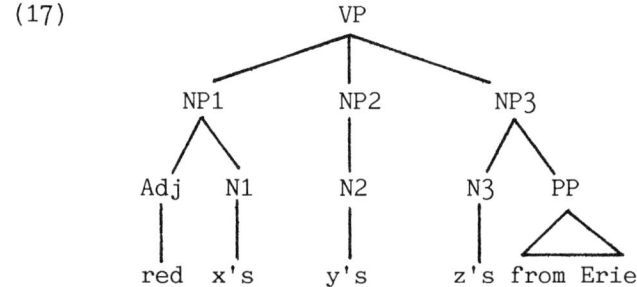

Hindle and I are assuming here an analysis of
conjunction that's rather different than the traditional
assumption of Chomsky-adjunction. We assume that conjoined
structures have a kind of three-dimensional syntax, similar
to proposals that various people have been playing with
recently (e.g. Goodall 1983), although no one seems to have
all the details straight yet, including us. The basic idea
is that a conjunction forms a stack of the conjoined items
which gets treated as if it were a three dimensional pile
that forms a single entity, as long as there's an and
around.

Now, let's be a little more careful than I've just
been. A D-theory analyzer doesn't build trees at all; it
builds descriptions of trees. So a D-theory analyzer won't
build this tree (17), but rather a description of it, part
of which will look like (18):

(18)   D (vp, np1)
                D (vp, np2)
                D (vp, np3)
                np1 < np2
                np2 < np3

Note that D here means 'dominates,' not 'directly
dominates'. So (18) says that the VP named vp dominates the
NPs named np1, np2, and np3, and that np1 precedes np2,
which precedes np3. Ultimately, we assume, on the way to
computing the semantics of the utterance, somebody further
down the line will reinterpret this predicate as 'directly
dominates', but at that point this just involves taking the
circumscriptive reading of the 'dominates' predicate. So if
you don't know any differently, if you know that some node a
dominates node b and there's nothing in between, then in the
circumscriptive reading a directly dominates b. Actually,
it isn't clear that one wants explicit predications about
the order of internal constituents at all, because one knows
from the speech, from the physical world, that red precedes
x's, x's precedes y's, and y's precede z's. By this
account, all the precedence information follows from lexical
items, although the precedence relations of internal nodes
can be derived as theorems, if one needs. And that's all
that's crucial.

So the analyzer knows all this. It knows the order of
the words in the utterance, and it knows (18). Now the
question is, are the names np1, np2 and np3 coreferential or
aren't they? And the answer is, as always, that if the
descriptions in terms of each name are incompatible, then
the names name different entities, but if the descriptions
are not incompatible then you can't tell. Well, you can
play this out formally for (18), and it turns out that the
descriptions in terms of np1, np2, and np3 are all
compatible. First of all, the nodes referred to by these
three names are all dominated by the same node.
Furthermore, if I take these names as being coreferential,
then the entity that they all turn out to be alternate names
for has the internal phrase structure 'adjective followed by
three nouns followed by a prepositional phrase', which is
just fine. So I can't tell which of the two readings of
(16) (18) describes, and this is just what I want. A D-
theory parser will create only one description, what it
might take to be a description for the multiple NP structure
(to the extent that it makes sense to talk of the parser

believing anything), but later processes will simply note
that this structure is ambiguous between the two readings,
and will bring to bear the world knowledge necessary to
resolve the ambiguity. (There's a kind of 'across-the-board'
effect that must be brought to bear by the semantics, but I
don't have time to go into that.)

A real problem for the old deterministic theory that we
had - and this is a really crucial problem for us - was
presented by sentence pairs like (19):

(19a) Birds eat small worms and frogs.
(19b) Birds eat small worms and frogs eat ...
      [whatever].

Let me show you what the problem is. For (19b) an old-
fashioned parser might build a structure like (20) (the
details aren't important). The crucial thing is that frogs
is the subject noun phrase of the second coordinate clause,
which is conjoined with the preceding sentence birds eat
small worms. But for a deterministic parser to see if this
is the correct structure to build, then it must parse frogs
as an NP, to see if a verb follows. But this puts it into a
serious double bind, because parsing frogs as an NP may well
be incorrect if the sentence ends immediately after the
noun, as in (19a). The problem is that one perfectly good
reading of (19a) is the noun and noun conjunction in (21),
where both the worms and frogs are small.

(20)

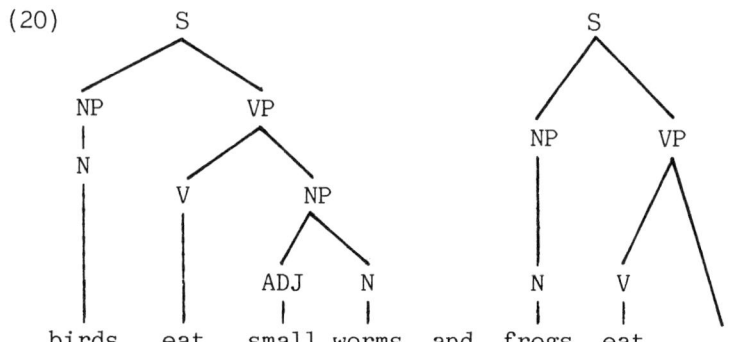

(21)

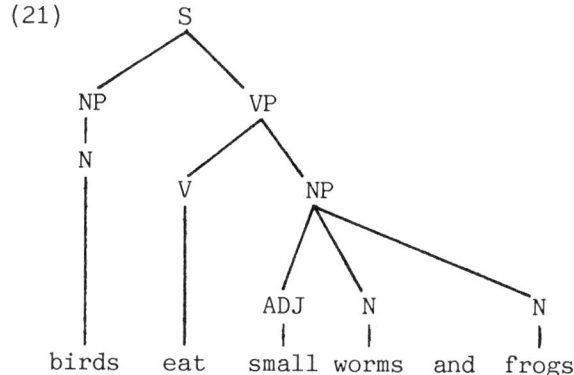

birds   eat   small worms   and   frogs

The problem is that no matter what analysis of conjunction you prefer for a noun-noun conjunction, whether Chomsky-adjoined N's or the three-dimensional stack approach we're taking, there is no second NP node over the noun <u>frogs</u> in the noun-noun case. So if you build the NP to see if a verb might be sitting in the buffer just past it, you lose. You can try to hack up some patterns to avoid creating the NP, but that's the way of perdition. From an engineering point of view, you can only hack the last ten per cent of local phenomena, and if you view conjunction as a local phenomenon, you're in real trouble. Of course, things are even worse than this, because (19a) is ambiguous between a noun-noun reading where both the worms and frogs are small, and a NP-NP reading where only the worms are small. So it looks like whatever a purely syntactic parser will do, it's going to lose.

Let me show you how D-theory makes this entire problem go away, as a result of viewing the structure that the parser builds for (19a) as a description, in particular the description summarized graphically in (22).

(22)

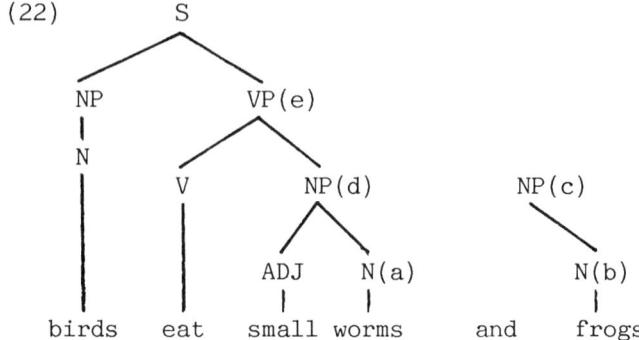

Here's what happens during the parsing of this
sentence, after worms. Let's just assume that the parser
knows that worms is a noun, which means that it must be
dominated by some noun or other, which the parser calls a,
and it knows that this noun must be dominated by some NP or
other, so it asserts that a is dominated by an NP which it
calls d. Now the parser sees frogs. (We're going to ignore
the and; the story about exactly how it gets parsed requires
a few extra facts that I don't have time to go into.) In
any case, the analysis of frogs is just the same; the parser
knows that frogs is a noun, so it says that the lexical item
is dominated by a noun which it calls b, and that this noun
must be dominated by an NP, so it asserts that b is
dominated by an NP which it calls c. At this point, the
parser will have the name c sitting in its buffer, with the
assertion that this node is an NP in its data base. If this
is the end of the sentence, then the parser knows that this
can't be a sentence-sentence conjunction, because it doesn't
see a verb after the NP (remember this is only a simplified
case), so it will attach the NP to VP, and it will go on its
way. (In fact it really doesn't attach to NP to the VP - in
a little while we'll see what it really does.) As it turns
out, this is really all very much like the behaviour of an
old-fashioned deterministic parser, except for the fact that
the parser runs with only names of nodes in its buffer and a
data base of propositions; this talk of "some NP or other"
is actually just a new alternate interpretation I'm putting
on the semantics of the same old operations.

And now we come to the point of this story, which is
just that the description that we end up with in (22) is
ambiguous between the two readings of (19a), but that if the
sentence had continued with eats, the parser would added

some predications to the description that would have described an unambiguous sentence-sentence conjunction. First of all, the description in (22) is ambiguous in just the same way that the description (18) is ambiguous between the readings of (16), with the two interpretations differing in whether c=d or not. But if the sentence had continued with eats, then the parser would have seen a node which was described as a verb following c in the buffer, so it would have created a new S node, and it would have asserted that c is dominated by that S node. Since the node named by d is dominated by the VP node named e, and the NP node named c is not, then the nodes named by c and d are dominated by different nodes, so c and d must name different nodes, so there is no ambiguity in this case.

One other part of the story that Don and I don't yet have: we'd like to be able to make a case ultimately that these descriptions are only ambiguous in those instances where pragmatic and semantic information is necessary to sort out the proper interpretation of the sentence. We're hoping the the parser's output representation, when viewed as a description, exactly highlights the cases in which semantic and world knowledge must be brought to bear to resolve alternate interpretations. We don't yet have such evidence, and I doubt that we will until we build a D-theory parser with a large grammar, and demonstrate the point by example.

The story I've been telling you is still oversimplified in a variety of ways; the real story is actually quite a bit richer that I've been letting on. I'd like to quickly sketch some of the other dimensions that we've been thinking about within the context of some work we're doing on the structure of Japanese. For example, we want to claim that the real input to the parser in your head consists of utterances chunked into intonation phrases. We've been working on the view that what the parser gets as input includes not only a lexical string - in fact some kind of morpholexical structure - but also some kind of symbolic representation of an intonation contour. On our current view, these two input representations are analyzed in parallel by two different mechanisms. One is something like the phrase-structure component I've sketched for you, and the other is a mechanism that enforces what we call 'rootedness'. Rootedness comes down to the constraint that everything within an intonation phrase must be part of the

same constituent, somehow. We believe that a particularly
simple representation of this rootedness constraint is
handed on to the subsystems that determine relations like
predicate/argument structure and information structure
(topic-comment structure, including the analysis of topic
structures like wa-phrases in Japanese).

We want to argue that the phrase structure component
itself uses an incredibly impoverished form of X-bar theory,
that if some traditional part of speech doesn't go to a
maximal projection (that is if a part of speech Q doesn't go
to a full Q-phrase), then it isn't in the category system.
We're also working with a very impoverished phrase structure
notation; with phrase structure rules written like (23a):

> (23) a. unexpanded: I' -> P V h
>   b. expanded: I' -> P'* V'* I

These rules, by the way, are for Japanese, not English.
We're going to assume one bar level, not because it's
clearly right but because it usefully simplifies the
examples. In this notation, only maximal projections can
appear on the right hand side of a rule, except for the head
of the construction, which is automatically one bar level
lower than the category the rule expands. As far as the
phrase structure is concerned, all categories can appear any
number of times. So (23a) means that I' (for INFL', i.e. S))
goes to the maximal projection of P, i.e. postpositional
phrase, any number of times, followed by any number of V-
phrases followed by the head of the INFL phrase, i.e. the
inflection itself. We're assuming that this is the only
phrase structure notation that the parser works on.

Each of these phrase structure rules is augmented by a
set of templates, which are local configurations describing
possible leading edges of that constituent, and which the
parser uses to trigger building that constituent. Here are
two templates for triggering the I' rule (24); the system
also always assumes automatically that the head of a
constituent is a template for that constituent.

> (24)   [P' +case]
>   [V']

So an I' (an S) in Japanese will be triggered whenever
the parser sees a postpositional phrase marked for case, or

a VP or INFL.

Now one key claim of our story is that any lexical item that doesn't appear as the head of a maximal projection is outside the categorial system, i.e. is no part of speech at all, or, as I'll say, is **extra-categorial**. For Japanese, we believe that the particle no is extra-categorial, as is the topic marker wa. One place that these extra-categorial elements do appear is in templates, where they can function as specified lexical items. So just as (25) says that a postpositional phrase consists of any number of NPs followed by the head, a postposition, and will be triggered by an NP, (26) says that an NP (which we'll assume here consists of only the head noun), can be triggered by the word no.

(25)   P' -> N h
        [N']

(26)   N' -> h
        [no]

So while the word no is not any part of speech, according to our analysis, it is used by the phrase-structure component. In particular, the particle no will always signal the beginning of an NP. The force of this will become clear in a minute.

I won't talk about this here, but we also believe that intonation breaks occur in the parser's input as entities like lexical items; we treat these as extra-categorial as well. Some of the evidence we have for this comes from the fact that in a variety of places where an intonation break is otherwise obligatory in Japanese, if wa occurs there, the intonation break is optional.

Some comments on rootedness: As the parser runs, whenever two elements appear in the buffer, or at least whenever two pre-terminal elements appear in the buffer, a mechanism separate from the phrase structure analyzer (although using its buffer data structure) enforces the rootedness constraint. It does this by adding a pair of statements that assert that some previously unmentioned node, about which nothing else is known, dominates each of the pair. So as the preterminals shown in (27) come through the buffer, this rootedness mechanism will add the domination statements indicated here, and these domination statements enforce the rootedness constraint.

(27)

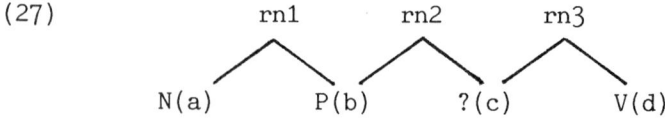

Why? Well, because if nothing else is known, i.e. if
the phrase structure analyzer adds no structure at all, then
later processes might as well assume that whatever names can
be coreferential are coreferential, minimizing entities, as
it were. They do this, of course, by adding a couple of
equality assertions (28), which results in the entire
intonation phrase having a single root (29), about which
nothing else is known.

(28)   equal (rn1, rn2)
         equal (rn2, rn3)

(29)

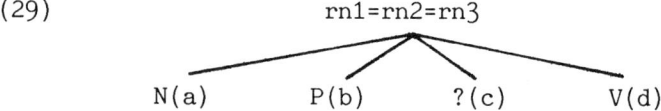

Let's look now at how a simple example from Japanese
(30) might be parsed within Description Theory.

(30)   John wa hon   o yonda.
          topic book acc read
       'John read a book.'

The interesting thing about this otherwise trivial
example is that wa is extra-categorial. So what happens
here is that the preterminal node A that dominates John
comes into the buffer and the parser starts with this phrase
structure rule (31). (Actually, what appears in the buffer
is the name of the node, not the node itself, of course.
But I'll be a little sloppy for the sake of brevity.)

(31)   N' -> h
       [N]

The template [N] gets triggered, creating the N' f and
the noun gets attached (32).

(32) stack: N'(f)

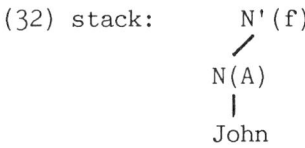

N(A)
|
John

The word <u>wa</u> comes into the buffer, but <u>wa</u> can't
continue an N', so the N' is complete, and is dropped back
into the buffer. The noun phrase now triggers a
postpositional phrase (33). The grammar that I just showed
you asserts that every noun phrase starts a postpositional
phrase.

(33) stack: P'

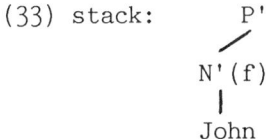

N'(f)
|
John

But now <u>wa</u> is in the first position in the buffer, so
it's the next lexical item the parser must use. The key
point here is that <u>wa</u> (unlike, say, <u>no</u>) doesn't occur within
the phrase structure grammar at all, even within templates.
This means that <u>wa</u> will always cause the parse to terminate
whatever it's building whenever the particle <u>wa</u> is
encountered. So the parser now discovers that <u>wa</u> cannot
continue this postpositional phrase, because <u>wa</u> is neither
of the two things that can continue a PP at this point,
either an NP or a postposition. So the parser concludes
that the postpositional phrase is done, and it drops the pp
into the buffer. But now nothing happens at all. None of
the phrase structure rules are triggered by the single PP,
and the <u>wa</u> now sitting in the second buffer slot totally
blocks any other templates from matching.

As I said before, deterministic parsers can handle
fragments by simply punting whenever they're stuck, and then
continuing on. All that's required to do this is for the
parser to simply eliminate the first thing in the buffer
whenever the stack is empty and no new constituent is
triggered. This is exactly what happens now. The parser
now takes the postpositional phrase (33), which is now
sitting in the buffer, and punts it out of the buffer. The
<u>wa</u> shifts into the first place in the buffer, but, again,
nothing happens, so the parser punts the <u>wa</u> as well. But
now the noun <u>hon</u> moves into the buffer, parsing starts up

once again, and continues till the end of the sentence. When the parser is done, it ends up with the string of fragments shown in (34): a postpositional phrase consisting of the word <u>John</u>, followed by the fragment <u>wa</u>, about which it knows nothing, followed by a sentence which consists of an accusative postpositional phrase and the verb.

While all this was happening, the rootedness mechanism was simultaneously adding lots of rootedness assertions as the preterminals streamed through the buffer, and all of these assertions (35) are available for later processes as well.

(34)

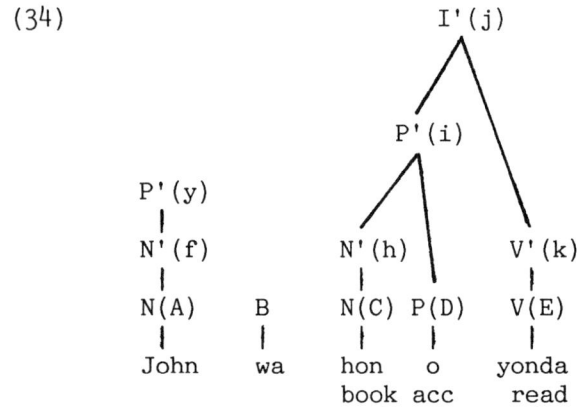

(35)

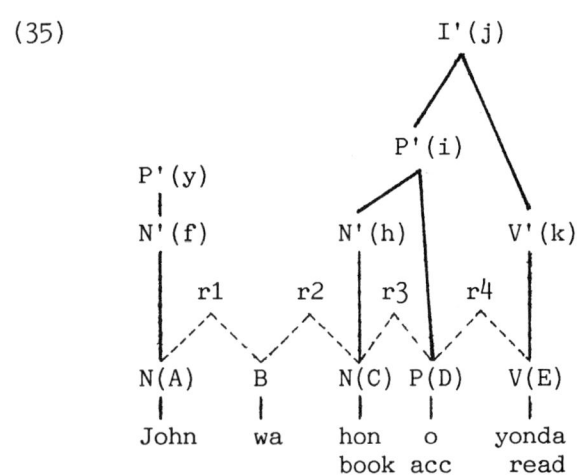

At the same time that the phrase structure analyzer and the rootedness mechanism are describing the syntactic structure of the terminal string, each predication is passed on to later components as soon as it's asserted. Among other things, these other components add equality statements and a few dominance assertions to further describe the sentence. For example, a mechanism that deals with topic/comment structure will trigger on the special configuration of 'rootedness node over wa' and add to the description some assertions that state that r1 dominates the PP y, and that r1 is the Topic Phrase of the utterance. Another mechanism, which handles the default case for rootedness, will equate the names added by the rootedness mechanism with phrase structure nodes, where that's possible, or else, where a rootedness node falls between two fragments, will float that node upward by the addition of two dominance assertions so that it dominates the two fragments. Actually, both of these processes on rootedness nodes can be viewed as two cases of a more general process that 'floats' rootedness nodes as high up the structure as possible. This process will assert that r4 is equal to j, and that r3 is the same as i. r2 will float up above everything and there's a special rule that's going to create a topic phrase out of it.

I'd really better point out one key distinction between the rootedness and phrase structure mechanisms on the one hand and the higher level processes that determine predicate/argument and information structures on the other. It turns out that the lower level processes that deal with rootedness and phrase structure have the special property that they can create node names. Higher level semantic processes cannot. But these higher level processes can use equality to make node names coreferent, while the low level processes cannot. Hindle and I would also like to hold to the position that only the parser can make domination statements, which leaves semantic processes only able to use equality, although at the moment we don't see quite how to pull it off.

Anyway, the resulting description, after all these processes are done, looks something like (36). As I said, we assume that Japanese has a rule, associated with the informational structure of the language, rather than phrase structure or syntactic structure per se, that will add assertions that say that r1 is a topic dominating both the

PP <u>John</u> and and the particle <u>wa</u>. And <u>r2</u>, which is floated
right out of the top of the structure, is going to be taken
as an utterance node. So when this part of the description
is added, the resulting description takes what has been
built as an utterance with <u>John</u> as topic, and a clause as
comment. This theory says that the topic is not the subject
of the sentence; some other component that determines
predicate/argument relations will later have to realise that
it serves as the agent of the predication. This same
component, or maybe the component that deals with case, will
have to realize that the PP <u>hon o</u> serves as a complement of
the verb, and that it should therefore be dominated by the
VP.

(36)

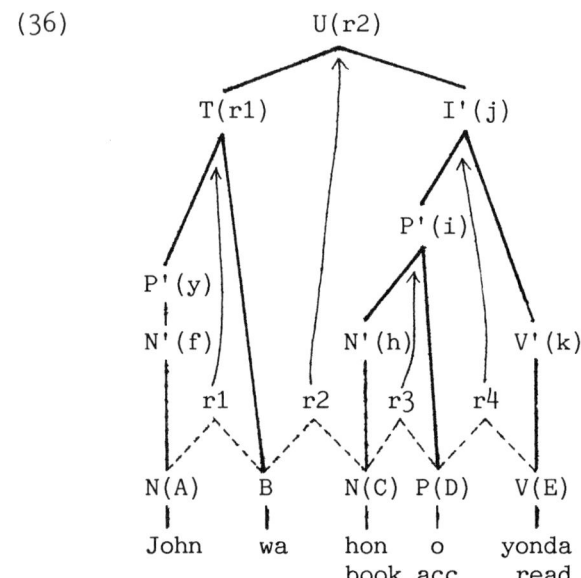

Now I'd like to sketch in a minute or two how D-theory
provides a unified account of the particle <u>no</u> in Japanese,
which is similar to the account of conjunction in English I
discussed before. So consider the phrase given here (37):

(37) isha   no sensei   ga ...
      doctor   teacher   nominative

Crucially, this is ambiguous between 'the doctor's
teacher', where <u>no</u> seems to serve as the genitive marker,
and an appositive meaning 'the teacher, that is the doctor'

where the first noun is in apposition to the second. (It's
the other way round in English.) So this phrase is utterly
ambiguous. Now it turns out that no has six other uses in
Japanese, and if I had enough time I'd tell you how to get
all of them, or at least most of them, to fall out of this
analysis.

The claim is that no is extra-categorial, but occurs in
an NP template, so no will trigger an NP whenever the parser
sees it. Here's the description of the phrase structure of
(37) that a D-theory analysis will create (38):

(38)

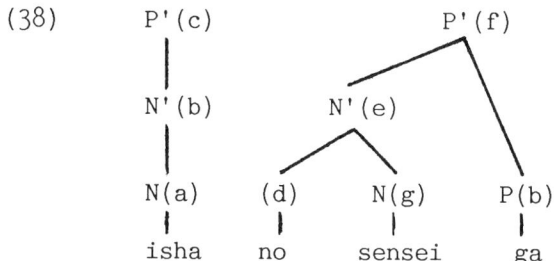

Because all NPs trigger PPs, given the grammar I showed
you before, isha, 'doctor', will trigger the NP b, which
then triggers a postpositional phrase c, which lacks a
postposition. The particle no triggers another NP which
picks up sensei, 'teacher', which then becomes a PP and
picks up the subject marker.

This configuration, with no attached to the leading
edge of the second NP initially, is all that we need, we
think, to get the proper analysis to work out. First of
all, among all the other rootedness nodes, there will be a
rootedness node r1 between the two PPs which by the default
rule is going to float off the top. And so you get this
structure (39) which has a stack of two PPs, one of them
lacking a postposition.

(39)

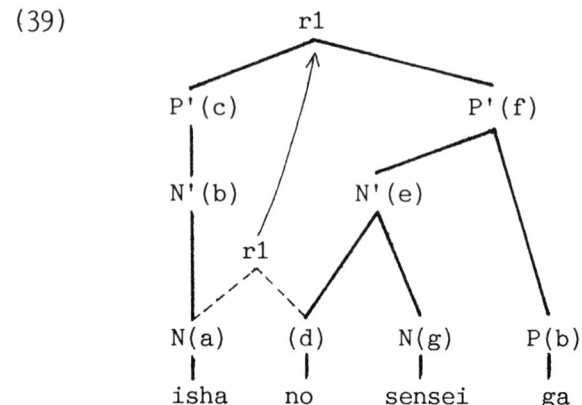

After the description of this much structure is output
by the phrase structure mechanism, a stack-interpretation
mechanism is going to be triggered - one assumes by the
particle no - that can use equality assertions to reduce
this stack. How can it fix things up? Well, one thing that
it can do is assert that c = f. That gives you essentially
this structure (40), with a stack of two NPs under the
postpositional phrase.

(40)

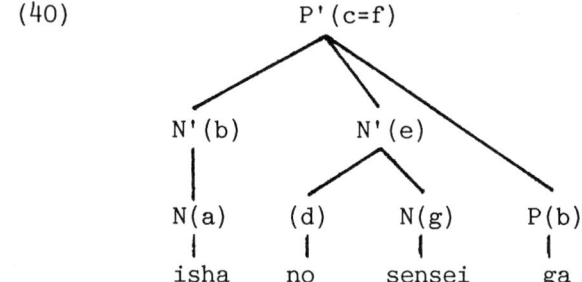

One natural interpretation of two stacked NPs is that
they form an appositive structure. The only question not
resolved is why isha is taken as being in apposition to
sensei, rather than the other way around.

Another move that the stack-busting mechanism can make
is just to assert that b = d (41). If this is done, then no
ends up as a particle of N'(d), which is the traditionally
assumed constituency. But because in fact d was dominated
by N'(e), asserting b = d puts N'(b) under N'(e), leaving
N'(b) a modifier of N'(e). And this yields the reading 'the

doctor's teacher'.

So the crucial claim is that the phrase-structure does just what it can, and no more, resulting in a description that includes these funny stack configurations. We assume that these stacks can't be interpreted <u>per</u> <u>se</u> by later semantic processes, but that they can be interpreted after processing by later components - and the choices that are open, using equality, seem to allow just the configurations that are legal for Japanese. Of course, this is just a fast sketch of the story, but hopefully you've seen enough to get the flavour, at least, of our analysis.

(41)

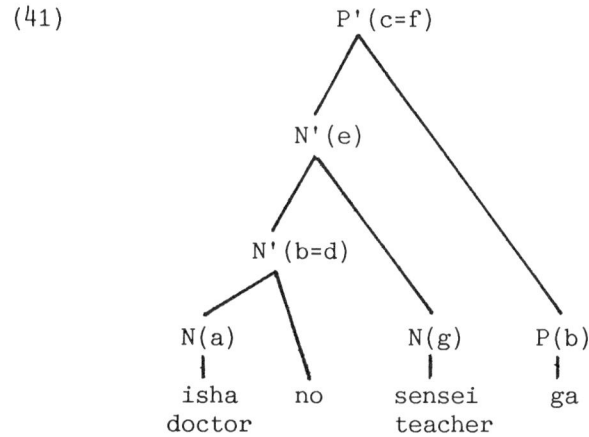

I want to finish with an extremely fast look at gapping, in even less detail than the last example. Consider something like (42). Well, what a D-theory parser might build is something like this: Showing just the structure after <u>ball</u>, the NP <u>a</u> <u>ball</u> would be part of the VP of the sentence <u>John</u> <u>bought</u> <u>a</u> <u>ball</u>, followed by two noun phrases (43).

(42) John   bought a ball and Mary a book.

(43)

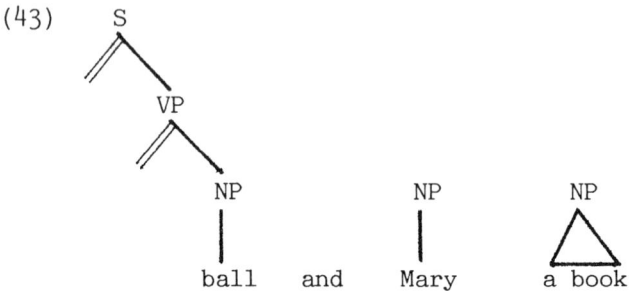

The extra-categorial element <u>and</u> is going to completely
break off the structure after <u>ball</u>.   The parser will   then
build and output the descriptions of the two NPs, without
being able to say anything else about them. But at the same
time, the rootedness mechanism will have introduced a number
of rootedness nodes; we'll focus on three in particular
(44).   One of these nodes, <u>r1</u>, will float right off the top
of the structure, and another, <u>r3</u>, will float above both <u>and</u>
and the two NPs.   A rule a bit like the rule for <u>wa</u>
interpretation, but that handles <u>and</u>, will equate the node
<u>r2</u> with <u>r3</u> as well, but never mind that.

(44)

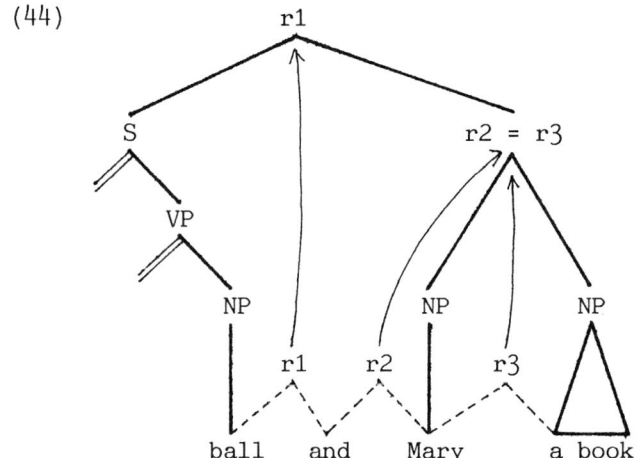

What's the resulting structure?   It's just (45).   What
does it say?   Well, it says that <u>John bought a ball</u> is an S,
which is in a stack with some other node ['?'] about which
nothing can be said - by phrase structure - except that it

dominates two NPs, preceded by the word a̲n̲d̲. This
essentially informs later stack-busting mechanisms that
there's a conjunction here, and that the mystery node will
be of whatever category its predecessor turns out to be.

(45)

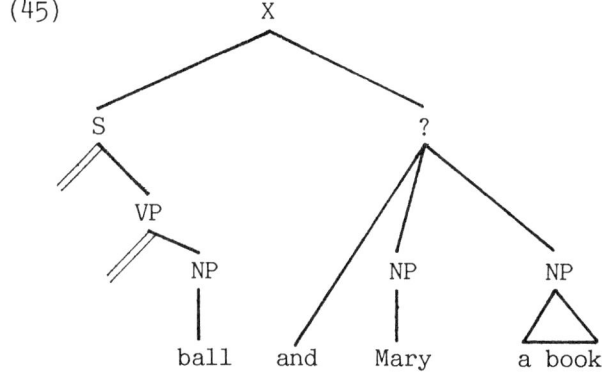

So no matter whether the preceding context was in fact
(46a) or (46b), determining the appropriate structure is
left open for later, leaving open all the options that are
necessary. Now of course this leaves rather too much open,
but you get the flavour of the analysis, at least.

    (46a) I gave Mary a book and John a box of ice-cream.
    (46b) John bought a ball and Mary a book.

Let me stop here. This work is in early stages
certainly, and is rather speculative. The point is that from
an engineering point of view Don Hindle and I would like to
believe it holds out a kind of panacea that may allow a
rather radical separation of syntax from semantics in just
the places where it might seem that the kitchen sink really
needs to be brought to bear to make syntactic decisions.

Doug ARNOLD: Clarification, I think: you said at various
times in the talk 'we can't handle PP attachment' and
'semantics is constrained not to introduce nodes'. Are
those two remarks related?

MARCUS: No. Though that actually looks like a case where
you may need domination statements to work things out. One
of the nice things about this 'dominates' predicate is that,
when you see a prepositional phrase, you say it's dominated

by the highest thing in sight, which is of course all you
can say about it. I really mean it when I say that this
thing is impoverished.

By the way, you may have noticed in the Japanese
parsing case that all the NPs were dominated by S and that
nothing was dominated by this V'. Now you might think that
I wanted to claim that Japanese doesn't have a VP. In fact
I'm not sure what we want to claim. The point of the
example is that you can't ever do any better than to attach
complements under S, because any kind of complement **could** go
under S. And the complementation component, the theta-role
component, is going to have to make sense of this. So it
looks as if this component is going to have to add
domination statements to lower the complements back under
again. Similarly with prepositional phrase attachment. I
think for prepositional phrase attachment it seems rather
sensible; for complementation structure it seems rather more
radical than one might like.

Bob MOORE: In your discussion of parsing of notionally ill-
formed utterances, it seems to me that there must be
something more going on than simply saying that there really
are rules that govern the form of the input, because of the
fact that we have very little or no trouble in understanding
dialects with ill-formed input, or - this is a bit more of a
global issue - how is it we understand dialects that differ
somewhat from our own?

MARCUS: Two comments. The first is that whatever this
ability is, it's not unlimited. Those truly ungrammatical
sentences [(12)] were truly ungrammatical, right? That was
not a dialect you don't speak. So the first comment is that
whatever's going on, there's got to be some distinction
between the two.

One point that I didn't have time to make - and it's a
point I could have made this afternoon, in terms of limiting
the power of syntactic representations - is that it may well
be the case that you actually need a constantly active
learning component which will tell you what kind of things
are possible, and which you can use to, as it were, 'learn'
dialects almost on the fly. It's a very vague statement but
it's valid in some ultimate world or other. Then of course
I'll argue that Berwick's thesis (Berwick 1985) shows that
you can also do learning in our model, which is another

piece of evidence for it. But the claim would be that ultimately you're going to need a learning mechanism, and it's interesting what you'd like it to learn. You clearly keep learning new lexical items throughout your life, and picking up the meaning of things. You clearly - it seems to me - don't keep learning radically new kinds of semantic entities. You clearly can learn very superficially different syntactic patterns. And you clearly can't learn a different language very well just by listening to it being spoken. So there's some range of what you want this thing to learn, it seems to me. That might be one solution to this problem. At least it's consistent.

MOORE: It strikes me that there might be some other general mechanisms other than this speech-editing business. One of the examples suggested to me that the guy had started the sentence and had a very long noun phrase in the middle, and then he continued as if he'd started the sentence with a noun phrase, and that suggests that maybe the stuff before the noun phrase just falls off the buffer or something like that.

MARCUS: Typically when people do that in speech, when it's the subject position, they use the resumptive pronoun: 'The guy I was telling you about two weeks ago who did so-and-so, he did such-and-such.' That's the standard pattern.

Stu SHIEBER: In the previous discussion I think we agreed on at least one necessary condition for calling something 'deterministic', that being the characteristic of being built up. Now it's clear that this impoverished syntax does have this characteristic, but it wasn't clear to me whether the part that enforces rootedness and does the identities and that kind of thing, has that characteristic. Well either it does, or if it doesn't ...

MARCUS: ... then the whole system isn't deterministic?

SHIEBER: Well, no. Either there's a weakening of the determinism hypothesis, or only a portion of it is deterministic. The kind of stuff that some of the older systems used do deterministically is now being split between something, one part of which is deterministic and one part of which isn't. Now that sort of leads you down a slippery slope where you start dumping stuff off to other things which don't have to be deterministic. Where does that stop?

MARCUS: Let me restate that in the strong form. I think you meant what you said. But someone else might have said 'Oh I see - you can't make this determinism thing work. You're just pushing off the hard part and only solving the easy problem.' The first comment is that for the simple straightforward cases where there's not much magic going on - we had a summer student last summer, Robert Fow, who implemented a system which had most of a proof (it wasn't utterly formal but it looked like it was going to go through) that the thing was linear timed. In fact it had the same real-time property that the old parser had. And it did the rootedness stuff. So you take this rootedness thing and for the situation where the things just float off the top, not for any sort of magical cases, but for the simple ones, it is linear timed, that much we know.

As for the rest of it, let me make your question a little worse. One might have also said that it looks like the semantics is really going to have to consider two alternatives, and in considering the two alternatives, i.e. whether z's are red or not [cf. (16)], pragmatically somehow, it looks like the thing is in fact building a structure that it's not going to use. So it might turn out to be terrible, i.e. not linear timed. And the other problem is that it may build structure which is indelible.

The answer to both of them is I don't know at the moment how it's going to go. My guess is that for a lot of the kinds of things that we need to do, there aren't going to be many combinatorics involved, although we need to show that. I think the combinatorics aren't bad for these cases, there really are only a couple. To stop being linear timed it has to be the case that you need to consider unboundedly many choices; if there's some bounded number of things you can consider then you're all right. And my suspicion is that that's the way it's going to remain.

The second thing I think is going to go against us. In some sense or other I don't see any way that the pragmatics can not work by considering, say, if $x = y$ then it's coreferential so then this description isn't going to go through because these aren't red. Just to make it a little more concrete, take (47a) versus (47b):

(47a) They sell red apples, pears and oranges from
      local orchards.

(47b) They sell ripe cheese, bread, and cider from local orchards.

Now for those two things pragmatically it's utterly clear which is which, and yet I can't see any way not to think about whether the cider is ripe or the bread is ripe. On the other hand I think that the number of such things that need to be considered per sentence is very small. I do not believe that the mind is deterministic, so that once you get into pragmatics of this kind it doesn't bother me too much that the determinism thing goes away. I think that it's not unreasonable at that point. You're off in the periphery. I consider most of this stuff - the rootedness business, the phrase-structure stuff - pretty close to peripheral processing, whereas the pragmatics is clearly something more complex.

SHIEBER: Two quick problems. First of all I don't follow the argument that you're building in boundedness in the first place.

MARCUS: I didn't offer an argument, that was just an assertion.

SHIEBER: The second point is your use of 'determinism'; it's become a strategy as opposed to some sort of claim about processing.

MARCUS: First comment is that if the depth of the zippering that you need to do is a function of the total length of the string, then you're still OK - you've got linear zippering to do with the length of the string.

SHIEBER: Yes, in real time, as I understood it.

MARCUS: Well, there's more to be said about this, but lets go on. Let me turn to another point which gets at this. Let's take a parody of the position: you give me instructions in English to do something, e.g. 'Go write a program that does a quick-sort'. I understand what you said, and it takes me three tries until I get my quick-sort algorithm to work right. Clearly I'd backed up, and therefore language understanding isn't deterministic, right?! Now it seems to me that there is a line to be drawn somewhere between that aspect which is to be taken as language understanding or parsing or whatever, and that

which is to be taken as something much richer. My belief is
that once you bring real-world knowledge to bear then you're
not doing the first. A corollary of that, which you might
find objectionable, is that this thing that I would call
narrowly 'language understanding' never builds a parse tree.
But I have no trouble with that.

Henry THOMPSON: You said at some point that the behaviour
of Hindle's (1983) parser, Fidditch, was notable inter alia
because of its robustness with respect to fragments,
something which you asserted in passing was not obviously
possible in non-deterministic parsers.   I found that
somewhat surprising as I would have thought that any left-
corner or bottom-up invocation style non-deterministic
parser would produce just about exactly the same set of
fragments or parse forests, given the approximately
translated grammar. So I wasn't clear about what it was
about the mechanism that you thought gave you better
leverage.

MARCUS: First of all, any purely bottom-up parser is going
to find every fragment you could possibly find everywhere.

SHIEBER: Well, that depends on your definition of what a
bottom-up parser is.

MARCUS: Well your standard CKY bottom-up parser (Younger
1967) will find all possible fragments. That's what I mean
by 'bottom-up'. So clearly you get the ones you wanted
among all the other ones, but you get lots of others as
well.

THOMPSON: Surely there's a filter which is 'maximal
fragment over a particular region'.

MARCUS: I'm not sure that it works out straightforwardly.
My problem with that, though it may work out that way, is
that it's actually an engineering point. You could build
one that did the right thing. But one wants to build
grammars for non-deterministic systems that fail as quickly
as they possibly can. So they tend to be built fairly
conservatively. You tend for efficiency reasons, if you
actually build one of these grammars, to build something too
narrow. So the fragments that you get tend to act as an
empirical statement rather than a theoretical one.

THOMPSON: This is now something about grammars rather than parsers, which seems to me to be fair, although empirical and therefore we need evidence.

MARCUS: But you see there's a good motivation to be strict about it, because it depends on how long the thing takes. There's a nice property of these deterministic systems, which is that they go as far as they can and then they just stop, whereas the non-deterministic ones spend a lot of time doing a lot of work and hence you need a very fast machine in order to loosen things up.   But I agree with you that it's an empirical statement rather than a theoretical one.

Nick OSTLER: Perhaps I haven't understood it right, but if you take the two particles wa and no in Japanese and you say that they are extra-categorial - and yet you can have sentences which differ only in having wa instead of no and they will clearly have different interpretations imposed on them, for example:

> (48a) John no hon o yomimasita. 'I read John's book'
> (48b) John wa hon o yomimasita. 'John read the book'

Wouldn't your theory predict that they should both be ...

MARCUS: No!   What it predicts is that the output of the phrase-structure analyser for the two is identical.

THOMPSON: In fact it doesn't even predict that, because as you pointed out no is a noun-phrase initiator ...

MARCUS: Yes. The claim is that it always initiates a noun phrase.   It's the head of a noun phrase.   It initiates one and it's also the end of one.

OSTLER: So the point is that although it's extra-categorial in some sense, it does have a piece of structure attached to it. Could you say what you mean then by 'extra-categorial'?

MARCUS: I tried to do this in the talk, and I see that it wasn't sufficient.   'Extra-categorial' means narrowly that the item can serve in the grammar in exactly one way.   I call it 'extra-categorial' because the grammar consists of three components.   The phrase structure component consists of two parts.   One is the set of X' rules, and the things that participate in those are categories, and all of those

go to maximal projections, and that's what I mean by
'categorial'. The other part of it is these extra-
categorial elements which don't appear anywhere in the
templates, and all those behave identically with respect to
the phrase-structure analyzer. They can serve only as
initiators of structure, so they can serve at the leading
edge of structures, and they can serve to initiate things.
So they can serve as flags.

It may be for example that English complementizers are
extra-categorial (I'm actually speaking a bit wildly here,
and this is the kind of thing we need to look into). What
would follow from that? Well, you'd expect them to occur
only at the leading edge of constituents, only as triggers.
Check. And you'd expect them to be involved in the kinds of
things that would occur if their only role in the grammar
was the very surfacey kind of thing that you get with these
templates, which are very weak, i.e. the grammatical things
that involve them would be not only finite state but weaker
than that. There's a possibility, although we see a couple
of problems with it right now, that we can make it go
through eventually. But in fact surface structure filters
fall from exactly this kind of interaction. You also
wouldn't get an unbounded number of them in a row, and for
the templates there **aren't** an unbounded number of these
things. I think it would be highly marked to find more than
one instance of one of these things in a constituent. So
there's a whole story that goes with them.

OSTLER: But in the case of <u>wa</u> and <u>no</u>, it's clear that they
are syntactically different from each other, and you can say
certain things like "<u>no</u> is connected with noun phrases", and
you have actually got that as a minimal statement in your
second component, as you said. Would you generally think
that if you **can** make a clear syntactic statement about
something, it should be represented in the parsing system?

MARCUS: No. For example, <u>wa</u> by and large marks noun
phrases that only occur at the beginning of utterances.
There are exceptions to that: <u>wa</u> **can** occur phrase-
internally, but then it has to be preceded by an obligatory
intonation break, and we argue that that is parenthetical.
But let that go for the moment. Say it were just the case
that <u>wa</u> occured sentence initially. You might want to say
that that ought to be part of the phrase-structure, but we
say no, it can't be. Now topics in English, intonation

aside, occur only phrase initially, roughly.   Do you want
to capture that in the phrase-structure of the language?   I
think not.   And I think that the story in both languages is
roughly the same: that you say topics first, even if you
mark them in some way or other.

OSTLER: Does that mean that something that looks just the
same as a topic but goes to the end doesn't count as a
topic?   Because both wa-phrases in Japanese come after, as I
say, and there's all this right dislocation stuff.

MARCUS: We have a whole story about wa, and the story
hinges crucially on the fact that a non-initial wa-phrase
has to be preceded by an obligatory intonation break.   We
also have a whole long story about obligatory intonation
breaks.   But the upshot of it is that we find it utterly
consistent to take non-initial wa-phrases, as I said, as
being parenthetical.   We think that that's a consistent
statement, and that it goes through.   So that's the kind of
story that one tells about that.   Sure there's more to say
about topicalized elements: there are other things going on,
and intonation carries a lot of information, and that's got
to be taken into account.   And we think it's not taken into
account by the phrase-structure mechanism.   But the wa thing
in Japanese doesn't bother me at all - we think we've got a
pretty full story on that.

OSTLER: Does it by any chance deal with the wa
characteristic of women's speech as well, which doesn't seem
to have any meaning at all?

MARCUS: No, and we think that's a problem!   Let me tell you
why.   One thing that we discovered with no, and one
principle that we want to hold to and that we don't in this
case for Japanese, is that any analysis of a particle in
Japanese that claims that it's extra-grammatical ought to
handle every instance of it.   Now if I'm correct the wa in
women's speech is a problem because it's a sentence-final
particle, is that correct?

OSTLER: Yes.   It's the same with sentence-final no as well,
which is also a characteristic of women's speech.

MARCUS: In those cases I think it's not going to be too
much of a problem for us.   The uses can clearly be very
different from each other, so I think this other wa case

won't be a problem for us: we want to take a hard line on particles in general. A principle has to be that there's only one lexical item of that kind, and it's always the extra-grammatical one. It doesn't have to be true, but I think methodologically that's the kind of line one has to take for the sake of honesty. And I think we've made it work out on no and wa.

References

Barwise, J. & Perry, J. 1983. **Situations and Attitudes.** Cambridge, Mass.: MIT Press.

Berwick, R.C. 1985. **The Acquisition of Syntactic Knowledge.** Cambridge, Mass.: MIT Press.

Goodall, G. 1983. A Three-dimensional Analysis of Coordination. **Papers from the 19th Regional Meeting of the Chicago Linguistic Society,** 146-154.

Hindle, D. 1983. Deterministic Parsing of Syntactic Non-fluencies. **21st Annual Meeting of the Association for Computational Linguistics** (Cambridge, Mass.), Proceedings. 123-28.

Labov, W. 1978. **Sociolinguistic Patterns.** Oxford: Basil Blackwell.

Marcus, M. 1980. **A Theory of Syntactic Recognition for Natural Language.** Cambridge, Mass.: MIT Press.

Marcus, M., Hindle, D. & Fleck, M. 1983. D-theory: Talking about Talking about Trees. **21st Annual Meeting of the Association for Computational Linguistics** (Cambridge, Mass.), Proceedings. 129-136.

Simon, H. 1981. **The Sciences of the Artificial.** Cambridge, Mass.: MIT Press.

Younger, D.H. 1967. Recognition and Parsing of Context-free Languages in Time n^3. **Information and Control** 10, 189-208.

Montague Grammar and Machine Translation

Jan Landsbergen

Introduction

In this paper I will examine the possibilities of using Montague Grammar for machine translation. I will discuss briefly the various ways in which this theory could be used, but most attention will be given to one actual application: the Rosetta translation system. The paper is organized as follows. After a short introduction to Montague Grammar, its strong and weak points with respect to computer applications will be discussed. Then a syntactically powerful and computationally viable version of Montague Grammar, called M-grammar, will be described. Subsequently I will discuss various ways in which Montague Grammar may be used directly for machine translation and pay special attention to the problems that arise in these cases. Finally I will outline the isomorphic grammar approach to machine translation, followed in the Rosetta project, in which the compositionality principle of Montague Grammar plays an important role.

Montague Grammar

It is not possible to give in a few words a fair account of Montague Grammar and this holds in particular for

---

The Rosetta project is partially sponsored by NEHEM (Nederlandse Herstructureringsmaatschappij).

I would like to thank Jeroen Groenendijk, Kees van Deemter, Rene Leermakers and Jan Odijk for their comments.

LINGUISTIC THEORY AND COMPUTER APPLICATIONS
ISBN 0-12-747220-7

its semantic power. In this section I will restrict myself
to introducing some basic concepts and the corresponding
terminology, which are needed for a good understanding of
the rest of the paper. The terminology and the notation may
deviate a little from "standard" Montague Grammar.

Montague's most important papers on language are 'The
Proper Treatment of Quantification' (1973), 'Universal
Grammar' (1970a), and 'English as a Formal Language'
(1970b). They have been collected together with other papers
in Thomason (1974). A good introduction to the theory is
Dowty et al (1981). The 1973 'PTQ' paper, as it is usually
called, is the best known and contains the most influential
example of a Montague grammar. The paper 'Universal
Grammar' describes the general algebraic framework (cf
Janssen 1986 for a better insight into and an elaboration of
this framework). 'English as a Formal Language' (EFL) is
interesting because it shows how natural language can be
interpreted directly, without intervention of a logical
language.

The main characteristic of Montague Grammar is the
attention that is given to semantics. Montague grammars
have to obey the **compositionality principle,** which says that
the meaning of an expression is a function of the meaning of
its parts. What the parts are has to be defined by the
syntax, so the principle prescribes a close relation between
syntax and semantics.

The syntax of a Montague Grammar specifies (i) a set
of basic expressions and (ii) a set of syntactic rules. The
basic expressions are the smallest meaningful units, the
syntactic rules define how larger phrases and ultimately
sentences can be constructed, starting with the basic
expressions. The rules are applied in a compositional
("bottom-up") way.

A simple example:

The basic expressions are: the noun boy and the verb sleep.

The rules are:

R_1 : this rule is applicable to a noun, e.g. boy, and makes
a definite plural noun phrase, by adding the article the
and the suffix -s; e.g. the boys.

R_2 : this rule is applicable to a noun phrase and a verb and makes a sentence with the NP as its subject, in the present progressive tense, e.g. the boys are sleeping.

The process of deriving a sentence from basic expressions by recursive application of rules can be made explicit in a **syntactic derivation tree**. In (1) an example of a syntactic derivation tree is given: it shows the derivation of the sentence the boys are sleeping according to the example grammar.

(1) S (the boys are sleeping) - - - - R_2

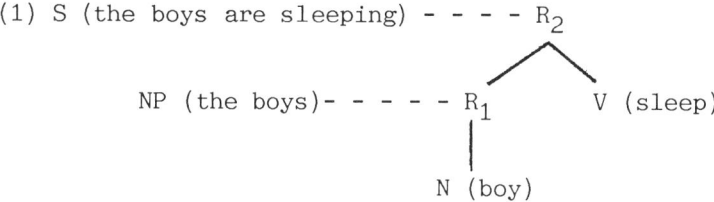

In Montague's example grammars the basic expressions and the expressions generated by the rules have a syntactic category, but no explicit internal structure, they are just symbol strings. Actually, Montague used a version of categorial grammar. However, these restrictions are in general not considered essential properties of the theory. Already in the seventies Partee (1976) proposed an extension in which the rules operate on syntactic structures (or - equivalently - labelled bracketings) in which syntactic transformations may occur.

The semantic component of Montague Grammar assigns a semantic interpretation to the language as follows. First a semantic domain is defined, consisting of individual entities, truth values, special indices and functions defined in terms of these objects. Characteristic of Montague Grammar is the use of a special kind of indices, usually called "possible worlds". They are important for the power of the semantic system, which is often referred to as "possible-world semantics", but will not be discussed here.

The assignment of semantic values to expressions of the language can be done in two ways: directly and indirectly. In a direct interpretation (a method explored in the paper EFL) basic expressions and syntactic rules are immediately interpreted in terms of the semantic domain; each basic expression is associated with an object in the domain (e.g. an individual, a function from individuals to truth values, etc.) and with each rule an operation on objects in the domain (e.g. function application) is associated. The semantic value of an arbitrary expression is then defined with the help of the syntactic derivation tree. In parallel with the application of the syntactic rules the semantic operations associated with these rules are applied to the semantic values of their arguments, starting with the values of the basic expressions. The final result is the semantic value of the complete expression. So the process of derivation of the semantic value runs parallel with the syntactic derivation process and can be represented in a tree with the same geometry as the syntactic derivation tree, but which is labelled by names of semantic values and semantic operations. This representation, called **semantic derivation tree**, is introduced here because it will be useful in the sequel; it is not explicitly used by Montague. If we assume that the rules of our example grammar correspond to meaning rules, named M_1 and M_2, and the basic expressions to meanings with the names C_1 (for boy) and C_2 (for sleep), the relation between syntactic and semantic derivation tree is as in (2).

(2)   syntactic derivation tree --> semantic derivation tree

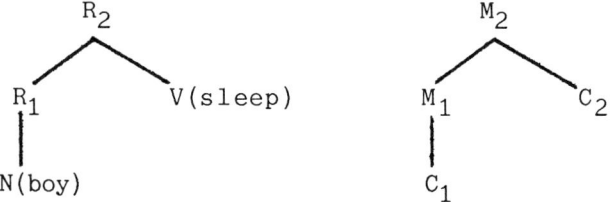

A simplified example:

C_1 is a property of individuals (equivalently: a set of individuals), i.e. the property "being a boy".

C_2 is also a property of individuals, i.e. the property "sleeping".

M_1 operates on a property P and yields the set of properties that all individuals with property P have, in this case the properties all boys have. (In this example it is assumed - wrongly - that "the + plural" can be interpreted as universal quantification.)

M_2 operates on a set of properties S and a property P and yields <u>true</u> if P is in S, else <u>false</u>.

So the semantic value of the sentence is <u>true</u> if the property of "sleeping" is a property that all boys have, else it is <u>false</u>.

The more usual way of assigning interpretations (pursued in PTQ) is the indirect one, which proceeds in two steps. First an expression of the language is translated into an expression of a logical language (in PTQ higher-order intensional logic). Then the logical expression is assigned a semantic value by interpreting the logical language in the standard way.

The translation from natural language into logical language is defined in a similar - syntax-directed - way as the direct interpretation. For each basic expression its translation into the logic is given, each syntactic rule corresponds to a (possibly complex) operation on logical expressions. In parallel with the application of the syntactic rules the logical operations associated with these rules are applied to the logical expression associated with their arguments, starting with the logical expressions corresponding to the basic expressions.

The final result is the logical representation of the complete sentence. Note that in the indirect way of assigning interpretations, the form of the logical expressions themselves is not relevant; they are only a means to express in a convenient way the model-theoretic interpretation.

In (3) I illustrate this process by showing in parallel the derivation of the sentence <u>the</u> <u>boys</u> <u>are</u> <u>sleeping</u> and of its (extensional) logical representation, but without further explanation. The derived logical expression for the complete sentence is equivalent to the reduced form: $\forall x$: boy' (x) --> sleep' (x)

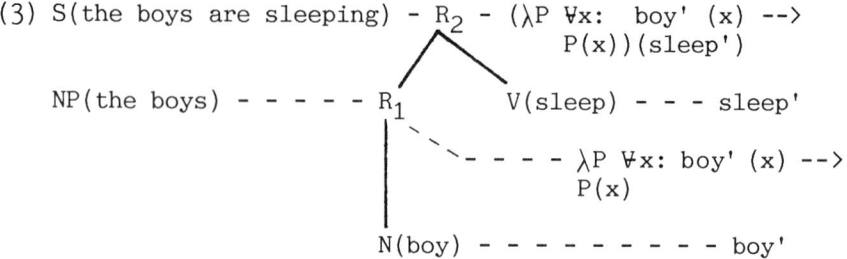

(3) S(the boys are sleeping) - R_2 - (λP $\forall$x: boy' (x) -->
                                                              P(x))(sleep')

    NP(the boys) - - - - - R_1 V(sleep) - - - sleep'

                                  - - - - λP $\forall$x: boy' (x) -->
                                              P(x)

                N(boy) - - - - - - - - - boy'

Montague Grammar and computer applications

What are the strong and the weak points of Montague Grammar with regard to its use in computer applications that involve natural language processing?

Two important application areas in the field of natural language processing are natural language question-answering and machine translation. A strong point of Montague Grammar in these two areas is the attention that is given to semantics. In both application areas a sound semantic base is needed for determining what a correct answer or a correct translation is.

Another advantage of Montague Grammar in comparison with some other linguistic theories is its exactness and its "constructiveness". By "constructiveness" I mean that there is a clear step-by-step construction of phrases and - in parallel - of their meanings, thanks to the compositionality principle. Since for each rule both the syntactic and the semantic operation must be defined, the correctness of the rule can - to a large extent - be judged locally. This advantage is lost in a grammar with several syntactic levels, where the semantics is defined at the deepest level (whatever other virtues these levels may have). Local correctness criteria are important in the design of large systems in general and in particular in the design of large grammars.

A supposed weak point of Montague Grammar is that it treats only small fragments of language in a syntactically simplistic way. As for the fragmentariness, this is a consequence of exactness. Dealing with small - but non-trivial - fragments completely, in full detail is to be preferred - from the point of view of computer applications - to making interesting, but imprecise claims about natural languages in general. The syntactic simplicity of the framework is certainly a weak point, but it is more an incidental property of Montague's example grammars than an inherent property of the theory. The problem is not a lack of formal power, but a lack of linguistic power: the rules operate on strings and not on structured objects, e.g. syntactic trees. I have already referred to the syntactic extensions proposed by Partee (1976), and other work has been done in this direction, but nevertheless it is a correct observation that most workers in the field are primarily interested in semantics and less in syntax.

Another objection against Montague Grammar is that intensional logic and possible-world semantics are complicated and therefore hard to put to practical use in large systems. This is a correct observation. Montague needed the power of intensional logic to solve several difficult semantic problems, but these problems do not necessarily occur in all applications. For instance, in most data base question-answering systems a simple extensional semantics is sufficient. It is not in conflict with the spirit of Montague Grammar to use a simpler logic, as long as there is a compositional and model-theoretic semantics. The specific system of intensional logic may indeed be difficult, but model-theoretic semantics in itself is very easy to understand and to use; by imagining a particular interpretation it is possible to get a fast insight into the semantic correctness (and especially the incorrectness) of a particular rule or of a larger part of the grammar.

The most important obstacle to the application of Montague Grammar is that it is a purely generative framework. The theory defines how sentences and their meaning representations are generated in parallel, but it does not define how for a given sentence a meaning representation can be constructed effectively. This weakness can only be overcome by restricting in some way the class of possible Montague grammars. This will be the topic of the next section. There I will define M-grammars, which are less powerful than unrestricted Montague grammars from a purely formal point of view, but more powerful from a linguistic point of view, in the sense that the rules operate on structured objects instead of strings.

M-grammars

To my knowledge, two different ways of defining parsers
for Montague Grammars have been described: by Friedman and
Warren (1978) and by Landsbergen (1981).   The approaches
differ strongly in what they consider to be a Montague
grammar.   Friedman and Warren remained as close as possible
to the PTQ grammar and designed a parser which can be
characterized as a context-free parser with some specific
extensions for phenomena falling outside the context-free
framework, in particular the quantification rules.   My own
proposal defines a parser for a class of grammars, called M-
grammars, which are syntactically more powerful and which
are in accordance with Partee's transformational extensions
(Partee 1976). Since 1981 a few changes in the definition of
M-grammars have been made, of which the most important is
the introduction of a separate morphological component. The
new version is described in Landsbergen (1985).   I will
recapitulate it here briefly.

An **M-grammar** consists of three components: a syntactic
component, a morphological component and a semantic
component.

The **syntactic component** of an M-grammar defines a set
of surface trees of sentences.   The specific kind of surface
trees generated by M-grammars - and the intermediate results
- are called **S-trees**. An S-tree is an ordered tree of which
the nodes are labelled by syntactic categories and
attribute-value pairs and of which the edges are labelled by
syntactic relations.

Formally, an S-tree t is an object of the form

$$N [r_1/t_1, \ldots, r_n/t_n], \quad (n \geq 0)$$
$$\text{with } N = C \{a_1: v_1, \ldots, a_k: v_k\}$$

where N is a node,

$t_1, \ldots, t_n$ are S-trees, the immediate constituents of **t**,

$r_1, \ldots, r_n$ are syntactic relations, between t and its
constituents (if n = 0, t is a terminal S-tree)

C is a syntactic category,

$a_1, \ldots, a_k$ are attributes,

$v_1, \ldots, v_k$ are values of these attributes.

An example of an S-tree in the more familiar graphical representation is given in (4). It is a - simplified and unrealistic - example of a surface tree, for the sentence the boys are sleeping.

(4)

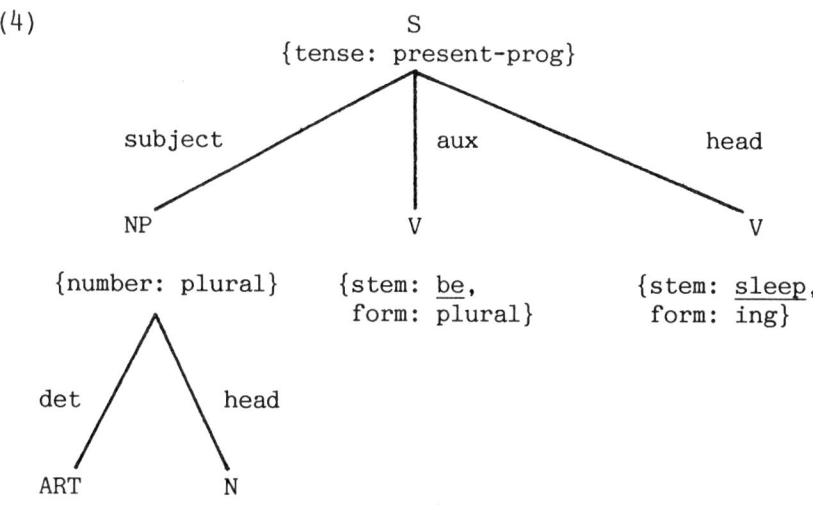

In the sequel I will often use an abbreviated notation, as in (5).

(5)   S (the boys are sleeping)

The leaves of an S-tree correspond to words.   For example, the terminal node

N {stem: boy, number: plural}

corresponds to boys. This relation between terminal nodes and words as symbol strings is defined by the morphological component.

An M-grammar defines a language (in this case a set of

surface trees) in the same way as a Montague grammar, i.e.,
by specifying a set of basic expressions and a set of
syntactic rules. But here the basic expressions are S-trees
(in general S-trees consisting of one node) and the rules
are defined for S-trees as arguments and yield S-trees as
their results.

The derivation process of a surface tree from basic S-
trees by application of rules can be represented by a
syntactic derivation tree in the way described earlier. If
we reformulate the example grammar of the previous section
in terms of S-trees, the syntactic derivation tree of the
boys are sleeping (i.e. of its surface tree) is the same as
(1).

In principle all rules of an M-grammar have
"transformational power": they can perform fairly arbitrary
operations on S-trees. However, this power is restricted by
three conditions that M-grammars have to obey in order to
make effective parsing possible: the reversibility
condition, the measure condition, and the surface syntax
condition. I will describe them here informally (cf.
Landsbergen 1985 for more precise definitions).

The **reversibility condition** states that a rule should
not only define a compositional ("generative") function
(with a tuple of S-trees as argument and an S-tree as
result), but also an analytical function (which operates on
an S-tree and yields a tuple of S-trees). The compositional
and the analytical function should be each other's reverse
(the term reverse is used instead of inverse, because a rule
produces a set of results, possibly the empty set, if the
rule is not applicable). If the compositional function is
applied to a tuple $(t_1, ..., t_n)$ and t is in the set of
results, then application of the analytical function to t
must yield a finite set containing the tuple $(t_1, ..., t_n)$,
and vice versa.

Given a set of basic S-trees and a set of reversible
rules, two functions, M-PARSER and M-GENERATOR, can be
defined:

M-GENERATOR operates on an arbitrary syntactic derivation
tree (i.e. an arbitrary tree labelled by rules and basic
expressions) and yields a set of S-trees, by applying the
compositional versions of the rules in the derivation tree,

in a "bottom-up" way. The resulting set may be empty if some rule is not applicable.

M-PARSER operates on an arbitrary S-tree. It tries to apply the analytical versions of the rules in a "top-down" way until it arrives at basic S-trees. If this is successful, the result is a syntactic derivation tree (more than one derivation tree in case of ambiguities; the empty set if the input was not a correct S-tree).

M-GENERATOR and M-PARSER are each other's reverse: they define the same relation between S-trees and derivation trees.

In order to guarantee that M-PARSER is a computable function, an M-grammar has to obey the **measure condition**. It says: there is a measure on S-trees (a function from S-trees to integers, with a minimum) such that application of an analytical rule to an S-tree t yields S-trees smaller than t with respect to this measure. An example of a measure is the number of nodes in an S-tree, but in practice more subtle measures are needed. Thanks to the measure condition, application of M-PARSER always ends after a finite number of rule applications.

As it is our purpose to generate and analyze sentences, not surface trees, additional functions are needed. In the generative direction this is no problem: a function LEAVES can be defined which yields the sequence of leaves (the terminal S-trees) of an S-tree. For analysis purposes we need the third condition on M-grammars, the **surface syntax condition**. It says that for each M-grammar a set of "surface rules" must exist which define for each sentence a finite set of surface trees of which the set of correct surface trees is a subset. So this surface syntax has to be "weaker" than the real syntax and the surface rules can be simpler than the actual syntactic rules. A surface rule is applied in a bottom-up way to a sequence of S-trees; if it is applicable, the result is an S-tree with a new top node and with the input sequence of S-trees as its immediate constituents. Thanks to this, conventional parsing strategies can be used for the application of the surface rules, e.g. a variant of the CKY or the Earley Parser. The function applied by the parser is called S-PARSER.

The **morphological component** of an M-grammar relates

terminal S-trees to actual words, symbol strings. It makes use of a dictionary and of various kinds of morphological rules, not to be discussed here. The morphological component defines two functions:

A-MORPH converts words into (sets of) terminal S-trees.

G-MORPH converts terminal S-trees into (sets of) words.

A-MORPH and G-MORPH are each other's reverse.

The syntactic component and the morphological component together define a function SYNTACTIC ANAYLYSIS and a function SYNTACTIC GENERATION, which are each other's reverse. The function SYNTACTIC ANALYSIS is the composition of A-MORPH, S-PARSER and M-PARSER, the function SYNTACTIC GENERATION is the composition of M-GENERATOR, LEAVES and G-MORPH. In (6) the two functions are shown with example expressions. Note that the examples are a bit misleading as they suggest that these functions always give a unique result, which is the case for our example grammar, but not in general.

The **semantic component** of an M-grammar defines for each syntactic rule a "meaning rule" and for each basic expression a set of "basic meanings". As it depends on the application what the most appropriate way is to express these meanings - in an intensional logic, in an extensional logic or in some other way - this is left open here. A minor difference from standard Montague Grammar is that in an M-grammar a basic expression may have more than one meaning. This has the practical advantage that during analysis purely semantic word ambiguities can be "postponed" until after the syntactic analysis.

(6)   the boys are sleeping

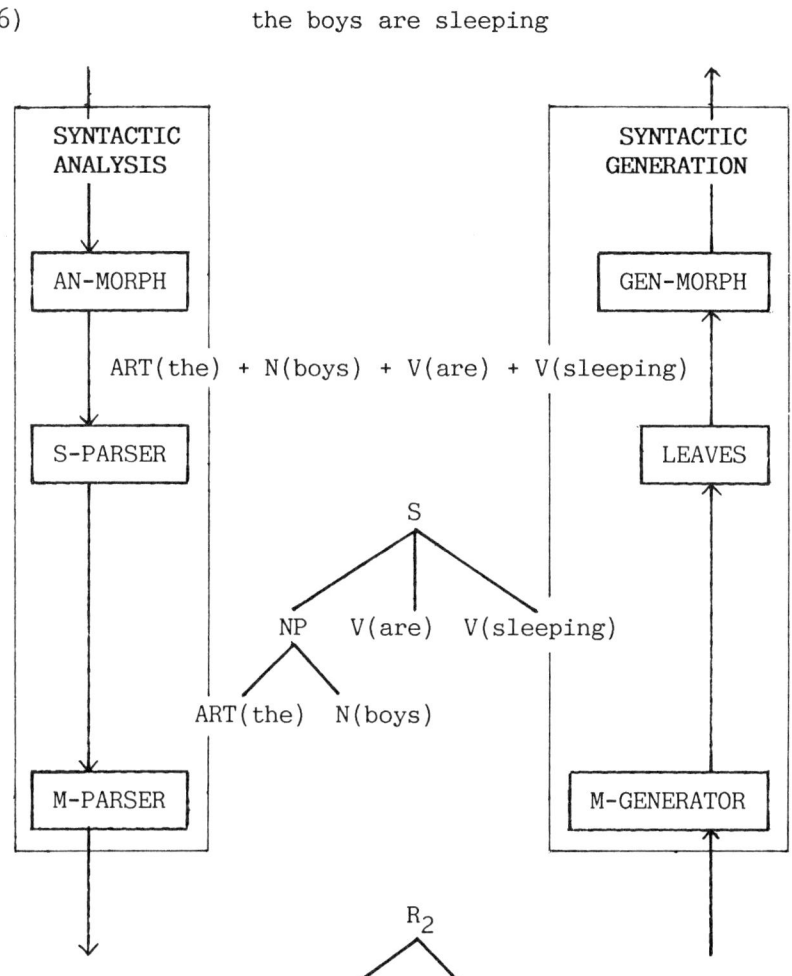

Montague Grammar and machine translation

I arrive now at the central topic of my paper: the use
of Montague Grammar in translation systems.   In the previous
section I have defined M-grammars, syntactically   powerful

versions of Montague grammars, for which an effective analysis procedure can be defined. In what way can they be used in a translation system? In order to be able to discuss the application of a linguistic theory in a translation system, I assume that in such a system the linguistic aspects can be clearly separated from the other aspects (e.g. the use of extra-linguistic information, robustness measures, etc.). Then it is possible in principle to consider a "stripped" system that makes use of linguistic information only. In addition I restrict the discussion to systems that translate isolated sentences. Such systems are in general not able to translate sentences unambiguously, but they define a set of **possible translations**. I define the function F-PTR as the function that operates on a sentence of the source language and yields the set of possible translations into the target language. F-PTR has the property that it is reversible: if s' is a possible translation of s, then s is a possible translation of s'.

(7)   s' in F-PTR(s) <--> s in F-PTR'(s')

The "correct" or "best" translation of s (chosen on the basis of extra-linguistic information) should be an element of the set F-PTR(s). Obviously, the function that yields this best translation is not reversible.

I would like to impose the following requirements on such a "possible translation" system.

1. It must be defined clearly what are correct sentences of the source language (SL) and the target language (TL). In other words, the system must be based on explicit grammars of SL and TL.

2. The translation function F-PTR must be defined in such a way that correct sentences of SL are translated into correct sentences of TL.

For me these requirements define the domain in which a theoretical discussion on machine translation makes sense. It is hard to compare - on a theoretical level - translation systems that do not obey them or at least try to obey them.

3. There must be some definition of the information that has to be conveyed during translation. Only if there is a

clear definition of information content that a sentence and
its translation should have in common, is it possible to
evaluate a translation system in this respect.
Unfortunately, there appears to be no theory of translation
that offers a satisfactory definition.

The obvious way to use Montague Grammar (i.e.   M-
grammar or some other analyzable version) in a "possible
translation" system appears to be the following.   Define a
Montague grammar for the source language and for the target
language.   From these grammars analysis and generation
components are derived. Then we extend the analysis with a
component which translates a syntactic derivation tree into
the logic according to the semantic component of the
grammar. The generation component is extended with a
component which performs the reverse function.   So in this
approach Intensional Logic is used as an interlingua.   This
type of system is outlined in (8).

(8) SL   TL
     sentence   sentence

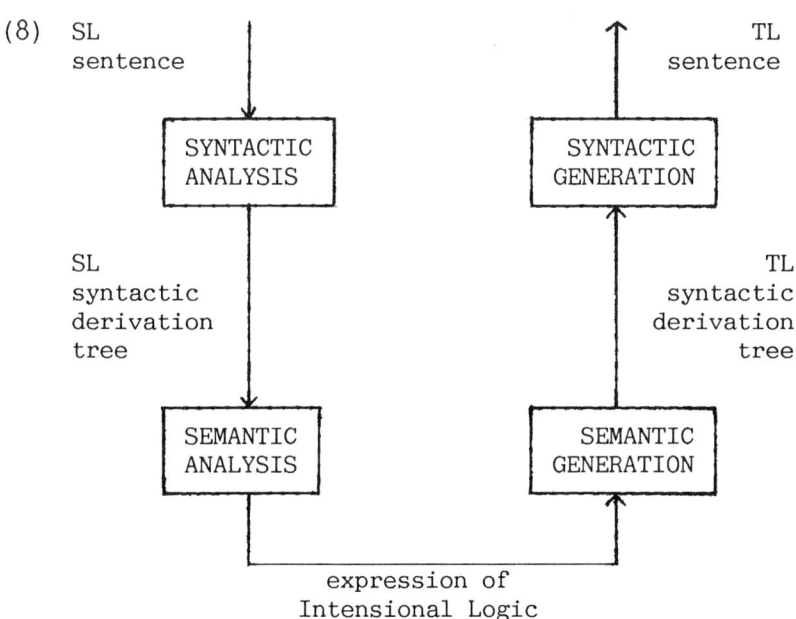

This approach obeys the three requirements: a correct
sentence of SL is translated into a correct sentence of TL
according to explicit grammars and the information that is

conveyed is the meaning in the model-theoretical sense. At
first sight this is a very attractive method. It has the
additional advantage that knowledge of the world can in
principle be formulated in the same logical language as the
interlingua, that inferences can be made, etc. I think that
long-term research along these lines would be very useful.
But in the Rosetta project we have chosen a different
approach. Why? Because of the following problems with
intensional logic as an interlingua.

1. Montague Grammar has been successful in defining the
semantics of a number of natural language constructions, but
a lot of work has to be done yet. For translation purposes
it is in general not necessary to define in detail what a
certain term or construct means, it is sufficient to know
that a term or construct of one language means the same as a
term or construct of another language. For example, the
semantics of belief-sentences may be a problem, but the
translation of the verb believe into the Dutch geloven is
probably not at all problematic. This is not really a
fundamental objection against the use of some kind of
intensional logic. The problem is mainly that there is a
discrepancy between the actual research in the field of
Montague Grammar (directed to a detailed semantic analysis,
for small fragments) and what is needed for machine
translation (a fairly superficial analysis, with a wide
coverage).

2.   The second problem is more fundamental. In this
approach the information that is conveyed during translation
is the meaning in the model-theoretic sense. This is a nice
basis for machine translation and certainly preferable to a
purely syntactic approach, but there is other information to
be conveyed as well, e.g. information on pragmatic and
stylistic aspects. In general it seems to be wise to stay
as close to the original form as possible (in some sense of
the word "form"). Intensional logic is not adequate for
carrying this information. One might object that the form
of the logical expression expresses information about the
form of the sentence too, and this is correct to a certain
extent, but making use of the form of logical expressions is
in fact in conflict with the spirit of Montague Grammar. As
I already mentioned in the introduction, the logical
expressions are only a way to define the model-theoretic
meaning, their form is not relevant.

3.   The third problem is the most delicate one: Montague
grammars translate natural languages into a **subset** of
intensional logic.   There is no guarantee that two Montague
grammars for two languages map them onto the same subset.
In (9) the situation is sketched.   The grammar of SL maps
onto a subset IL_1 of IL.   The grammar of TL maps onto a
subset IL_2, and consequently the generation component based
on this grammar is only applicable to expressions of IL_2.
So translation is only possible for the sentences that are
mapped onto the intersection of IL_1 and IL_2.

(9)

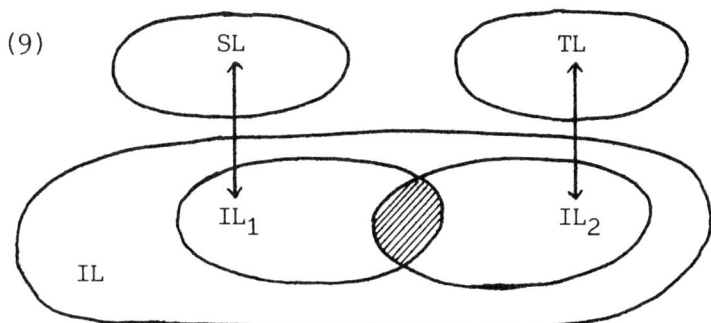

Notice that there is no independent definition of IL_1
and IL_2. They are only defined indirectly by the mappings
that follow from the grammars of SL and TL.   Therefore it is
very difficult to get to grips with this problem.   For
solving it, it is not sufficient that the terms of IL_1 and
IL_2 are the same, but in addition sentences that are to be
translated into each other should get exactly the same
logical structure and not just equivalent logical
structures.

This "subset problem" arises in some guise in all
systems - both interlingual and transfer sytems - that
translate via deep structures of some kind.   In general it
is not possible to define the translation for all "possible"
deep structures (many of them will not correspond to any
sentence at all), but on the other hand it is not possible
to characterize what the subset of relevant deep structures
is and to guarantee their translation.   (Of course this
problem does not arise in systems where the correct
translation operations cannot be distinguished from the
robustness measures.)   The only fundamental way to solve
this problem appears to be that the grammars of SL and TL
are not developed independently, but in close cooperation.

This possibility will be exploited in the next section, but will be left out of consideration here.

There are various other ways in which Montague grammars can be used for machine translation. One of them is to make a transfer system at the level of the intensional logic. In terms of figure (9) the transfer component has to translate from IL_1 into IL_2. Godden (1981) has done work along these lines for Thai to English, making use of Friedman and Warren's parser. The transfer rules have the status of meaning postulates, which gives them a sound semantic foundation. This is very interesting, but has only been worked out for the small fragment grammar of PTQ and does not appear to be easily extensible to larger fragments. Godden wrote in fact a PTQ-like grammar for Thai (i.e. the grammars for the two languages have not been written independently of each other) and added transfer rules for the small set of discrepancies betwen this grammar and the English PTQ grammar. Apart from the problem of the growing set of discrepancies for larger grammars (which ultimately comes down to the earlier-mentioned problem 3), problems 1 and 2 with regard to the use of intensional logic in machine translation are valid here too.

Another possibility of basing a translation system on Montague Grammar is to design a transfer system as outlined in (10) with transfer at the level of syntactic derivation trees.

(10)

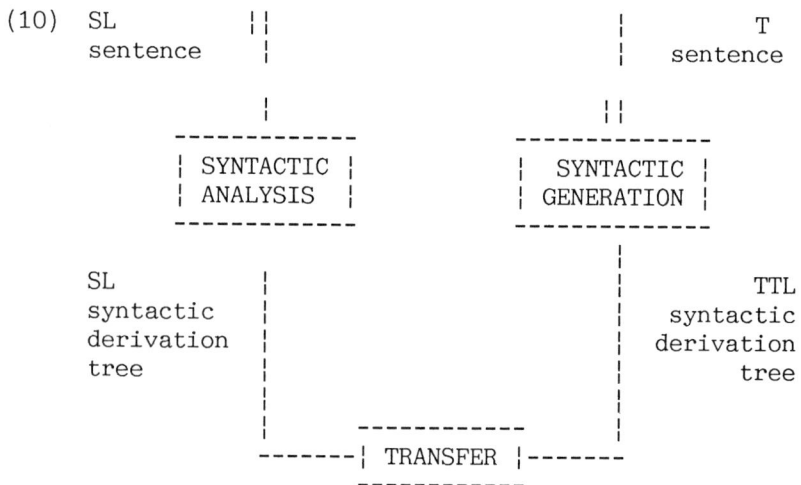

In this approach there is an analysis component based on a
grammar of SL and a generation component based on a grammar
of TL; the transfer component converts syntactic derivation
trees of SL into syntactic derivation trees of TL. In the
most general version of this approach the transfer rules
would convert arbitrary parts of SL derivation trees into
arbitrary parts of TL derivation trees. Problems 1 and 2 do
not arise here, as intensional logic is not used explicitly.
However problem 3, the subset problem, returns here in a
different form. The point is that the rules of the TL
derivation tree that is yielded by the transfer component
need not be applicable.

A different type of Montague-based transfer system is
described by Nishida and Doshita (1982). In this system the
transfer component converts the logical expression yielded
by the analysis component (of which the terms are source
language dependent) into a function-argument structure of
which the application (in the generation component) yields
target language expressions. There is no separate grammar
of the target language in this approach.

I discussed the various Montague-based approaches under
the assumption that the grammars of source language and
target language are developed independently. Some of the
problems are alleviated or disappear completely if these
grammars are coordinated in some way. One, rather drastic,
way of doing this will be discussed in the next section.

Isomorphic M-grammars

After the introduction of M-grammars, compositional
grammars that can be used for both analysis and generation,
only a relatively small, but essential, step has to be made
to arrive at the isomorphic grammar approach. This step is
that the grammars of the various languages are not developed
independently, but more or less in parallel and are attuned
to each other as follows.

For each basic expression in one language there must be
at least one corresponding basic expression in the other
language with the same meaning. For each syntactic rule in
one language there must be at least one corresponding
syntactic rule in the other language with the same meaning
operation. Grammars that are attuned in this way are called

isomorphic grammars, if the rules obey applicability conditions to which I will come back later.

Given two isomorphic grammars, the translation relation is - informally - defined as follows: two sentences are translations of each other if they are derived from corresponding basic expressions by application of corresponding rules.

Before giving more precise definitions, I will give a simple example of isomorphic grammars for English and Dutch, in (12). The grammar is the same as the one described before. In the middle column of (12) the names of the basic meanings and meaning rules that the two grammars share are given. The grammars define a translation relation between sentences (11a) and (11b).

> (11a)   The boys are sleeping.
> (11b)   De jongens slapen.

(12)   DUTCH   ENGLISH

basic expressions   basic meanings   basic expressions

N(jongen) c_1 N(boy)
V(slaap) c_2 V(sleep)

syntactic rules   meaning rules   syntactic rules

NR_1: M_1 ER_1:
N(jongen) -> NP(de jongens)   N(boy) -> NP (the boys)
NR_2 M_2 ER_2:
NP(de jongens) + V(slaap) ->   NP(the boys) + V(sleep) ->
S(de jongens slapen)   S(the boys are sleeping)

In the example grammar I use the abbreviated notations for S-trees; the rules are characterized by means of an example application.

Note that the relation between basic expressions of Dutch and English need not be one-to-one, although the example may suggest this. For each basic meaning there is a set of basic expressions in each language. The same holds for the rules. For example, NR_2 might also correspond to a rule ER_3, which generates a sentence in the simple present tense. Then the grammars would also define a possible translation relation between de jongens slapen and the boys sleep.

The definition of the translation relation given above can be reformulated more precisely as follows. Two sentences are each other's translation, if they have the same semantic derivation tree, i.e. if they have syntactic derivation trees with the same geometry, of which the nodes are labelled by corresponding rules and basic expressions. The syntactic derivation trees of the example sentences and their semantic derivation tree are given in (13).

(13)

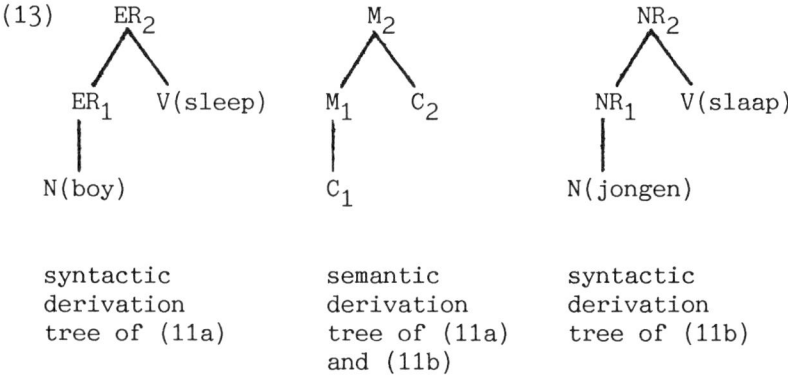

syntactic	semantic	syntactic
derivation	derivation	derivation
tree of (11a)	tree of (11a)	tree of (11b)
	and (11b)	

There are several possible ways of using isomorphic grammars in a translation system; one of them is a transfer system like the one sketched in diagram (10). The global design is the same, but the difference is that the TRANSFER component is now much simpler. The syntactic derivation tree of the source language can be converted into a derivation tree of the target language by a straightforward node-by-node transfer of basic expressions and rules.

Here I will discuss another possibility: the use of semantic derivation trees as interlingual expressions. This lies at hand, since a semantic derivation tree is exactly what translations have in common according to our definitions. In the section on M-grammars I described how a function SYNTACTIC ANALYSIS and a function SYNTACTIC GENERATION can be defined on the basis of the syntactic and the morphological component of an M-grammar. The semantic

component of an M-grammar relates basic expressions to basic
meanings and syntactic rules to meaning rules. On this
basis two additional functions can be defined:

A-TRANSFER applies to a syntactic derivation tree and yields
the set of corresponding semantic derivation trees.

G-TRANSFER applies to a semantic derivation tree and yields
the set of corresponding syntactic derivation trees.

Both A-TRANSFER and G-TRANSFER are simple functions, defined
in terms of local operations on nodes.

The result is an interlingual system as outlined in (14) for
Dutch to English.

(14) de jongens   the boys are
      slapen   sleeping

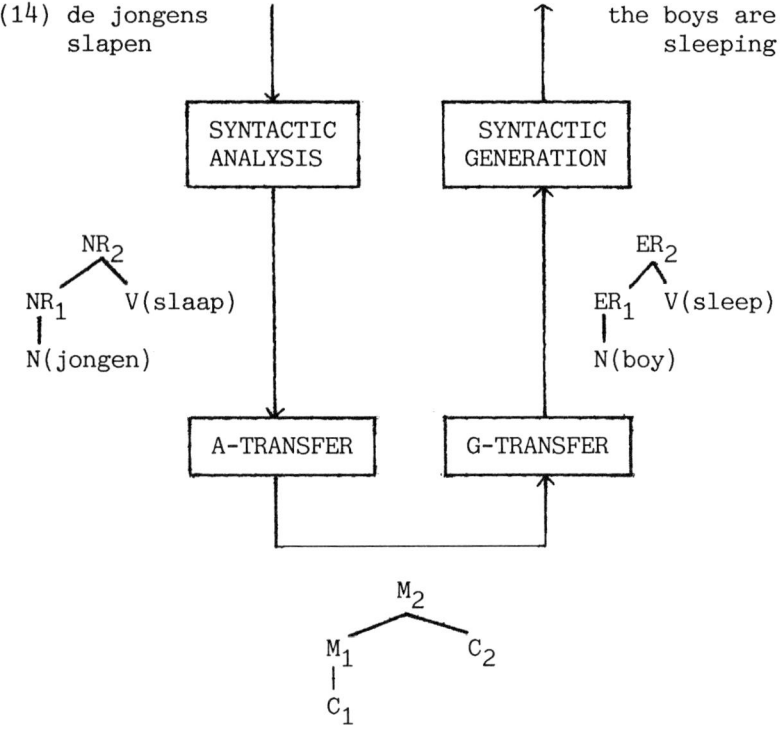

I will now give a more precise definition of isomorphy.
First, a syntactic derivation tree is called **well-formed** if
it defines at least one sentence (i.e. the rules in the

derivation tree are applicable). A semantic derivation tree
is called well-formed if one of the derivation trees to
which it corresponds (according to the semantic component)
is well-formed. Two grammars G and G' are called **isomorphic**
if each semantic derivation tree that is well-formed with
respect to G is also well-formed with respect to G', and
vice versa. Note that isomorphy is an equivalence relation
between grammars and that the definition can be extended
easily to sets of more than two grammars.

The definitions imply that if a translation system as
outlined in (14) is based on isomorphic grammars, we know
that the analysis of a sentence in the source language
yields a semantic derivation tree, the generation component
will always yield a correct sentence of the target language.
Translations defined in this way have the same meaning, they
have the same semantic derivation tree, they have similar
syntactic derivation trees, and they may have completely
different surface trees. So in this framework the
information that is conveyed during translation is not only
the model-theoretical meaning, but also the way in which
this meaning is derived. This could be called the
compositionality principle of translation.

This approach avoids the earlier mentioned problems
with intensional logic as an interlingua. The hardest of
these problems was the "subset problem", which arises not
only in a system with a logical interlingua, but also in a
system with transfer on syntactic derivation trees (as in
(10)), if the grammars of source and target language are
developed independently. In principle this problem is
solved in a system based on isomorphic grammars, but it
would be somewhat misleading to state it that way. A
remaining problem is that in the syntactic framework we use,
it is not yet possible to prove **formally** whether two
grammars are isomorphic or not. For various kinds of
grammars a formal proof is possible, but not yet for
grammars with the syntactic power of M-grammars. However,
even without a formal proof the approach is an important
step forward.

In practice the process of grammar writing proceeds as
follows. A set of compositional rules $\underline{R}$ is written for
handling a particular phenomenon in language L, a
corresponding set of compositional rules $\underline{R}'$ is written for
handling the corresponding phenomenon in language L'. The

rules R should be complete for the expected set of input expressions, the rules R' should be complete for the corresponding set of input expressions of L' (their "translations"). The most important practical difference between this and other approaches may be that here the grammars are written with translation in mind. Because of the reversibility of the grammars the rule writers can focus their attention on writing compositional (i.e. generative) rules in parallel and on the applicability of these rules to the expected inputs.

Diagram (14) shows the global design of the systems which are being developed in the **Rosetta project.** This is a research project on machine translation at Philips Research Laboratories, Eindhoven. A few years of preparatory research resulted in the isomorphic grammar approach outlined here and in two experimental systems based on this approach, Rosetta1 and Rosetta2. A fairly large six-year project has started this year (1985), in which more sophisticated systems, Rosetta3 and Rosetta4, will be developed, for Dutch, English and Spanish.

The Rosetta approach is interlingual. Since interlinguality can be defined in various ways, this statement may cause misunderstandings. Therefore I will give three possible definitions of interlinguality and indicate which of them are applicable here.

1.   A system is interlingual if there is an intermediate meaning representation which has the "same distance" to the sentences of the source language and the target language. Note that according to this definition even a bilingual one-direction translation system may be interlingual. This definition is clearly applicable to the Rosetta systems.

2.   A system is interlingual if an interlingua is defined for a given set of languages in such a way that for each of these languages an analysis component can be defined that translates from that language into the interlingua and a generation component that does the reverse. So the combination of an analysis component for language L and a generation component for language L' is a translation system from L into L'. This definition is also applicable to the Rosetta systems.

3.   A system is interlingual if it uses an interlingua

which is "universal", i.e. which can be used for expressing any meaning of any sentence in any natural language. Obviously, the Rosetta approach is not interlingual in this sense.

In the Rosetta project we aim at developing an interlingual system, according to definition 2. This is certainly more ambitious and more difficult than developing a purely bilingual system. Rosetta3 is being developed for three languages in order to find out what the price of this multilingual approach is, in comparison with the bilingual approach according to definition 1.

Concluding remarks

In the section on Montague Grammar and machine translation I formulated three requirements on translation systems: explicit grammars of source language and target language, translation of correct sentences into correct sentences according to these grammars and a definition of what has to be conveyed during translation. The isomorphic grammar approach satisfied the first two requirements; with respect to the third requirement a step forward has been made in comparison with using Intensional Logic as interlingua. In the Rosetta systems it is not only the model-theoretical meaning that is conveyed, but also the way in which this meaning is derived from basic meanings.

I mentioned three problems with using Intensional Logic as an interlingua. The first problem was that a meaning representation in Intensional Logic may require a more detailed meaning analysis than is needed for translation purposes, because for translation we are mainly interested in equality of meanings. This problem is solved by using semantic derivation trees as interlingual meaning representations, in which the unique names of basic meanings and meaning rules serve exactly to express the equality of meaning of basic expressions and syntactic rules, respectively. The second problem was that expressions of Intensional Logic only convey the meaning in the strict model-theoretical sense. As I pointed out, semantic derivation trees indicate in addition the way in which the meaning is derived. They may also be used to convey other information than the meaning. If two basic expressions or two syntactic rules (of the same language) have the same

meaning, but differ in some other aspect which is relevant
to translation, we may assign different names to the
corresponding basic meanings and meaning rules. The
solution of the third problem, the subset problem, has been
the main motivation for the isomorphic grammar approach. If
the grammars of the source and the target language are
isomorphic, each interlingual expression generated by the
analysis component can be processed by the generation
component.

In this paper I have illustrated the isomorphic grammar
approach by means of very simple examples. This may leave
you with the impression that isomorphic grammars can only
define very trivial translation relations. The following
remarks should indicate the potential power of the approach.

1.   First and foremost it is important to notice that the
rules and the basic expressions of the grammars are chosen
with translation in mind.

2.   Syntactic rules may perform powerful operations on
syntactic trees, e.g. permutations, substitutions and
deletions, as long as the conditions on M-grammars are
obeyed. So the correspondence between syntactic rules of
different grammars as required by the isomorphy relation
does not imply similarity of the surface structures.

3.   Basic expressions need not be terminals (i.e. S-trees
consisting of one node), but may also be complex S-trees.
This is especialy useful for idiomatic expressions (e.g. to
make up one's mind), which are primitive from a semantic
point of view, but complex from a syntactic point of view.
The same mechanism is used in the case where a word in one
language corresponds to a complex expression in the other
language, even if this complex expression would not be
considered as an idiom in that language (e.g. the
translation of the Spanish verb madrugar into the English
expression to get up early). On the other hand basic
expressions may correspond to "deeper". possibly more
abstract, notions than those denoted by words.

4.   Corresponding basic expressions of two languages need
not have the same syntactic category, under the conditions
that these different categories correspond to the same
semantic type. Obviously allowing such a mismatch of
categories imposes conditions on the rest of the grammars

which are not always easy to fulfill. In Landsbergen (1985) I dealt with a particular example of this: the translation of the English verb <u>to</u> <u>like</u> into the Dutch adverb <u>graag</u>.

I hope that these points make it clear that the isomorphic grammar approach is in principle quite powerful. The practical feasibility should be shown and has to a certain extent been shown already by the actual systems developed in the Rosetta project.

In conclusion, I hope to have shown that application of Montague Grammar in machine translation may yield the best results if it is applied in a "creative" way. The main influence on the Rosetta systems has been exerted by the compositionality principle. This plays an important role in Rosetta, not only by relating form and meaning of one language, but also by inspiring us to formulate a compositionality principle of translation which relates form and meaning of various languages. These principles should not be interpreted as refutable theories of language or translation (cf. Partee 1982 on the status of the compositionality principle), but as **guiding** principles for the construction of grammars and translation systems.

And there I would like to stop.

Pete WHITELOCK: Well, I would like to ask a question. In your approach, if you have a sentence which is ambiguous in translation but non-ambiguous in the source language as far as we can tell, do you have to essentially give it two analyses so that you can get the two translations?

LANDSBERGEN: If a sentence is ambiguous in translation, i.e. if it has more than one translation, there are two possibilities. The first one is that these translations are paraphrases, corresponding to the same meaning. In that case there is only one analysis of the SL sentence and the ambiguity arises only in the generation component. The second possibility is that these translations correspond to different meanings. In that case there must be two analyses of the SL sentence. It is not always easy to decide if for a particular phenomenon we have to create a semantic ambiguity or if it can be described as having one "encompassing" meaning. In Rosetta this decision will not only depend on what is most elegant in one language, but it will also be influenced by the other languages.

Doug ARNOLD: The language that the grammar defines is
something rather close to the surface of the languages -
it's something, I imagine, like morphologically and
syntactically analyzed English, or morphologically and
syntactically analyzed Dutch, and so on. That's right,
isn't it? You have only one set of ...

LANDSBERGEN: One level of representation, yes. However,
during the generation process of a sentence, we start with
rather abstract representations, which are gradually
transformed into surface representations. But they are all
S-trees, so essentially there is one level of
representation.

ARNOLD: What is your feeling about having more levels of
representation, so that in fact the 'tuning' of the grammars
would be between grammars that essentially generate semantic
representions of appropriate languages or, let's say, F-
structures of the languages, logical forms of the languages,
something like that? Do you have an argument against using
other levels of representation, for instance?

LANDSBERGEN: Well, in the first place it is the other way
round. There should be arguments for having more levels.
But leaving that aside: in Rosetta the syntactic rules have
a clear effect on both the form and the meaning. If there
are more levels between form and meaning the effect of the
rules may be harder to understand. But the main problem
with having more levels is the "subset problem" I discussed
in my presentation. If there are more levels, the
representations at the deepest level will be the result of a
number of translation steps between the various levels. It
is hard to charaterize independently the subset of deep
representations that correspond to sentences. This makes it
difficult to guarantee that this subset is actually
translated.

ARNOLD: I think that the subset problem is one of the major
problems. Could I just say what the argument for having
other levels is: there are more superficial differences
between languages than there are non-superficial ones; so
languages configure differently, let's say. So a non-
configurational representation makes translation easier.
You can phrase that within a different theory if you want,

but there is that sort of intuition around. That would motivate having other levels than one.

LANDSBERGEN: I forgot to mention another objection against having deeper levels. After going to a deeper level of analysis, information that is useful for translation may get lost. E.g., at the F-structure level of LFG there is no information about the surface order of constituents, although this may be important for choosing the most plausible interpretation with regard to scope. Of course, the idea that languages have more in common at a deeper level of analysis than at the surface is an argument in favour of having more levels. But in our approach the derivational history is such a level; our assumption is that languages have much in common at the level of derivational history.

But I interrupted you - please continue.

ARNOLD: My point really relates to the subset problem. Why don't you just say, for the cases where there is a failure of intersection between source language and target language ILs, that there is no translation in those cases? Why don't you adopt a more restrictive view of translation, distinguishing, say, between translation and paraphrase?

LANDSBERGEN: There are two reasons. The first reason is a practical one. We make an interlingual system with interaction with the user during analysis, in case of ambiguities. If in such a system the analysis has been successful and has yielded an interlingual expression, one wants to be sure that the generation component provides a translation.

ARNOLD: Why? If what you are doing is translation why don't you ...

LANDSBERGEN: Well, I think of the application of this system in an electronic mail environment. It is unacceptable if an analyzed message is not translated.

ARNOLD: No, I was pressing you for a theoretical argument.

LANDSBERGEN: OK, that was a practical point.

ARNOLD: Why do you call the result of that sort of activity

'translation' and not something else? If the source text
and a target text don't share at least one IL
representation, why do you want to claim that they are
translations?

LANDSBERGEN: The theoretical argument is that if the source
text and the target text do not share an IL representation,
it may still be the case that they have logically equivalent
representations. So in that case they have the same meaning
and may be called each other's translations, but due to
fairly arbitrary differences in the two grammars, they are
not recognized as such by the system.

Henry THOMPSON: I suspect that really the right place to
get an answer to this is in Partee's work, but on a quick
understanding of what you said, can you disabuse me of the
notion that a Montague grammar with constraints imposed on
it which you refer to to ensure parsability is any different
from a context-free grammar? Is there an obvious way to
characterize the difference between a Montague grammar so
restricted, particularly the S-rules that are associated
with it, and something that I would think of as a context-
free grammar with a rule-to-rule relationship between the
syntactic rules and some compositional semantics? Is there
anything that really remains of Montague in this? That is,
I guess, what it comes down to.

LANDSBERGEN: Montague's own example grammars are more or
less context-free, but in Rosetta we use a transformational
extension of Montague Grammar (cf Landsbergen 1981). Our
rules are powerful, they can perform permutations, deletions
etc. Indeed, our surface grammar is context-free in its
weak generative capacity, but the grammar as a whole defines
a non-context-free subset of this. Actually, our formalism
is undergoing some changes at the moment. We are going to
make a distinction between meaningful rules that contain
information relevant for translation and on the other hand
purely syntactic transformations. These transformations are
not involved in the isomorphy relation and can be defined
for each language separately.

THOMPSON: What does the parser then look like as a result of
all this?

LANDSBERGEN: The parser consists of two parts: the surface
parser and the M-parser. The surface parser produces a set

of candidate surface trees for the input sentence. The M-parser applies the analytical rules of the M-grammar to a surface tree and breaks it down into smaller parts, ultimately into basic expressions. If the M-parser is successfully applied, i.e. if the surface tree is correct, the result is a derivation tree. The surface grammar is weakly equivalent to a context-free grammar, it is similar to a recursive transition network grammar. The rules of the M-grammar are more powerful.

THOMPSON: Thank you.

Graeme RITCHIE: Could I ask you about idioms? I'm a bit puzzled about what you said about idioms. It sounded from what you said as if, if one of the languages had a phrasal, idiomatic expression of some concept, there had to be a basic concept in the logic and a basic expression in the semantics corresponding to that which had that semantic compositional structure.

LANDSBERGEN: No no no. Not that.

RITCHIE: Well you said that idioms may have whole semantic derivation trees.

LANDSBERGEN: I said that idioms correspond to compound basic expressions. I am sorry about all these different kinds of trees, but here we have to make clear distinction between S-trees and derivation trees. All basic expressions are S-trees, but usually they consist of one node. An idiom is a compound S-tree, consisting of more than one node. It is a basic expression from a semantic point of view, but it is a compound expression from a syntactic point of view. For example, to lose one's temper will be represented as an S-tree with lose and temper in it, but its meaning is not derived compositionally from these parts.

RITCHIE: For the semantics that's derived from it, to do the translation the other language has to have some expression which has that as its semantics?

LANDSBERGEN: Yes, the expression in the other language may be atomic or may be an idiomatic expression. It may also be a compound expression that one would not be inclined to call an idiomatic expression in that language. For instance, a possible translation of to lose one's temper into Dutch is kwaad worden, an idiomatic expression of Dutch, but in the translation system it has to be treated in the same way as an idiom.

RITCHIE: I can understand that. I didn't see what the adjective 'compound' implied with your various levels.

Karen SPARCK JONES: You said quite explicitly you're not dealing with ill-formed text at the moment, fragments and things like that. Is it perfectly obvious how, when you've got around to it, in principle you would do this in this kind of approach?

LANDSBERGEN: I did not deal with ill-formed input in my paper, but in the actual system Rosetta2 we try to deal with it. For sentences that do not fit into the system's grammar, there are several robustness measures, partially similar to those in other systems. For instance, if the surface parser is not able to make a complete parse, it will look for a "cover" of the sentence by the largest constituents it has found. It puts them together under a special node with category UG (for "Ungrammatical"). In the next phase, the M-parser, there is an analytical rule that is able to cope with a UG. At the moment this rule is very simple: it splits up the tree into its immediate subtrees. Each of the subtrees is then analyzed and translated further in the usual way. In the generation component the translated subtrees are combined again by a rule corresponding to the beforementioned analysis rule for a UG. So the net result of all this is that an incorrect sentence is split up into correct parts which are translated separately.

Nick OSTLER: Do you have any experience of working practically with, say, three languages? I don't know whether it's only in the future that you are going to bring in Spanish, but it seems that you envisage a real-time interaction between linguists working together drafting these grammars, and presumably that's just about feasible when you've got two languages. If you've got three, establishing your isomorphisms will be twice as difficult again, I suppose, and if you were to add more languages of course it would rapidly become completely infeasible.

LANDSBERGEN: I have some experience with writing isomorphic grammars for Dutch, English and Italian, for Rosetta1, but these grammars were small and I did that on my own, so there

I did not encounter the problems you are talking about. The second version of the system, Rosetta2, has larger grammars, which have been designed for the same three languages, but they have been worked out only for Dutch and English, due to a change in our planning. We are now working with a group of linguists and the actual writing of the rules has to start yet. We will first make global isomorphic schemes for the three grammars. Then these grammars will be worked out in detail, separately. If serous problems arise in that phase, there may be feed-back to the isomorphic scheme.

OSTLER: But you haven't done it very much as yet? This is your plan for the six-year project.

LANDSBERGEN: Yes. The six-year project itself is very young. It started at the beginning of this year [1985].

OSTLER: So your experience is just of doing English and Dutch. There has been the PHLIQA project (Landsbergen 1976).

LANDSBERGEN: That was in a way the predecessor of this project.

OSTLER: Did that involve multilingual or just bilingual ...

LANDSBERGEN: No, it was just English. PHLIQA was a question-answering system. So we have experience with building large systems, but not with building a large interlingual translation system with a group of linguists. Note that the isomorphic approach is also feasible for bilingual translation. We have chosen to work on three languages, because we are interested in interlingual applications and want to investigate to what extent the multilingual approach is feasible. One of the goals of the project is to find out what the price of this multilinguality is. I hope to report on this in a few years.

References

Dowty, D.R., Wall, R.E. & Peters, S. 1981. **Introduction to Montague Semantics**. Dordrecht: D. Reidel.

Friedman, J. & Warren, D.S. 1978. A Parsing Method for Montague Grammars. **Linguistics and Philosophy** 2, 347-372.

Godden, K. 1981. **Montague Grammar and Machine Translation between Thai and English.** PhD dissertation, University of Kansas.

Janssen, T.M.V. 1986. **Foundations and Applications of Montague Grammar, Part I.** CWI Tract 19. Amsterdam: Centre for Mathematics and Computer Science.

Landsbergen, S.P.J. 1976. Syntax and formal semantics of English in PHLIQA1. In L. Steels, ed., **Advances in Natural Language Processing.** Antwerp: University of Antwerp.

Landsbergen, S.P.J. 1981. Adaptation of Montague Grammar to the Requirements of Parsing. In Groenendijk, J.A.G., Janssen, T.M.V. & Stokhof, M.B.J. **Formal Methods in the Study of Language, Part 2.** MC Tract 136, Mathematical Centre, Amsterdam, 399-420.

Landsbergen, S.P.J. 1985. Isomorphic Grammars and their Use in the Rosetta Translation System. In King, M., ed., **Machine Translation Today.** Edinburgh: Edinburgh University Press.

Montague, R. 1970a. Universal Grammar. **Theoria** 36, 373-398. Reprinted in Thomason, ed., 222-246.

Montague, R. 1970b. English as a Formal Language. In B. Visentini et al, eds., **Linguaggi nella società e nella technica.** Milan: Edizioni di Comunità, 189-224. Reprinted in Thomason, ed., 108-221.

Montague, R. 1973. The Proper Treatment of Quantification in Ordinary English. In Hintikka, J., Moravcsik, J. & Suppes, P., eds. **Approaches to Natural Language,** Dordrecht: D. Reidel, 221-242. Reprinted in Thomason, ed., 247-270.

Nishida, T. & Doshita, S. 1982. An English-Japanese Machine Translation System based on Formal Semantics of Natural Language. In Horecky, J., ed., **COLING 82: Proceedings of the Ninth International Conference on Computational Linguistics**. Amsterdam: North-Holland, 277-282.

Partee, B.H. 1976. Some Transformational Extensions of Montague Grammar. In Partee, B.H., ed., **Montague Grammar**, New York: Academic Press, 51-76.

Partee, B.H. 1982. Compositionality. In Landman, F. & Veltman, F., eds. **Varieties of Formal Semantics** (Proceedings of the 4th Amsterdam Colloquium). Dordrecht: Foris, 281-312.

Thomason, R.H., ed. 1974. **Formal Philosophy: Selected Papers of Richard Montague**. New Haven: Yale University Press.

Three Seductions of Computational Psycholinguistics

Ronald M. Kaplan

Descriptive linguists, computational linguists, and psycholinguists have traditionally been concerned with different aspects of the formal study of language. Linguists want explicit grammatical formulations to characterize the well-formed sentences of a language and to indicate in some systematic way how the sequence of elements that makes up an utterance encode that utterance's meaning. They don't particularly care about specific processing algorithms that might be used to identify well-formed sentences or to associate them with their meanings, but this is a central concern of computational linguists. Computational linguists are interested in discovering the feasible algorithms that can interpret grammatical descriptions to recognize or produce utterances, and in understanding how the performance of these algorithms depends on various properties of grammars and machine architectures. Psycholinguists are also concerned with processes and algorithms, but not just with ones that are feasible within conventional computational architectures. They focus on algorithms and architectures that model or elucidate the language processing capabilities of human speakers and listeners.

These differences in concern have been the source of much debate over the years, and in some cases, suspicion, misunderstanding and confusion. The formalisms and methods of one approach have often seemed counterintuitive, if not totally inappropriate, for addressing the problems of the others. But it also happens that what seem like obvious and intuitive strategies for a given approach are actually inappropriate even for addressing its own problems. For each discipline there are certain compelling temptations or

LINGUISTIC THEORY AND COMPUTER APPLICATIONS
ISBN 0-12-747220-7

seductions that practitioners typically and frequently fall
into. In the metaphysical remarks at the beginning of my
talk I want to review some of the errors that have come from
paying too much attention to intuitions that come from any
of these domains. These are temptations that lead you into
doing things that you wouldn't really want to do if you
understood what was really going on. I have picked out
three particular seductions that might spark some discussion
later.

Having outlined some of the way in which one can get
off the track, I want to tell you a little bit about Lexical
Functional Grammar and how it is organized to avoid some of
these seductions. I'll present some fundamental formal
concepts that we use in LFG but which I think can be
abstracted away from the details of our formalism. I think
these mechanisms are common to a variety of formalisms and
perhaps represent the right level at which to define a
linguistic meta-language.

1. The procedural seduction: a computational temptation

The first seduction is what I call the procedural
seduction, the mistaken belief that you know what to do next
and that you can gain computational efficiency by saying
what it is. This comes from your intuitions about
computation, about how you would actually go about
recognizing and generating utterances with specific,
concrete algorithms and programs. This kind of seduction
had a valid justification in its day. Starting out in the
'60s, everybody thought that non-procedural formalisms, such
as context-free gammars, were too weak. You couldn't
express the generalizations you wanted to express about
natural languages in a context-free formalism. If you
tried, you would end up with thousands of incomprehensible
rules, and merely storing such a grammar would take a major
amount of the available memory. You were running on a 1620
that had approximately 2 bytes of memory and this was very
important.

Despite the general appeal of declarative systems,
there was widespread acceptance in the computational
community, if not also the linguistic community, of
Chomsky's (1963) arguments that context-free grammars were
too weak to support either natural language descriptions or

computations. But then what the noncomputational linguists were using at the time - transformational grammar - did not seem to offer a reasonable computational alternative. Transformational grammar was neither fish nor fowl: though developed by noncomputational linguists with what we might now call a declarative orientation, the formalism nonetheless relied on an implicit sequential ordering of operations to define valid deep-structure/surface-structure correspondences. This implicit derivation procedure was not regarded as crucial to the theory of grammar - any mathematically equivalent technique for enumerating valid correspondences would do just as well - but in point of fact it was extremely difficult to devise alternative procedures that accurately computed the proper results. Nobody could do any reasonable computations with the transformational grammars that the linguists were actually using. A number of restricted forms of transformational grammar, more or less in the spirit of Chomsky's proposals, were implemented and explored in some detail, but they were not really accepted as serious candidates by a large number of computational linguists.

The solution to that kind of thing was to add more general operations to a simple declarative base. That's what the ATN (Woods 1970) was. Take a very simple thing like a context-free grammar or recursive transition network and add on a way of managing more information by virtue of registers containing information that persisted across a rule or network. You didn't just have a feature value or category value that you could test against some literal locally in the grammar, but you could actually carry information through a network and even up and down the tree. As we saw this morning, Woods did this in the obvious way, given that he was working in Lisp. He said 'let's put a list of forms on the arc and we'll simply EVAL them'. He defined a list of primitive forms that you could use - SETR and GETR etc., but of course everybody who wrote ATN grammars realized that he had provided an escape hatch, a route to arbitrary Lisp evaluations. This also provided a seduction to go out and write your own functions, to explore alternative ways of manipulating grammatical, and frequently, process-control information.

Initially people would write actions that were compositions of the primitive functions. But then of course people starting using other random woolly types of

computations. It was a reasonable move at the time but it
led down the slippery slope (see Figure 1).

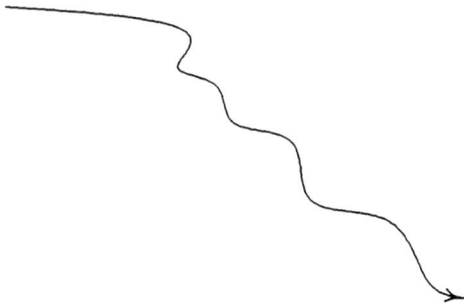

Figure 1. The slippery slope

Richer formalisms basically allow outputs to be
determined by intermediate process steps, intermediate
operations and intermediate data that are not theoretically
committed. In any linguistic system there are certain kinds
of structures that really have some theoretical
significance, that you'd like to argue about with somebody
and say that that's the way language is, that that's what's
in somebody's head or that's what a possible human language
can have. Those are the things that you are theoretically
committed to.

But in these richer procedural formalisms you get the
possibility of determining inputs and outputs by things that
you don't really care about, that have to do with particular
details, either of your specification or your
implementation. You have various combinations of indexing,
caches, strategies, extra registers, and the ability to look
at the internal implementation state of the parser. You can
control what sentences get recognized and what structures
can be associated with them by virtue of information that
you really don't have a good theoretical grasp on.

The outputs begin to depend on the details of a
particular, usually complicated, implementation or
interpreter. Complexity is really the key here. The ATN
parser in the LUNAR system (Woods, Kaplan, and Nash-Webber,
1972), for example, was a 40-page Lisp function, each line
of which had some particular motivation - perhaps some
argument that somebody had made, a process-control feature

that somebody might take advantage of, or an accident that somebody left in the code. Because it was trying to allow for various kinds of information flow upwards and downwards through the tree, it was very difficult to understand what the formalism actually meant. The same is true of other powerful procedural systems. The only way you could figure out the input/output behaviour of the formalism was to run the one particular program that implemented it. As a scientist, you couldn't get an independent grasp on it, and I regard this as a serious theoretical, if not practical, problem.

The major computational motivation for this was to obtain some degree of fine process control. Let's enrich our grammatical notation a little bit more so that we can actually say, 'do this under these situations but not under those situations', or appeal to pragmatics and say 'we've been going on long enough on this path and it's not worth it, let's cut it off'. By letting process-control specifications into the grammar, you thought you were going to get something that ran more efficiently - you thought you as a grammar writer knew enough about the global parsing situation to give detailed instructions about what to do next. If you looked at ATN grammars you saw people beginning to invent new ways of doing that kind of thing - suggesting constructs for splitting configurations and merging them back together, having exclusive OR instead of inclusive OR etc.

The reason I claim that this approach is seductive is because it doesn't get you where you want to go, whether you're a linguist or a computer scientist. In hindsight it seems that whenever the sequential, procedural facilities of the ATN formalism were used, some sort of linguistic error was being committed, in the sense that generalizations were not being expressed. You ended up with a grammar which could be correctly describing all the sentences of the language but would have replication and redundancy, would be patched all over the place to make up for some basic deficiencies.

To give you just one example of that, take the interaction between passive and tag questions. The traditional way of doing passive in an ATN is to find the initial noun phrase and call it the subject as a first guess. Then as you go from left to right, if you later discover that there is a form of the verb 'to be' and a passive participle, you swap the registers around. You take what was the subject and make it be the object and then if you later find an animate by-phrase you make that the subject. That was seen as a smooth move in those days and became, in fact, one of the intuitive successes that ATN advocates (including Woods 1970; Woods, Kaplan, and Nash-Webber 1972; and Kaplan 1972) could point to.

One of the reasons was that the only alternative that people could conceive of was to say 'active and passive are nondeterministic alternatives; you take the one that corresponds to active and if that doesn't work out then you fail all the way back to the beginning. Starting again at the initial state, you go off on another path corresponding to passive'. The procedural perception of the way a parser would behave with a grammar of this sort is that it would have done a lot of work recognizing that initial noun phrase, which could have been a complicated, elaborate structure. Upon determining that the sentence isn't active, all the information about the initial noun phrase is thrown away, and the parser goes off on a completely separate nondeterministic path, rediscovering exactly the same internal structure of that initial noun phrase.

Thus register swapping was the canonical technique for doing the active and passive in the ATN. The problem with this strategy is that it loses track of the surface subject. When you consider tag questions, such as

(1) John saw the girl, didn't he?
    The girl was seen by John, wasn't she?

you see that the tag pronoun agrees with the surface subject, not the deep subject, and the identity of the surface subject was lost in the passive register swapping. The grammar would have to be expanded, either by listing separate transitions for passive-tags and active-tags, or by also keeping track of the surface subject in addition to the deep one. But then the intuitive advantages of the ATN analysis begin to disappear. This is not the only example where register swapping is associated with a loss of generalization - in fact, in retrospect I think that all instances of register swapping in my original LUNAR grammar suffered from linguistic defects of this sort.

Process-control specifications in the grammar also cause you to lose what I call an 'ideal-convergent language characterization'. This is discussed briefly in Bresnan and Kaplan (1982) and is really a separate talk, so I'll say just a few words about it now. The basic idea is that you can evaluate theories of grammar-based processing as to whether their behaviour corresponds to the behaviour of an ideal native speaker, in the limit as the amount of available processing resources goes to infinity. Of course, the behaviour of an ideal native speaker, one who knows his language perfectly and is not affected by restrictions of memory or processing time, lapses of attention, and so forth, is difficult to observe. But as psycholinguistic methods and technologies improve, we can imagine doing experiments in which we somehow vary the cognitive resources of real speakers and hearers, by removing distractions, giving them scratch-pad memories, etc. We can then take the limiting, asymptotic behaviour of real speakers as approximations to the behaviour of the ideal. A grammar-based processing model which, when given more and more computational resources, more and more accurately simulates the behaviour of the ideal has the 'ideal-convergent' property. But when you have things like cutting off paths and heuristically destroying options in the grammar you lose the ability to converge on this fiction of the ideal native speaker. Similarly, Marcus' deterministic parsing system is also not ideal-convergent: if the grammar explicitly indicates how many buffer cells to use, the behaviour of the system will not change if more memory resources are added.

More seriously from the perspective of natural language processing, just when you think that you're getting computational efficiency, in fact you might be losing it. This is because you're committing yourself to more specific details of implementation by letting constraints on the step-by-step order of execution sneak out into your grammar specification. So you lose the ability to have alternative implementations that might be suitable for some purposes but not for others. A case in point is island-driving with an ATN (Bates 1976). The idea is that in speech recognition you might not want to start at the beginning of a sentence but instead start processing outward in both directions from an island of reliability, a word in a speech wave that's easily and reliably identified, and use that as a a pivot point for your analysis. The order of computation thus differs markedly from the order defined by the canonical

interpretation of left-to-right register-setting operations
and top-down sending and lifting. It's possible but very
difficult to vary the order of execution and still get the
correct results. John Carroll (1983), one of Karen Sparck
Jones' students at Cambridge, did an implementation, and it
was also tried in the BBN speech system. Martin Kay and I
looked at the problem and decided there has to be a
different way of thinking about things. The ability to tune
an implementation to take advantage of heuristically
available information is drastically reduced if your
grammatical specifications are committed to particular
execution orders, as was the ATN.

You can also get a loss of efficiency, because your
specification language now is so complex and is trying to
describe so much about the process that you lose the ability
to have automatic compile-time and run-time optimizations.
You're really relying on the grammar writer to put in the
optimization. But in many cases the grammar writer really
doesn't know what's going on, doesn't have a sense of the
global structure of the grammar. But there may be
algorithms that can systematically reorganize the grammar in
various ways, compile it in various ways, if there's a lot
of freedom of implementation and not a lot of over-
specification of exactly what the flow of control should be.
If the flow of control is over-specified then rearranging it
can change the input-output relations in ways that a
compiler can't figure out. So you can actually lose the
possibility of performing significant compile-time
optimizations.

One kind of run-time optimization that you lose in the
ATN is the use of a well-formed substring table that can
save exactly the work that the grammar writer was trying to
save in doing the passive as outlined above. With a well-
formed substring table, that initial noun phrase would be
remembered as a noun phrase, independent of the role it
plays in the larger sentential context. But because the ATN
formalism allows information to be passed around in such
complex ways, it was difficult and costly to simulate even a
simple well-formed substring table in the original ATN, and
there were no net efficiency advantages.

In sum, it's not necessarily the case that when you
want to get efficiency you should allow yourself more
procedural specification. That's the point of the first

seduction.

2. The substance seduction: a linguistic temptation

The substance seduction is the mistaken belief that you know what you're talking about. This is a typical pitfall of linguistic approaches. We had some discussion of this yesterday, that linguists are interested in restrictions, imposing substantive constraints. They take the driving metatheoretical goal to be to characterize all and only the possible human languages.

But the problem is that, at least in the current state of the art, they don't know which generalizations and restrictions are really going to be true and correct, and which are either accidental, uninteresting or false. The data just isn't in; indeed, the definitive data may in fact be psychological and not linguistic in nature. So if we try to restrict our formalisms by taking substance into account, what we think is true of possible languages, we're apt to make a number of mistakes, some of which have undesirable consequences. Premature identification of substantive generalizations may lead to grammatical descriptions that complicate, or even defy, formal specification. I have a little picture here to illustrate the point (Figure 2).

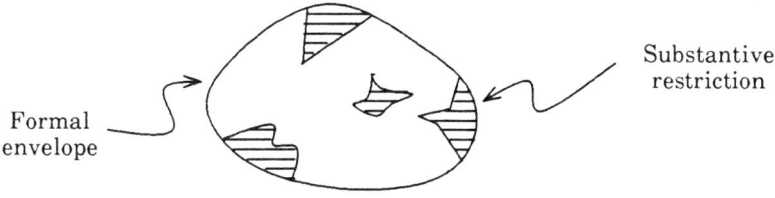

Figure 2. The shape of a linguistic theory

A formal theory might have a relatively smooth outline and be easy to implement, well-behaved mathematically, and so forth. Then you start taking chunks out of it (shown shaded) because you claim that no human language or no grammar has such and such a property. The functional locality restriction that was proposed for LFG is an example. This stipulates that no functional designator can be specified with more than two function applications, and

thus introduces a notational complication into the
formalism. But it doesn't really restrict the kinds of
sentences that can be accepted or the kinds of structures
that can be assigned to them. It is thus a theoretical
complication for which direct empirical support is
difficult, if not impossible, to come up with.

With restrictions like these, you may end up with a
formalism that has very bizarre and irregular contours, that
is very difficult to understand mathematically or implement
correctly. This is because it has all sorts of special
'don't do this in this situation, do do this in that
situation' conditions that are not directly visible in the
grammar itself. By imposing restrictions on the basis of
what you think can or cannot happen, you're in effect adding
special conditions to the notation's interpretation,
complicating its definition. Often these restrictions turn
out to be computationally or mathematically inconsequential,
in that they impose no true restriction on what may be
computed, as in the case of functional locality.
Substantive hypotheses about the nature of human language,
even inconsequential ones that complicate our formalisms,
are important to pay attention to if they have some
convincing empirical support. But I don't think we should
regard three examples in one language or one example in each
of three languages as particularly convincing, and this
exaggerates only slightly the kind of evidence behind many
constraints that linguists have proposed.

It's a mistake to carry premature and unjustified
substantive hypotheses into our computational and
mathematical work, especially if that leads to
mathematically complex, even if more restrictive, theories.
We should let considerations of mathematical and
computational simplicity have higher priority in defining
the formal envelope in which to do our work. Until we can
more clearly recognize the true substantive generalizations,
we should be wary of the seduction of substance.

3. The interaction seduction: a psycholinguistic/ computational temptation

People have been proving the obvious for years now,
that people don't process modularly. If you look at very
fine time grains in human sentence processing, one way or

another, you will likely find out that pragmatic information is being processed while you're still trying to figure out what the first phoneme is, before you've figured out the noun phrase, before you figure out what the predicate is and so forth. Many studies have been done to demonstrate this unsurprising point. The conclusion that computational linguists and psycholinguists have often drawn from these demonstrations is that no modular theory, no theory that, for example, separates out syntax and semantics or morphology and syntax, can possibly provide an accurate psychological model. This is the interaction seduction: the mistaken belief that just because information from all linguistic levels can be shown to interact in human language processing, modular theories of that process should be rejected as incorrect and undesirable.

As computational linguists you might or might not care about having an accurate psychological model. But whether or not you're interested in psychology, your intuitions about what's good and what's bad are informed by your psychological world-view, your own intuitions about how you process. You might also conclude that reasonable computational frameworks must therefore have syntactic specifications and processes mixed-up and integrated with, for example, phonetic and semantic specifications and processes. This kind of intermixing of constraints from what are typically thought of as different linguistic levels is just what you find in so-called semantic grammars. These grammars embody the view that different kinds of linguistic constraints must be intermixed because the information that they deal with can be shown to interact in observable language processing behaviour.

But this is a confusion of two quite separate issues, simulation and explanation. As scientists, we are not merely interested in simulating human behaviour - in constructing a black box that behaves exactly as people behave, has the same profiles of complexity and so forth. What we're really interested in as scientists is explanation - in developing models that help us understand how it is that people behave that way, not merely demonstrating that we can build an artefact that behaves similarly. We don't want to replace one black box, namely a person, by another black box, namely the artefact that we've built. We should look for modular theories that account for the observed interactions in terms of the interleaving of information from separate, scientifically comprehensible subsystems.

In the interaction seduction we fail to distinguish the static specification of a system from its execution behaviour. It should be an obvious point that in principle you can have separate specification of syntax and semantics and pragmatics and still, at run-time, have those operations interleaved and depend on one another in a very intricate way. But it has been difficult to come up with modular formalisms and theories that have enough descriptive power and yet also allow for run-time integration of constraints.

I think this is sometimes confounded with the procedural seduction. If your syntactic theory is very very complex - because it has lots of procedural specifications or its interpretation is basically a complex procedure - then it's going to be very difficult to see how interleaving can take place. You have to be able to understand in a kind of abstract and mathematical way, in a manipulable way, the structure of your formalism in order to be able to use compilation techniques or even run-time interpretation techniques that will interleave the syntax and semantics.

Those are some of the issues that I think have been confused, and are confusing, in the development of computational and linguistic theories. There are many many more. What I want to do for the remainder of my time is to get a little bit more concrete about the strategy that we took in developing the LFG theory, to try to get at the primitive mechanisms that I think are implicit in many, if not all, linguistic theories.

4. The grammatical mapping problem

The basic problem that we are confronting is what I call 'the grammatical mapping problem' - the problem of characterizing and computing the mapping between the surface form of an utterance and its meaning (the claims that it makes about the world, the discourse, the speaker, and so forth) (Figure 3). This is a very simple and abstract view - that what linguistics is about, what we're trying to do in computational linguistics, is to be able to map back and forth between form (the external representation) and meaning.

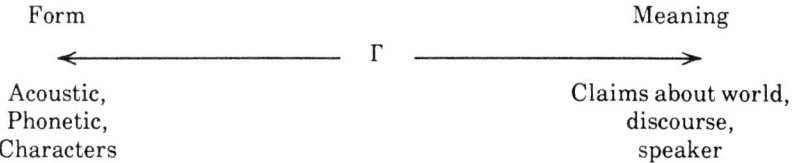

Figure 3. Grammatical mapping between form and meaning

It is an obvious observation that the external forms
vary. They vary from language to language. The same thing
said in different languages is totally different. Even
within a language you have different ways of saying
basically the same thing. Internal representations from
language to language presumably are the same, they have a
universal character that doesn't vary. Moreover, it seems
that this mapping is in some sense simple and transparent,
since, by virtue of perceiving an external form, human
beings seem able to quickly and easily discover what its
meaning is. Yet it also seems that the mapping is quite
complex. There are ambiguities and paraphrase relations and
dependencies that operate over long stretches of an
utterance, and these have defied clear and simple
specifications in any number of explicit theories over the
years. The challenge for linguistic theories is to give a
transparent account of these mapping complexities.

Once you characterize how forms and meanings relate to
each other, there's something else that you want as well.
You want effective procedures for mapping back and forth
between form and meaning, both for practical purposes -
natural language processing - but also for the theoretical
purposes, to account for the fact that people can do this
kind of thing. If you have a formal system that describes
what the relationship is, but it's not computable, you
haven't really approached the psychological question of how
it is that people can do this sort of thing.

We suggest that the fundamental computational
linguistic problem is what we call 'structure mapping'.
Generative linguistics tends to think of generation as the
thing that grammars are supposed to do - generate all and

only the acceptable sentences of a language. I don't think that's right, particularly if you take the view that grammatical mapping is what we're after. What we really need to be concerned with is not the generation of structures but the correspondences or mappings between structures. What I claim is that there is a nice way of thinking about structure mappings that, to use the terms that came up in discussion yesterday, is not only simple and general but also useful, and that it's common to all the various theories and formalisms that Stuart [Shieber] talked about and some others as well. (Henry [Thompson] observed that the notions of generality and usefulness are distinct and there has been some confusion about that. But Turing machines are simple and general but not useful, that is they don't really illuminate the problems that we would like to solve.)

The notion of structure mapping also gives us a basis for comparing theories at a more refined level. Theories can differ in the kinds of mathematical structures - trees, strings, functions, etc. - that they allow, the kinds of mappings between structures that they support, and the empirical interpretation they give to these structures and mappings. You can have mappings between similar kinds of structures - trees to trees as in transformational grammar and for which there's a fair amount of technology. But you can also have mappings between dissimilar structures, between strings and trees as in context-free grammars, or between trees and functions, strings and functions, and so on.

Theories can also differ in the kinds of specifications of these mappings that they provide. You can have procedural specifications that tell you how to construct the output from the input by a particular sequence of operations, but you can also have declarative specifications that tell you what the output is given the input but don't necessarily say what you should do to compute it. If somebody gives you an input and says 'I think this is an output', then you can verify whether or not that's the case. But given the input you can't necessarily go and construct the output. That's what I take to be the major difference between procedural and declarative specifications.

5. Lexical Functional Grammar

I'm going to use LFG as an example of these things but again I think that the ideas generalize beyond that. Basically what we have is very simple - the formal notions of structure in the abstract, structural description and structural correspondence. Those are the three aspects of this notion of structure mapping that I want to get at.

Now I'm going to make it a bit more concrete. In LFG there are at least three kinds of structures, levels of representation, for a sentence. There's the word string that makes up the external form of the sentence, for example (2). There's the constituent phrase structure, which varies across languages, where you have traditional surface structure (3) and parts of speech labelling categories, perhaps a feature system on those categories (although in the case of LFG if there is one it's a very weak one).

(2)   I saw the girl.

(3)

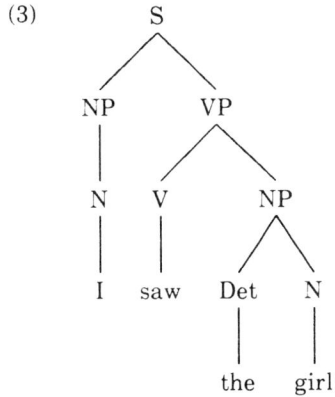

The third kind of structure is the 'functional structure' (f-structure). We claim this is nearly invariant across languages and is a formal representation of notions like subject and object and case and so forth (4).

Structure (4) is a mathematical function that takes atomic attributes into values that might also be functions, structure (2) is a tree, structure (1) is a string. Here are three kinds of structure, and the reason why LFG illustrates the issues of structure mapping better than

transformational grammar is that we really are consciously
mapping between structures of different formal types.   You
can't rely on the same kinds of predicates being applicable
both to the input and the output.

(4)

$$
\begin{bmatrix}
\text{SUBJ} & \begin{bmatrix} \text{PRED} & \text{'PRO'} \\ \text{PERSON} & 1 \\ \text{NUMBER} & \text{SG} \end{bmatrix} \\
\text{TENSE} & \text{PAST} \\
\text{PRED} & \text{'SEE<SUBJ,OBJ>'} \\
\text{OBJ} & \begin{bmatrix} \text{PRED} & \text{GIRL} \\ \text{DEF} & + \\ \text{PERSON} & 3 \\ \text{NUMBER} & \text{SG} \end{bmatrix}
\end{bmatrix}
$$

6. Structures and structural descriptions

Well, very abstractly and simply, what is a structure?
The simplest mathematical notion of a structure is a set of
elements with some defined relations and properties.
Strings are one example: for a string like abc, the
elements are the set of words and the only relation is the
linear precedence relationship.   For trees (or 'c-
structures') you have (5):   the elements are a set of nodes
N, you have a mother function M that takes nodes into nodes,
a precedence relation < and a labelling function λ that
takes nodes into some other finite labelling set L.

(5)   N : set of nodes
      M : N -> N
      < $\subseteq$ N x N
      λ : N -> L

And for f-structures you have (6), where F, the set of
f-structures is defined as the solution to these recursive
domain equations. Something is an f-structure, it belongs to
the set, if it's a symbol or if it's a function from symbols
into that set.

(6)   S : set of symbols
      F : S + (S -> F)

Basically, the set of f-structures is the set of hierarchical finite tabular functions - sets of ordered pairs satisfying a uniqueness condition where the value itself can be a set of ordered pairs also satisfying a uniqueness condition, and so on. The only defining relation for these structures is function application. A function f applied to a symbol s has some value v if and only if the pair $\langle s,v \rangle$ is in that set f, as in (7) (using Lisp parenthetic notation).

(7) (f s) = v iff $\langle s\ v \rangle \in f$

So those are some examples of structures. They happen to be, as I said, the ones that we use in LFG.

We next observe that structures can be described in terms of the properties and relations by which they are defined. So if I have a tree (8),

(8)

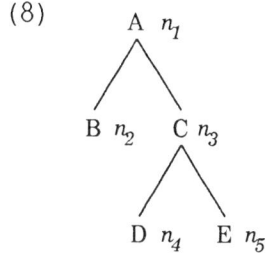

I can write down a description of that tree (having given the nodes some sort of names, n_1, n_2 etc.): the mother of n_2 is n_1, the label of n_1 is A, and so forth. A complete description of this tree is provided by the set of equations (9):

(9) $M(n_2) = n_1$ $M(n_4) = n_3$
        $\lambda(n_1) = A$ $M(n_5) = n_3$
        $\lambda(n_2) = B$ $\lambda(n_4) = D$
        $M(n_3) = n_1$ $\lambda(n_5) = E$
        $\lambda(n_3) = C$ $n_4 \prec n_5$
        $n_2 \prec n_3$

Given a tree I can write down a set of propositions that that tree satisfies. I can also write down a set of propositions that a given f-structure satisfies. For the f-structure in (10), where the names f_i are marked on the opening brackets, I can write f_1 applied to q is the value f_2, f_2 applied to s is t, and so forth (11).

(10)

$$f_1 \begin{bmatrix} q & f_2 \begin{bmatrix} s & t \\ u & v \end{bmatrix} \\ w & x \end{bmatrix}$$

(11) $(f_1 \ q) = f_2$
       $(f_2 \ s) = t$
       $(f_2 \ u) = v$
       $(f_1 \ w) = x$

Structures can thus be described by their properties and relations. Conversely, given a consistent description, the structures that satisfy it may be discovered - but not always. It depends on the complexity of the description language. For the simple functional domain of f-structures descriptions that involve only equality and function application can be solved by an attribute-value merging or unification operator (e. g. Kaplan & Bresnan 1982). But one could imagine algebraic systems with complex uninvertible operators where the algebraic descriptions are just not solvable. One would like to know when one crosses into that kind of space, or at least when one would cross into it so that one doesn't. It's not always obvious. But in the simple domains that seem to appear in linguistic work it is decidable whether any structures exist that satisfy a given description and there are algorithms for producing these satisfying structures.

A set of propositions in a given structural description is usually satisfied by many structures. The description (8) is satisfied by the tree (8) but it is also satisfied by an infinite number of larger trees [e. g. (12)]. It is true of this tree that the mother of n_2 is n_1 and, indeed, all the equations in (9) are true of it. But this tree has nodes beyond the ones described in (9) and it satisfies additional propositions that the tree in (8) does not satisfy. Similarly, for the description (11) of the f-structure (10), there are infinitely many larger f-structures, such as (13), that also satisfy the same set of equations.

(12)

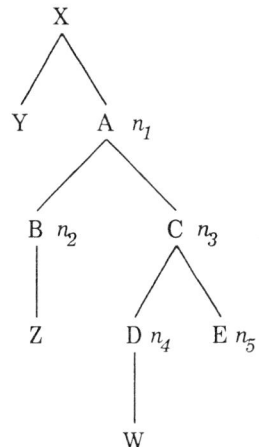

(13)

$$f_1 \begin{bmatrix} q & f_2\begin{bmatrix} s & t \\ u & v \\ a & b \end{bmatrix} \\ w & x \\ c & f_3\begin{bmatrix} d & e \\ g & h \end{bmatrix} \end{bmatrix}$$

In general structures that satisfy descriptions form a semi-lattice that is partially ordered by the amount of information they contain. The minimal structure satisfying the description may be unique if the description itself is determinate, if there are enough conditions specified, enough equations and not too many unknowns. The notion of minimality figures in a number of different ways within the LFG theory, to capture some intuitions of restriction and constraint, but unless there are questions I don't think I'll go into that. Minimality also enters into LFG's definition of grammaticality: we reject a string as ungrammatical if its functional description does not have a unique minimal solution.

7. Structural correspondences

Having made some straightforward observations about

structures and structural descriptions, we now turn to the last important idea, the concept of a structural correspondence. Structures of different types can be set in correspondence by a piece-wise function. If you have structures of any two types, it doesn't matter what they are, then you can define a piece-wise function that goes from the elements of one of the structures into the elements of the other structure. In (14) I've given the example of a function ϕ that goes from the nodes of a tree into f-structure space.

(14)

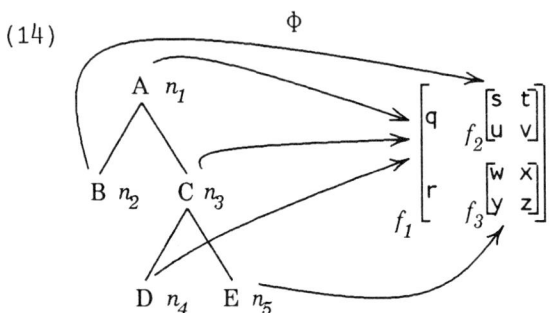

Node n_1 maps onto f_1 and node n_2 maps onto f_2, and so forth. You have two structures and a function that connects them, that sets them in correspondence. This is just a mathematical function, there's no procedure attached to it. But once you assume this sort of correspondence, then the descriptions of elements in its range can be defined in terms of the elements and relations of its domain. Previously we described an f-structure by specifying only f-structure properties and elements. Now, with the f-structure elements assumed to correspond to tree nodes, we can describe the f-structure in terms of the mother-daughter relationships in the tree.

In (14) for example, if we take the mother of node n_2 in the tree and take its functional structure and apply it to q, then we get the functional structure corresponding to node n_2. If we take the functional structure of node n_2 and apply it to s we get t, the functional structure of node n_5 applied to y is z, and so forth (15).

(15) $((\phi \ (M \ n_2)) \ q) = (\phi \ n_2)$
       $((\phi \ n_2) \ s) = t$
       $((\phi \ n_5) \ x) = z$

Thus the f-structure is characterized in terms of function-
application in the f-structure description language, but
also in terms of the mother function and possibly other
relations in the tree.   Our notions of structural
description and structural correspondence combine in this
way so that the description of a range structure can involve
both its own native relations but also the properties of a
corresponding domain structure.

A structural correspondence set up in this way has to
be a function but it doesn't have to be one-to-one. We can
have several nodes in the tree that map onto the same f-
structure; the correspondence ϕ in (14) maps the nodes n_1,
n_3, and n_4 all onto the same f-structure f_1. When we have
several nodes mapping onto the same f-structure, that f-
structure in some sense becomes an equivalence class or
quotient of nodes induced by the correspondence.   It
represents the folding together or normalization of
information carried jointly by the individual nodes that map
onto it.

A structural correspondence also may not be 'onto'.
This is illustrated by (16), which shows the c-structure and
f-structure that might be appropriate for a sentence
containing a gerund with a missing subject.

(16)

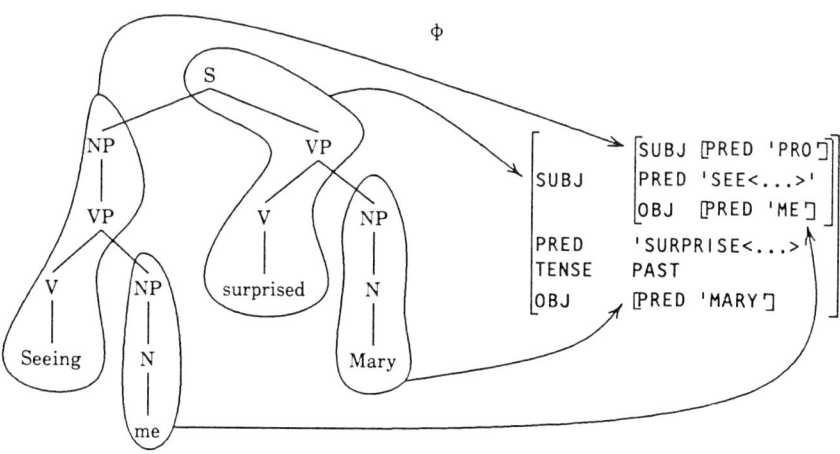

In most phrasally-based theories you would postulate an empty node on the tree side in order to represent the fact that there is an understood subject, a dummy subject, because subjects (and predicate-argument relations) are represented in those theories by particular node configurations. In LFG, given that the notion of subject is defined in the range of the correspondence, we don't need the empty node in the tree. Instead, the f-structure's description, derived from the tree relations of the gerund c-structure, can have an equation that specifies directly that the subject's predicate is an anaphoric pronoun, with no node in the tree that it corresponds to. This account of so-called null anaphors in terms of the non-onto nature of the structural correspondence has a number of interesting mathematical consequences, but I won't go into them here.

I have been presenting some very very simple ideas. I want to keep coming back to this notion of simplicity because if it's simple you can see alternative implementations, you can begin to understand some mathematical properties. Yet I want to claim that this is a basis for much of what we do, not only in LFG but in other theories as well.

Continuing on, we note that a correspondence may induce non-native relationships in its range. For example, the precedence relation is a native relationship in the constituent structure - it is a defining condition of c-structure that nodes may be linearly ordered. But f-structures are functions, they don't have a precedence relationship defined on them. But we can construct an f-structure precedence relationship as a natural image of c-structure precedence. For two f-structures, f_1 and f_2, f_1 f-precedes f_1, if and only if for all nodes n_1 in the inverse image of f_1 and for all nodes n_2 in the inverse image of f_2, those nodes are in the proper c-structure relationship (17).

$$(17) \quad f_1 <_f f_2 \text{ iff}$$

$$\text{for all } n_1 \in \phi^{-1}(f_1), \text{ and}$$
$$\text{for all } n_2 \in \phi^{-1}(f_2),$$

$$n_1 <_c n_2$$

We have already seen that there is a deformation of the

distinctions in the domain structure as you go through the many-to-one mappings to get into the range quotient classes. Defining relations also get deformed in the same way - you get quotients of the relations as well. That turns out also to be useful - it seems that f-precedence as a degraded image of c-precedence gives a nice account of certain constraints on anaphoric relations (Bresnan 1984).

Let me now summarize the formal architecture of LFG. In LFG the c-structure trees are the external syntactic structures representing surface phrase configurations. They are very concrete, highly constrained by the actual words in the string, in contrast to the more abstract phrase-structures of some other theories. There are no empty nodes in LFG c-structures, for example. The f-structures represent the abstract, internal grammatical relations, the notions of subject and object and predicate and so forth. There is a structural correspondence that maps the c-structure nodes to f-structure units. This mapping is many to one, and this fact gives us a way of accounting for intuitions of control, headedness, and some cases of feature propagation. It is also not onto, and that's how we represent zero anaphora.

The allowable c-structures for a sentence are specified by a context-free grammar. The grammar doesn't generate the f-structures directly: it generates a functional description, and the minimal f-structures, if any, that satisfy it represent that sentence's grammatical relations. Thus we have a generative system for descriptions of f-structures based on an independent, context-free way of describing c-structures. This way of looking at things differs conceptually, even if not in mathematical power, from other approaches in which, intuitively, the internal structures, not descriptions of them, are directly generated.

Notation is a very important issue in the design of a linguistic theory, particularly if what you're trying to do is to get other people to use it. If you just want to use it yourself then perhaps it's not such a big deal because you know what you mean.

In LFG, the way descriptions of the f-structure are derived is this: you start with an ordinary context-free rule such as (18) which tells you what phrase structure you

can have - it defines allowable phrase structure
configurations. This can be used to generate nodes in an
acceptable tree or to match against nodes of an existing
tree to verify that it is acceptable. We let the symbol *
stand for the node that is generated by or matches against a
particular element in the right-side of the rule. Then,
using that symbol, the mother function, and the structural
correspondence, we can write general propositions about the
f-structures that correspond to the nodes in any tree
configuration that satisfies this rule. In (18) we specify
that the f-structure corresponding to the NP's mother
applies to 'subject' to give the f-structure corresponding
to the NP, and that the f-structure corresponding to the
mother of the VP, namely the S node, is also the f-structure
corresponding to the VP. The terms of this notational
system are category-equation pairs.

(18) S ->   NP   VP
          (($ o M *) subj) = ($ *)   ($ o M *) = ($ *)

We then simplify to a more convenient notation. We use
up-arrow (↑) to stand for the composition of the structural
correspondence with the mother function, and down-arrow (↓)
to stand for the structural correspondence applied to the
current node *. This reduces the annotation on the NP to
(19), which you can read as 'my mother's f-structure's
subject is my f-structure'.

(19)   (↑ subj) = ↓

Having such an intuitive natural language paraphrase is very
important, if what you're trying to do is to export a
notation or formalism.

This brings up a point that I was talking about to
Karen [Sparck Jones] at lunch and that she said I should
mention: the 'Trojan horse' theory of computational
linguistics. This relates to what Gerald [Gazdar] said [in
his presentation]. Linguists don't really design
formalisms, or at least, they don't seem to design very good
ones. It is the business of computational linguists to do
this, and this is what we're skilled at. But we've got to
design formalisms that linguists will use, to make sure that
they don't come up and start using formalisms that are
unimplementable. Then they'll do all their work finding out
all these wonderful facts about language, even writing them

down, in a way that we can't deal with. We want to come up with formalisms that we can get linguists to adopt, as a Trojan horse, to attract them to what we believe is the right way of doing things, to ways which will help us to do our work. It takes a fair amount of care and attention to design appealing formalisms; we actually spend a lot of time worrying about these issues as we developed the LFG framework.

(20) is just to give you an example of a little bit more of an LFG grammar. This shows that the equations that describe the f-structure in terms of the c-structure come not only from rules in the grammar but also from entries in the lexicon, and these have exactly the same interpretation. We don't make a distinction between the syntax and the lexicon in a theory like this. If you have a language like Eskimo where all the work is done in the lexicon and the morphology, you can do it within this framework just as well as you can handle a language like English.

(20) **the:**   Det   ($\uparrow$ spec) = def

    man: N   ($\uparrow$ pred) = 'man'
                      ($\uparrow$ pers) = 3
                      ($\uparrow$ num) = sg

    walks: V   ($\uparrow$ pred) = 'work<($\uparrow$ subj)($\uparrow$ obj)>'
                      ($\uparrow$ subj num) = sg
                      ($\uparrow$ subj pers) = 3
                      ($\uparrow$ tense) = pres

The LFG notation is thus based on the simple notions of structure, structural description, and structural correspondence.

8. Extensions and variations

There are various extensions, generalizations and restrictions that one might consider once you have this as the space you're working in. You can think about extending the structural domain, that is, allowing in structures that have more properties, more kinds of relations. In the original version of LFG (Kaplan & Bresnan 1982) we allowed slightly richer structures than I've discussed so far in this talk. We also allowed sets of f-structures to be

values in f-structure ordered pairs. That was done
originally so that we could have a representation for
multiple adjuncts, but we mentioned in a footnote that if we
only understood how to do conjuncts we would do it that way
too.   Since then we've actually done a lot of work on
conjunction and in fact do use sets to represent the
conjoined items.   It is worth noting that there is no
obvious encoding of membership relations in the PATR
formalism, which goes against Shieber's claim (this volume)
that LFG is reducible to PATR.

You can fiddle around with the description language
without actually changing the domain that you're describing.
Take the set of trees as your structures and the description
language that I gave in (5) which had a mother function and
a precedence relation.   You can say 'look, what we want is
the left daughter function, that's the thing that we want to
use to describe trees'.   Or 'we want to take the closure of
the mother function' to express some long-distance
dependencies.   You want to be able to refer to some node
arbitrarily far above some other node, as Mitch [Marcus] has
been doing in his D-theory (this volume). You invent some
new notation to be part of the description language but it's
describing structures that are the same sort as you had
originally. This is different than the set-membership case,
where new kinds of elements were added to the structural
domain.

As another example of changing the description
language, we are now proposing to allow regular expressions
over attribute names in our function application
specifications, thus formalizing a notion of **functional
uncertainty**. Under this proposal you can specify the result
of applying an f-structure to comp* object, where the Kleene
* indicates that you can go down through an arbitrary chain
of complements to get to one with an object that you can
then say something about.   This provides an alternative to
the LFG account of long-distance dependencies given in
Kaplan and Bresnan (1982:231 ff.). Originally we did it in
terms of the mother* relationship - this was implicit in the
double-up and double-down metavariables - but I now believe
it was a mistake to define long-distance dependencies in
terms of c-structure configurations.   We were misled by our
phrasal, transformational linguistic upbringing.   If you
look carefully at the old data and also at some new data,
you find that a much better account can be given in terms of

a long-distance relationship on f-structures, specified in this regular extension to the language of functional descriptions. It's a question of which side of φ you have the long-distance relation on. I now think you should have long-distance relations in the range of φ instead of its domain. This makes the claim that properties of the c-structure, such as category, that don't carry through the structural correspondence are irrelevant to long-distance dependencies.

You can also fool around with the way that descriptions of structures can be generated. To a certain extent I think this is what Mitch [Marcus] is doing in D-theory. We can think of a context-free grammar, for example, as involving a structural correspondence between strings and trees. We can write it down in terms of the concatenation relationship and perhaps lexical information about the words, which carry descriptions of tree relations like the mother of the mother of this node is the mother of that node, and so forth. You can take a context-free grammar and re-represent it in that kind of descriptive language, although the notation would probably be quite inconvenient. What I think Mitch is saying is 'if you think of descriptions as the thing that you're operating with, there are other ways of generating descriptions than the full set of context-free rule formalisms'. He introduces templates and other new notational conventions (e. g. the expression i -> p v is to be interpreted as allowing p* v*). He's exploring the space of description generation mechanisms and how they might be restricted or constrained from other ways that you might think of for mapping between strings and trees.

You can also think about multiple levels of representation related by multiple correspondences. Clearly you can have a correspondence between any two levels of structure, but each of those can correspond to other kinds of structures by means of other correspondence functions. You might have correspondences among c-structures, f-structures, anaphoric structures, semantic structures, island structures, structures to represent the sharing of any kind of information among the elements of the word-string. If the range of one correspondence is the domain of another, the composition of the two correspondence functions might have interesting properties. If two correspondences are defined on the same domain, you have independent mappings representing notionally different equivalence classes of information. Either way, it is possible to give modular specifications of different kinds of linguistic information with interactions encoded implicitly by the requirement that the different structural descriptions be mutually or simultaneously satisfied. If no collection of related structures exists with all the specified properties, that might be reason to mark the sentence as ungrammatical.

This is what we do in LFG, of course. The f-structure description mechanism serves as a filter because the described f-structure does not exist if the description is inconsistent. This would be the case if you said the subject's number was singular on the noun phrase node and the subject's number was plural on the verb phrase node. The verb phrase's f-structure is the same as the sentence's f-structure, so you're talking about the same attribute. You would have an inconsistency. There is no function that has subject with number with value singular and number with value plural, because f-structures are functions and functions have a uniqueness condition. So there is no f-structure that can satisfy that description and that is one of the formal characterizations of ungrammaticality.

I'll illustrate the use of multiple correspondences by going back to the problem I started out with, the problem of characterizing the grammatical mapping between form and meaning. We can use multiple correspondences to get a decomposition of the grammatical mapping into hopefully coherent and illuminating sub-mappings between linguistically interesting structures. One hypothetical arrangement of structural correspondences is shown in Figure 4.

Starting out with the word string, we assume a structural correspondence π that takes us to the constituent structure. The c-structure is then mapped by ϕ to the functional structure, in the usual LFG way. We might then postulate a further correspondence σ from f-structure to units of a semantic structure of the sort that Halvorsen (1983) has proposed. This is much closer to a meaning representation: it explicitly marks predicate-argument relationships, quantifier scope ambiguities, and so forth - dependencies and properties that don't enter into syntactic generalizations (at least as we currently believe and recognize) but do enter into meaning. We might also include another correspondence α defined on f-structures that maps them onto anaphoric structures: two f-structure units map

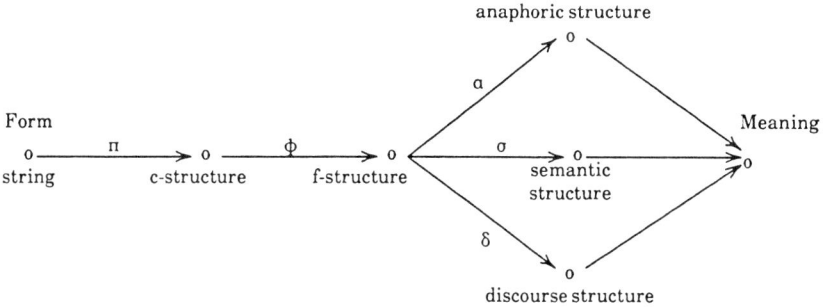

Figure 4. Decomposition of Γ

onto the same element of anaphoric structure just in case they are coreferential; this is how the intuition of coreference is formalized under this view. The figure also shows a mapping δ from f-structure to a level of discourse structure, which would give a separate formal account of discourse notions such as topic and focus. The patterns of correspondences would indicate how these are related to the grammatical functions, nodes in the phrase structure, and words in the string. The anaphoric and discourse structures, like the semantic structure, also contribute to meaning representations. By fitting these other systems of linguistic information into the same conceptual framework of description and correspondence, we can make use of the already existing mathematical and computational techniques and rich notations for structure specification. If we further defined a transfer component between source and target f-structures in terms of a correspondence, we might get the same conceptual advantages in configuring a machine translation system.

Although the structures related by multiple correspondences might be descriptively or linguistically motivated levels of representation, justified by sound theoretical argumentation, they are formally and mathematically, and also computationally, eliminable. The mathematical point is trivial: suppose we have a level of constituent structure and a structural correspondence that goes from the string to the constituent structure, and another correspondence that goes from c-structure to f-structure. Obviously there is a structural correspondence that goes from the word string directly to the f-structure, namely the composition of π with ϕ. It's a function that's not one-to-one, it's not onto, it has all the expected properties. So as a kind of formal, mathematical trick, you can say 'Those intermediate levels of representation are not real, they are just linguistic fictions, useful for stating the necessary constraints'.

This arrangement provides for some somewhat surprising descriptive possibilities. Looking at the mapping between f-structure and semantic structure, it might seem that the semantic structure may only contain information that is derivable from attributes and values present in the f-structure. This is what you would expect if you thought of the correspondence σ as an interpretation function operating on the f-structure to produce the semantic structure. The semantic structure, for example, could not reflect category and precedence properties in the c-structure that don't show up in the f-structure. But σ, as a piece-wise correspondence, does not interpret the f-structure at all. It is merely a device for encoding descriptions of the semantic structure in terms of f-structure relations. And since the f-structure is described in terms of ϕ and c-structure properties, we can take the composition $\sigma \circ \phi$ and use it to assert properties of semantic structure also in terms of c-structure relations, even though the correspondence isn't direct. Descriptions generated by the context-free grammar can use designators such as $(\sigma \uparrow)$ along with $\uparrow$ to characterize f-structure and semantic structure simultaneously. This compositional arrangement of correspondences permits the **codescription** of separate levels of representation. One effect of this codescription possibility is that semantic structure might contain certain attributes and values that are contingent on c-structure properties that have no f-structure correlates.

This organization also has some surprising computational consequences: cascaded correspondences and the intermediate structures they pass through can be constructively eliminated. One of many theorems that Kelly Roach (1985) has proved is that for any LFG grammar that associates f-structure and c-structures with a string, you

can construct algorithmically another LFG grammar that
assigns f-structures that are homomorphically related to the
first ones, but the second grammar has essentially a finite-
state base instead of a context-free base. For this second
grammar there is no notion of phrase structure as a separate
level with interesting properties. Instead, it enforces all
the constraints that the first grammar's c-structure
component imposes by additional attributes and values in the
f-structure in addition to those needed to carry the
original functional information. But you never have a phase
of context-free parsing, you never actually construct the c-
structure as a separate, coherent level of representation.
This result may have important practical consequences, since
the conditions that must be evaluated to analyze or produce
a sentence can now be stated in a uniform description
system. Though constraints come from independent, modular
specifications involving notionally different kinds of
linguistic information, this construction permits
interleaving them in online computation, to take heuristic
advantage of the most reliable sources of information. It
thus provides an answer to the interaction seduction; you
can construct, say, a semantic grammar, as the compile-time
composition of syntactic and semantic correspondences.

It is also a very illuminating result, because it
answers a basic question about where the power of this kind
of description system comes from. The recursive nesting
property of the context-free component may give rise to
nicer linguistic formulations, but it is not essential to
the expressive power of these systems. From a strictly
formal perspective, function-application and equality give
rise to the full power of the system. This result also has
a rhetorical use: when we're being attacked, as sometimes
we are, for having too many levels of representation, we can
say 'You're right, we do have too many levels of
representation, there's really no need for c-structure (or,
carrying the argument further along, for f-structure)'.

This proposed use of multiple correspondences to get
the interaction of modular specifications can be compared to
Bill Woods' (1980) cascaded ATN. The generalization that
Woods made to handle multiple levels of representation was
to consider a collection of ATNs as left-to-right procedures
feeding each other on some intermediate tapes. What we do
here is to set structures in compositional relationships to
each other. We don't have any left- or right-ness, we're

not inheriting any of the procedural properties of the ATN, all we have is transparent descriptions.

I want to finish up with an example to illustrate one other formal possibility. We have had some discussion of defaults, and whether default specifications should be procedural or declarative. In the spirit of the declarative, description-oriented approach I have been presenting, I propose handling defaults by adding an operator to the f-structure description language. The description language that we have so far is a very simple algebra, an algebra that has no operators in it. All it has is function application, equality, and set-membership. It doesn't have any devices, analogous to the plus or times of arithmetic, for combining two f-structures to get a third. But why should we confine ourselves to such a restrictive system? Maybe there are some operators that can be linguistically useful. One interesting possibility is what I've called 'priority union' (21):

(21)   / : (F x F) -> F

Priority union takes a pair of f-structures into an f-structure, and is defined the following way. For two f-structures A and B, 'A/B' is their priority union, perhaps read as A given B, or A in the context of B. It is the set of pairs ⟨s v⟩ such that v is equal to the value of the attribute s in the f-structure A, if s is in the domain of A, otherwise the value of s in the f-structure B. The operator gives priority to the values in A but anything that A doesn't include gets filled in from B. (22) shows what the priority union would be for a particular pair of operand f-structures:

(22)

$$A = \begin{bmatrix} q & r \\ s & t \\ u & v \end{bmatrix} \qquad B = \begin{bmatrix} q & m \\ s & t \\ p & 1 \end{bmatrix} \qquad A/B = \begin{bmatrix} q & r \\ s & t \\ u & v \\ p & 1 \end{bmatrix}$$

A/B gets ⟨q r⟩ from A, ignoring what would be the inconsistent value of q in B, not even noticing it. ⟨s t⟩ is common to both so A/B includes that. It also has ⟨u v⟩ from A and ⟨p 1⟩ from B.

The basic idea is that values found in A override the

values found in B, and B supplies the defaults. Note that this is not done as a procedure, it's done as an operator. It's simply a characterization of satisfactory structures.

This operator might be applied to specify default or unmarked values for morphological features. It might also be used in the description of various kinds of ellipsis constructions, for example, to assign proper interpretations for gapping constructions. A basic rule for sentence coordination is given in (23):

(23) S ->   S   and   S
        $\downarrow \in \uparrow$ $\downarrow \in \uparrow$

This has statements that involve membership instead of equality, indicating that the f-structures of the daughter nodes are members of the set that corresponds to the mother node. For ordinary conjunction the same statement appears on both daughter categories. A simple variation of this basic rule provides for gapping in the second conjunct. Instead of saying that the second daughter simply contributes its corresponding f-structure to the mother set, we can say that the mother set will contain the priority union of the second daughter's f-structure with defaults taken from the first daughter's f-structure. If, as is independently needed to handle English Aux-inversion, a verb is allowed to be optional in the VP that expands the second S, the predicate for the second f-structure will be inherited from the first if it is not carried by an explicit verb in the usual string position.

Now there are a lot of technical issues, as Stuart [Shieber] has and, I'm sure, will remind me of, concerning this particular operator and what its algebraic properties are. These are important questions that I at least have not yet worked on, and it may turn out that this is not the operator that we actually want. But the point here is to illustrate the spirit of this approach, that you can formalize notions like default, what you might think of as procedural notions, by thinking of operators that produce new structures, structures that are not directly in the image of the structural correspondence.

I think I will stop right there, having left about the right amount of time for discussion.

Doug ARNOLD: An appropriate answer to this question might be 'ask me afterwards and I'll explain it': I don't understand how the lines converge again, after anaphoric structure and semantic structure.

KAPLAN: That's a good question. It's the same kind of question that Mitch [Marcus] was talking about, there are various ways you could do it. One would be to have sharing of variables and do it in the description language, force it to be the case. But the observation that is true of LFG, and that I also interpreted Mitch to be talking about, is that you basically have a system that is underspecified; you might have a description of the meaning structure (meaning is not really a structure, it's out there in the world, but some structure very close to meaning), a specification of that meaning structure and pieces of it defined in this way, and a specification defined on other paths. Then if what you're asking for is the minimal structure that satisfies all the conditions on it, that implies certain kinds of equalities. So there are some properties of the model that you **can't** actually specify, that will cause things to come together, because you're asking for minimal models in that lattice; even though you can't write down the equations, because there is no way in the descriptive system of saying this thing relates to that thing.

You get the same kind of thing with sets. You say, 'Here's a set of f-structures'. You might think, 'I'm going to put these members in the sets, and they're all going to be distinct', but in fact all possible unifications of the elements that you put in the set may give sets that also satisfy all the equations, even though you couldn't have said that this is equal to that.

We originally discovered this when Jane Simpson, who was working on Warlpiri (Simpson 1983) said 'I want to be able to say that this is equal to that, but there is no way in the grammar that I can say it: I don't know how to name the thing that I want to make equal'. We realized that you don't have to say that, it's implied by what **can** be a solution to the equations, and whether or not it's the minimal one. That's why the model is very important. This is also a difference between LFG and FUG (Kay 1979) in spirit. Martin [Kay] really wasn't paying attention to the model - everything is in the description language. He has no notion of relations between structures other than the ones he can describe. He has the ANY feature, which is a way of saying 'take only the minimal models', but he has to encode it as a feature that has a special interpretation.

Rod JOHNSON: In your correspondence theory, you have this function φ that maps from some level of representation i to some level j. The domain of i is ... ? You can apply φ to any function that closes i. Isn't that a bit liberal, in fact?

KAPLAN: φ is defined on whatever is in the domain. You might have a restriction on your description language that says you cannot compose arguments to φ, that those can only be primitive functions for example. You might say that's the only kind of description that you're going to allow. And in the notation that we originally presented for LFG, with the up and down arrows, we picked out just two or three ways that you could compose the native relationships on the c-structure, and legislated. We didn't give you the ability to write down φ. That might have been too tight. For six years it's been fine, but there are some things we see we'd now like to do, where a little bit more notation would be useful. But the mathematical concepts allow you to compose things any way you want - it's just functions.

JOHNSON: You don't have any thoughts on restricting this?

KAPLAN: Well I have thoughts. But I think it's important to distinguish between what the basic mathematical space is - which is what I've been trying to get at here, using LFG as an example - and that space doesn't have restrictions in it - versus restrictions that you might impose, either for the sake of convenient notation, that would make these concepts easily usable by your target audience, be it machine or people, or that you think should be imposed because you have some beliefs about the general nature of language, and you believe this arbitrary method of composition is just too general.

Henry THOMPSON: A typically seductive substantive restriction might be to say that φ of the mother cannot be a proper subset of φ of the daughter. You might suppose that that might be true.

KAPLAN: Right. I have some intuitions about that, and Joan [Bresnan] certainly has a lot more, and some of those actually have computational consequences. E.g. if you knew such-and-such was the case, you could short-cut some of the branches of the code in your interpreter. Those might only be local to LFG, and I'm also trying to suggest that this kind of conceptual space is the space that PATR-II (Shieber et al 1983), and FUG, and GPSG (Gazdar et al 1985) ... It's just a matter of changing what the correspondences are, and changing what the relationships are, and it all comes out in the wash.

JOHNSON: A malicious person, which I'm not, might say that you could call this function EVAL, and then you claim that you're going to constrain EVAL so that it closes i̱, and the theory is still okay?

KAPLAN: It's a valid point. What I'm suggesting is this very general picture of structural correspondences with unaxiomatized function symbols; and leaving it to the consumer of this kind of conception to say what the domains are, what the relations are, what the correspondences are, and so forth. Obviously that's a very general picture. What I am also saying is that there are a couple of kinds of structures that are basically finite, like f-structures and trees and strings, that are the basis of what we want to do in linguistics. If you take the native relationships on those, even though it's more general than LFG or GPSG etc., then that's the right space to be in.

Mitch MARCUS: That sounds rather precisely like what PATR-II says. You get to work with two things, something very close to f-structures, and something very close to trees. PATR-II restricts you in some real sense to that. It seems that the mathematics is vastly general. Something that embeds PATR-II is the part that you suggest people live in, and then give them a formal basis, with model theory guaranteed, to go off and do truly bizarre things, claiming that it's mathematically well-founded every step of the way - off the edge. You're saying you post a sign saying 'pass down this path at your peril'. I think PATR-II builds a fence at that point, and that's extremely useful.

KAPLAN: LFG, all these things, build fences at roughly the same place. It depends how closely you look; but basically the fences are built with these objects, these kinds of relations. There are differences in the notation that you use for making up the descriptions. What I'm suggesting is that this is the mathematical basis for a variety of notations, and that we can explore their similarities and differences with respect to this kind of background.

The more substantive claim that is implicit in what I'm saying is this: if you want to do linguistics, and you take this general conception of things, and you start putting down the fenceposts you want, you will roughly put down the fenceposts of feature structures, functions, trees, strings. You won't put down a lot of other random, woolly topological spaces, and other things you might do with this very general thing. But in my mind that's a separate point. It's been important for me, and it might be important for other members of the community, to understand this kind of model for what we're all doing, in a very abstract way. Then the particular implementations, formalisms, and so forth, I'm not trying to say anything about here.

What's the difference between an LFG and a GPSG? With this backdrop, I think you can begin to say, 'this function is a such-and-such'.

MARCUS: But then you say you can reduce two structural correspondences to one, you can make all of this go away. It's powerful enough, that you have to base a theory on the substantives, otherwise you don't have anything you can talk about.

Stuart SHIEBER: I want to make two observations. I think you, Mitch, were claiming that what Ron had presented was a mathematical space in which any choice you made was going to end up giving you some kind of formalism that was 'semantically grounded' or 'mathematically well-founded', I don't remember the word you used. That doesn't follow, that that's necessarily so.

KAPLAN: It could be undecidable, for example.

SHIEBER: Or just incoherent. There's a lot of room there. Although I'm very sympathetic to the idea of placing these things in a framework to compare them, I think to get the differences between LFG and GPSG, for example, requires a finer grain than this level. That was exactly the kind of thing I was trying to do with notational reductions. This goes part of the way, but I think you need some finer tools to get at those distinctions.

One thing that Mitch pointed out was that if you look at things at this level of abstraction, the differences between one level and two levels goes away, which makes you wonder what all this philosophy in the literature, how important it is that LFG has two levels and GPSG only one, was about. They just disappeared on us. At one point, there was a psychological claim that this was significant.

KAPLAN: That's a linguistic claim.

SHIEBER: Whatever kind of claim it was!

KAPLAN: No, no! There's this point about simulation versus explanation coming back again. What this construction shows is that there is a simulation, there's something that behaves as if it had two levels, but it only has one. The level that it's behaving as if it had, but doesn't, is one that you make a lot of argumentation about, because it has certain important and significant linguistic properties - that's why you have it in the first place. But whether or not you need it to do this computation ...

Gerald GAZDAR: That shows how weak your claims were for having it in the first place!

References

Bates, M. 1976. Syntax in Automatic Speech Understanding. **American Journal of Computational Linguistics** microfiche 45.

Bresnan, J., ed. 1982. **The Mental Representation of Grammatical Relations.** Cambridge, Mass.: MIT Press.

Bresnan, J. 1984. Bound Anaphora on Functional Structures. **Proceedings of the Tenth Annual Meeting of the Berkeley Linguistics Society,** University of California, Berkeley.

Bresnan, J. & Kaplan, R.M. 1982. Introduction: Grammars as Mental Representations of Language. In Bresnan, ed., xvii-lii.

Carroll, J.A. 1983. An Island Parsing Interpreter for the Full Augmented Transition Network Formalism. **First Conference of the European Chapter of the ACL,** Proceedings, 101-105.

Chomsky, N. 1963. Formal Properties of Grammars. In Luce, R.D., Bush, R.R. & Galanter, E., eds., **Handbook of Mathematical Psychology,** Vol. II., New York: Wiley, 323-418.

Gazdar, G., Klein, E., Pullum, G. & Sag, I. 1985. **Generalized Phrase Structure Grammar.** Oxford: Basil Blackwell.

Halvorsen, P.-K. 1983. Semantics for Lexical-Functional Grammar. **Linguistic Inquiry** 14, 567-615.

Kaplan, R. M. 1972. Augmented Transition Networks as Psychological Models of Sentence Comprehension. **Artificial Intelligence** 3, 77-100.

Kaplan, R.M. & Bresnan, J. 1982. Lexical-Functional Grammar: A Formal System for Grammatical Representation. In Bresnan, ed., 173-281.

Kay, M. 1979. Functional Grammar. In Chiarrello, C. et al., eds. **Proceedings of the Fifth Annual meeting of the Berkeley Linguistics Society,** 142-158. Berkeley, Berkeley Linguistics Society.

Roach, K. 1985. The Mathematics of LFG. Ms., Xerox Palo Alto Research Center, Palo Alto, CA.

Shieber, S.M., Uszkoreit, H., Pereira, F.C.N., Robinson, J.J. & Tyson, M. 1983. The Formalism and Implementation of PATR-II. In **Research on Interactive Acquisition and Use of Knowledge** (SRI Project 1894 Final Rport), Menlo Park CA: SRI International, 39-79.

Simpson, J. 1983. **Aspects of Warlpiri Morphology and Syntax.** PhD dissertation, Massachusetts Institute of Technology.

Woods, W.A. 1970. Transition Network Grammars for Natural Language Analysis. **Communications of the ACM** 13, 591-606.

Woods, W.A. 1980. Cascaded ATN Grammars. **American Journal of Computational Linguistics** 8, 1-12.

Woods, W.A., Kaplan, R.M., and Nash-Webber, B. 1972. The Lunar Sciences Natural Language Information System: Final Report. Cambridge: Bolt Beranek and Newman, Inc.. Report No. 2378.

The Syntax-Semantics Interface

Steve Pulman

This is a discussion session on the interface between syntax and semantics. I've got twenty minutes or half an hour to fill before you get your turn, so what I'm going to do is make a quick survey of what the various theories that have been mentioned have to say about semantics, and then throw in one or two remarks about how you might set about implementing some of them, and by that time you'll either be so bored or so hopping mad the thing will look after itself.

Stu [Shieber] mentioned in his talk something which is going to strike us even more forcibly when talking about semantics, which is that linguists abstract away from anything to do with processing right at the very beginning. So the characteristic view of what a grammar in a wide sense, that is to say a syntax and a semantics, does in most linguistic theories is that it's a device: you have a grammar and it supplies a mapping between strings of words and logical forms. If you computational people want to use it, then what you do is tack it onto a parser and a bit of code for manipulating semantic structures. You throw a sentence at it and out the other end you get a lot of logical forms. The way in which you get the logical forms doesn't vary that much.

All approaches assume to a large extent that semantic structure or logical structure is derived from syntactic structure, that's to say the process of actually getting a logical form is syntax-driven, and this is especially so in what we can call the surface structure approaches, GPSG (Gazdar et al 1985), PATR (Shieber et al 1983), the Montague (1973) type of thing and various other theories that are around which haven't got names yet, the sort of thing that

LINGUISTIC THEORY AND COMPUTER APPLICATIONS
ISBN 0-12-747220-7

Robin Cooper (1983) and Emmon Bach (1983) have done. By and
large you've just got one level of syntactic representation,
and something which is either literally a version of the
rule to rule hypothesis or something equivalent to it, i.e.
that for every syntactic rule in a grammar there's an
associated semantic rule, and the process of getting to a
semantic structure is one which presupposes that you've got
a parse tree or something equivalent to it. Example (1)
says that the sentence is a noun phrase and a verb phrase,
and the way to get the meaning of the sentence is by taking
the translation of the noun phrase, for example, and
applying it as a function to the verb phrase. Somewhere or
other you've got meanings of the constituents. You apply
them and do whatever the appropriate operations are to
reduce it to some kind of normal form, which you then pass
to your theorem prover or whatever you're going to do with
it.

(1)   Syntax-driven

      S -> NP VP : NP'(VP')

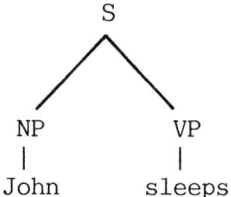

      [λP P (john')] (sleeps') => sleeps'(john')

      The same general scheme holds independently of
commitment to what the nature of the logical form is. It
might not even be logical form in the strict sense: the kind
of fragments that come out of Situation Semantics (Barwise &
Perry 1983) and so on are still using the same general
scheme where the syntax is used as a kind of key to pull out
the appropriate semantic operation. You do the syntax, then
you use the syntactic information to build the semantic
structure. That's a very literal interpretation of the
notion of compositionality that Jan [Landsbergen] was
talking about this morning because, in order to get the
meaning of the whole, you've got to work out the meanings of

the parts.

In GPSG (Gazdar et al 1985) in particular, a more recent alternative takes off from the observation that in a lot of cases what is stipulated in the rule, namely that you apply the noun phrase to the verb phrase in (1), is actually redundant. It couldn't have been any other way in fact. Because of the logical types of the constituents involved, you could only apply the one that's a function to the one that's an argument. It wouldn't make sense to do it the other way round. And that's the leading idea behind the type-driven translation system (2) which is sketched out in the last chapter of the book (Gazdar et al 1985).

(2) Type-driven

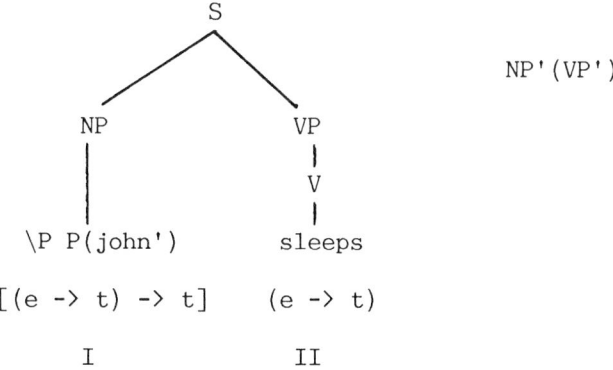

NP'(VP')

If the type of I is that of a function from types of II to truth values (it's actually more complicated of course), then you can only apply I to II, not the other way round, that wouldn't make sense. So the idea is that you're extracting a lot of redundancy out of the stated semantic rules, by letting the semantic types decide what can apply to what. You need to do some tricky stuff in a lot of cases to get this to work, so that actually information that occurs in the syntactic tree (a feature, usually) needs to get translated into some semantic operation, some kind of combinator or something that wraps all the lambdas round in the way that you need to get things to work out right in the end. But it's a powerful enough mechanism to do that, and provided you don't abuse it then it probably is an

improvement in terms of linguistic elegance over the simple
rule-to-rule idea.

I'm going to concentrate on one particular aspect of
constructing logical forms, which is that of getting
quantifier scope right, simply as a way of comparing
different approaches. There's a lot more to semantics than
getting the scope of quantifiers right, of course. If
you've only got one level of syntactic representation, and
you're using a strict rule-to-rule mechanism, then the only
semantic ambiguities you can get are those that correspond
to some syntactic ambiguity - at least if you're being
honest. So you need some extra mechanism for cases where
you're using some syntactic difference in the logical form,
like differing scopes of quantifiers, to reflect some
difference of meaning.

In the case of GPSG, and other Phrase Structure Grammar
approaches, this mechanism is a version of 'Cooper storage'.
This is, as you might expect, something that comes from
Robin Cooper (1975, 1983; cf. Gazdar et al 1985:243) (3).

(3)   Cooper storage

(3a) Every dog likes some cat.

(3b) ∀x:dog ∃y:cat (likes x y)
(3c) ∃y:cat ∀x:dog (likes x y)

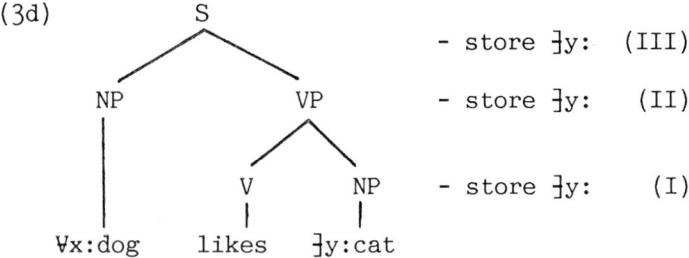

The basic idea is that when you're building up the
meaning of a sentence from the meaning of the parts, very
roughly speaking, whenever you come across a quantified NP
you've got two choices. You can either leave it where it
is, or, if there's still some stuff up there, you can take

it out and put it in a store and leave something which
ultimately is going to act like a variable in its place.
Consider (3a), which most people find has two readings,
representable by the different scopes (3b,c). One reading is
going to be straightforward: the one where the scope of the
quantifiers follows the order that they get in the syntax
(3b), and we don't need to say any more about that - though
of course you might hope that psychological evidence shows
that that's the reading that people actually prefer, given
no special context. Combining the verb and noun phrase, or
rather arriving at the meaning of the bottom-most noun
phrase, you've got the opportunity to stick it in the store
(I). The store can get carried up and associated with each
node (II) until you get to the top (III) when you've got the
option of taking it back out of store and plonking it in.
The result is that you can get the two readings there, in a
way which is faithful, as far as it's possible to be
faithful, to the requirement of compositionality. At every
stage we have a well-defined logical object: it's not a
complete 'kluge', the semantics of it is properly defined
the whole way up.

As a general device this is probably not going to be
satisfactory for representing all the kinds of differences
of meaning that scope of quantifiers and scope of logical
operators has traditionally been used to represent. As it's
defined in (Gazdar et al 1985:218) at least, Cooper storage
only applies to quantified NPs. But there are quite a lot
of examples which suggest that you're going to be able to
say the right things about some sentences. The first of
these (4) is one that Bob Moore suggested to me earlier on.

(4)   Some of the prizes may not be awarded.

I have trouble with this one but if the wind's blowing
the right way some of you can get three readings out of
that. The scopes of the three underlined things get flopped
over. I can only get two comfortably. You're not going to
be able to do that with Cooper storage, because there's only
one quantifier there and it's at the top already. An easier
one perhaps is the advertisement for the Alliance Building
Society which you may have seen on television, which ends
with sentence (5a), where the meaning of it is clearly not
(5a) literally. It's 'not all building societies are the
same'. It's easier to see if you take an analogous sentence

like (5b).

> (5a) <u>All</u> building societies are<u>n't</u> the same.
> (5b) All shoes aren't comfortable.

Now taken literally that means 'everything that is a shoe is not comfortable', but you've got the more natural reading of it that 'some shoes are comfortable and some are not'. Then there's well-known things like (6) where the natural representation of the various scopes is 'it seems to be the case that I am not able to finish it' rather than the modal, then the negative, then the sentence.

> (6) I can't seem to finish it.

We're assuming of course that shuffling the scopes around is the right way of doing this, and everybody has always assumed this, but it's by no means obviously true. People have suggested various non-scopal representations for at least some of this ambiguity, in Situation Semantics for intensional verbs (Barwise & Perry 1983), and in Discourse Representation theory for quantifiers (Kamp 1981). But as far as I'm aware, nobody has really got anything worked out in as much detail as the traditional quantifier scope treatments.

With theories that have more than one level of syntax, like LFG (Kaplan & Bresnan 1982), the situation is correspondingly more complicated, though we're still on the basic idea that it's the syntax that drives the semantics. As I understand it, the kind of approach to building logical forms in LFG goes through various stages (7).

We've got C-structures and F-structures. The information associated with F-structures in the lexicon gives you in effect the basic predicate-argument structure, and there are separate rules - not syntactic rules, separate semantic rules - which account for quantifier scope of the sort we've just been talking about, and things like control and the scope of various kinds of adverbial modifiers and so on. The basic idea is not a million miles removed from Cooper storage. It's just implemented slightly differently. The basic idea for quantified NPs is that when you've got a noun phrase, it can be in one of two modes: either it's really there, or it's not really there and there's a

variable in there instead, or something that acts
semantically like a variable. So by the time you get to
(7b), both possibilities can be realized and you can arrange
things so that the quantifier scopes are explicitly
represented as they are in (7c). I'm not doing this full
justice.

(7) LFG

      C-structures -> F-structures   (I)

               ↓

    rules for quantifier scope, control,   (II)
           modifiers etc.

            ↓

      semantic strutures   (III)

          ↓

  (formulae of intensional logic)   (IV)

(7a) Every dog likes some cat.
(7b) => likes {every dog} {some cat}

(7c) => (some cat)x (likes (every dog), x) or
      (every dog)x (likes x, (some cat))

Ron KAPLAN: This is Halvorsen's (1983) work. I think he
makes a very important point. He's not building the formulae
of the intensional logic. He's building descriptions that
characterize the formulae of the intensional logic. In
particular, he's not enumerating all the various quantifier
scopes. What he's providing is constraints on what those
scopes can be.

PULMAN: Yes, I haven't made that as clear as I ought to
have. The point of having the extra arrow here [between III
and IV] was to indicate exactly that what you got in the
semantic structures hasn't made up its mind one way or the
other. If you're going to make the whole thing explicit as

a formula of intensional logic, then the quantifier scopes are explicitly represented.

KAPLAN: The quantifier scopes that are not allowed are rejected at that level. The ones that are now in free variation are just classified as being in free variation: you don't know and you don't care.

PULMAN: And the other point is of course that [IV] is actually dispensable, because in principle you could eliminate it by going straight from [III] to the model-theoretic interpretation.

KAPLAN: Also there's an alternative version of it. We actually have a menu of semantic theories and one of them is situation schemata, so it's not just the intensional logic.

PULMAN: So those are roughly speaking the surface structure-ish theories.

GB theory (Chomsky 1982) is slightly different at least, and the general outline (though there are lots of variations on this theme and it changes every time you look at it) is that you've got D-structures which represent the basic predicate-argument structure of a sentence (8).

(8) GB

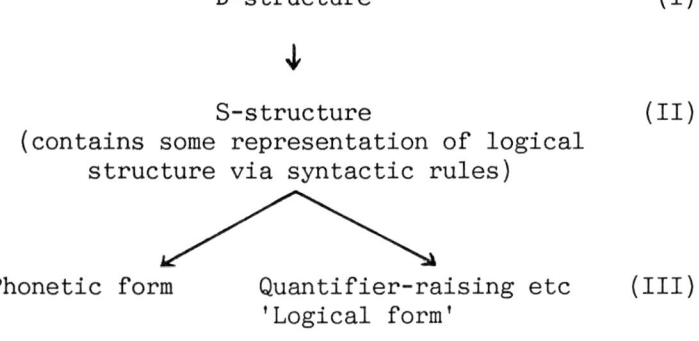

D-structure	(I)

S-structure   (II)
(contains some representation of logical
structure via syntactic rules)

Phonetic form   Quantifier-raising etc   (III)
                   'Logical form'

There are syntactic operations of various kinds, or more accurately there's a set of filters of various sorts, which allow you to get things that look more like sentences out, but they're still not sentences. In particular they

contain various kinds of bits of notation, traces and PROs
and such like, which are going to have semantic import.
Then there are rules which map from the sort of tree you get
out here at [II] to 'logical forms'. These rules are
specially there to build 'logical forms', and they're rules
all of their own, they have properties of their own, though
some of the properties are shared with syntactic rules.
'Logical form' is in quotes because, although it looks like
logical form, it's not really, because it's really just a
more abstract syntactic level of representation. In
particular it's not like other versions of logical form,
because it isn't necessarily going to support deduction or
inference, according to Chomsky (1980:143). Quantifier
raising does just what it says. In our sample sentence
(9a), quantifier raising is like any rule that simply
applies, and the results are either illegitimate or not,
depending on whether constraints have been violated.

(9a)   Every dog likes some cat.

(9b)

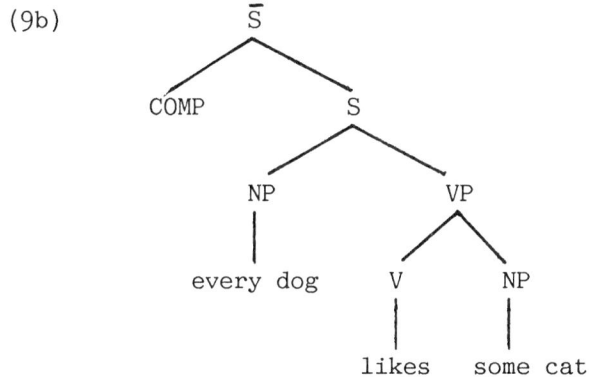

(9c)   => [every dog]x [some cat]y {x likes y}

(9d)   => [some cat]y [every dog]x {x likes y}

So with the sentence with the two quantifiers in it,
there's going to be two possibilities for the order in which
they get raised. That's how you get the two readings
(9c,d). So that's a purely syntactic manipulation in the
sense that there's no attempt to assign it any semantic
significance other than the fact it's getting you something
where some differences of meaning are represented by

differences of form. The justification for it, as with the other levels, is that it's supposed to have its own properties and generalizations which can't be stated in other ways.

All of these approaches, as I said, have embodied the assumption that what goes on inside a grammar is that you get a sentence, and a grammar characterizes the set of logical forms that are possible for that sentence. If you're a computational linguist and you're hoping to take some piece of linguistic theory off the shelf, then it's going to strike you that this is a rather funny way of looking at it. The literal implementation of that picture which is possible on a small scale is that you build your program and it's such that you throw a sentence at it and what you get out is a whole bunch of logical forms. Then you do some filtering to decide what the appropriate one for that sentence in that context is, and proceed. For any grammar that's of any size, that's not really possible. For a realistically sized grammar and a realistically sized lexicon, even quite simple sentences are going to blow up because there's going to be so many possibilities, and of course that's just a lot of wasted computational effort. Since that approach, that literal implementation, presupposes that you've got some process which is capable of choosing the correct alternative, then you might as well acknowledge that (10) is possibly a logical truth.

> (10) Any process which is powerful enough to choose
> among multiple analyses makes explicit computation
> of them **redundant.**

That's something which we can perhaps discuss. It's something that seems to me kind of obvious, but nobody else seems to think it's true, let alone obvious. So the suggestion here is that the literal implementation is actually not something that anybody's going to set about doing. But even if they did set about doing it, if you were anywhere near to getting it to succeed, then you would already have got to the point where you could do it all much more efficiently, because you would have this process that was capable of choosing among multiple analyses.

What then would a sensible implementation of these theories look like? Well we're changing mode here: this is

me pushing out junk at you to fall out over. There's lots
and lots of psychological evidence against this over-literal
picture, and really nobody is going to disagree with the
proposition that when people are interpreting sentences,
that's not the way they do it. To a large extent you're
working out the meaning of the sentence as you're going
along through it, and it would be nice if it were possible
for us to build programs that do the same thing. So let's
assume that that's a good thing, and we want our
implementations to try and do it. What implications does
that have for the kind of views of logical form and our
interpretation of views of logical form and the way that you
get logical forms out of a grammar, that we get from
linguistic theories? My suggestion is that it suggests at
least a two-stage construction of 'logical form' (now in
quotes because it's not quite the same as the piece we
started out with). Rather than throwing a sentence at a box
which grinds out loads of logical forms, the picture that
you get is that you have a sentence and a grammar which give
you some kind of partially built logical form, and other
aspects of it can't get filled in until you've actually
looked at the context in which the sentence is being
evaluated.

Let me try and give an example of how this sort of
thing might go, not because I think that this is the way
that you ought to handle this particular problem, but simply
because it's concrete enough for us to have an example - I
hope. This is a familiar one:

(11a) There were two men. One had a telescope.
      The other had binoculars.

(11b) John looked at the man with the telescope.

The problematic sentence is of course (11b), for which
everybody's parser finds at least two parses. Since we're
building a realistic system, (11b) is not the first thing it
ever sees. That's just an ill-formed beginning to a
discourse. So you might start your discourse with (11a),
because you want the discourse to set things up nicely so
that the parser's not going to break down later on. You
have extracted (11c), that there's a couple of men A and B,
there's a telesope C and some binoculars D, and the first
man has the telescope and the second man has the binoculars.

    (11c)   man(A)
             man(B)
             telescope(C)
             binoculars(D)
             have(A,C)
             have(B,D)

The crucial thing is of course that you don't want to have to build two parses for the sequence the man with the telescope.   So we get as far as John looked at the man   ... and the man just has the kind of analysis that derives from Russell (1905), that of some sort of contextually unique individual (11d).

    (11d) unique(x) (man(x))

We're doing incremental semantic interpretation, remember, so we're trying to build as much as we can of the meaning as we go along.   So we try to work out the man. (I'll describe it in a kind of Prolog-ish way, because it's natural to do it that way.) You get the meaning of **the man** which is (11d), assuming 'unique' is translated in the obvious way.   And what you do is to treat this as a little sub-goal which has to be satisfied before you can get on any further. So you throw that as a query against this little set of clauses (11c) that you've built. You can find two instantiations of x here, but of course that means that you're not going to find an instantiation satisfying 'unique', because the way that 'unique' is defined means that you've only got to find one of them.   So that's no good.   We haven't managed to properly work out what this noun phrase is referring to.   So we go along a bit further and we in fact build the semantic structure appropriate to the parse in which with the telescope is a restrictive modification.   At this point of course we've got enough stuff that when we re-submit the expanded goal (11e) that will get satisfied against the set of clauses because there's only one man with a telescope, so that's fine.

    (11e) unique(x) (man(x) $\wedge$ $\exists$y telescope(y)
      $\wedge$ have (x,y))

But of course now that we've in a sense used up this bit of logical form (11e) we don't necessarily need to have that kicking around any longer.   It is possible that all you

need then is <u>John</u> <u>looked</u> <u>at</u> ... then whatever notation your
system is using to identify the particular man you were
talking about (11f).

(11f) looked-at (John,A)

In other words, you are taking the logical form that
you would get from a standard linguist's description and
you're interpreting part of it procedurally. (Somewhere at
the bottom of this overhead it says "SHRDLU revisited"
(Winograd 1972)).

The other reading, of course, is where <u>the</u> <u>telescope</u>
is modifying the verb (12).

  (12a) There was a man outside. John picked up his
        telescope.

  (12b) man(A)
        outside(A)
        telescope(B)
        picked-up(John,B)

  (12c) He looked at the man with the telescope.

  (12d) => looked-at (John,A) ∧ used (John,B)

Well, there's a man outside, and we set that up nicely so
that we've only got one man. We've got these clauses in
(12b). Since we had to mention <u>John</u> in order to get a
reference to <u>telescope</u> there, we're not going to use <u>John</u>
again in the next sentence. We're going to use a pronoun
(12c). As everybody knows, we need to do inference to find
out what the reference of the pronoun is. This time <u>the</u> <u>man</u>
is going to succeed because there's only one of them.
You've got the interpretation for the noun phrase as
bracketed that far, so that's as much of the syntax of that
noun phrase as you need to do. You don't need to build any
more structure to it. You've found out what it refers to,
so you don't need to compute the other parse. So now with
the scope the only possibility left is that it's modifying
the verb as part of the verb phrase.

The details of this aren't terribly important. What I
wanted to do is to make the point that at least one obvious

way of interpreting current off-the-shelf approaches to
logical form within a framework like this is that at least
some aspects of logical form are instructions for building
up other bits of it, that it's not treated uniformly as one
long string of clauses and interpreted all at one go. I've
talked for too long now, so I'll stop.

Karen SPARCK JONES: That was a bit abrupt. Wouldn't you
like to make some rambling concluding remark?

PULMAN: What I'm trying to do I suppose is this: it's kind
of obvious that people do semantic interpretation
incrementally and everybody knows it would be nice for us to
be able to do it too. I'm trying to point to the kind of
views of standard logical form that you are led to if you
take that requirement seriously.

Graeme RITCHIE: Can I add a footnote to that example you
were working with: there are now students working on that in
the Centre for Cognitive Science in Edinburgh, and there'll
be a paper at the Linguistics Association [of Great Britain]
in two weeks' time on it (Haddock 1985), if anyone's
interested in following up that tradition of semantic
processing.

Henry THOMPSON: The further point to be made in conjunction
with that in the context of - oh what are we calling it? -
'Combinator Grammar' or 'Extended Categorial Grammar' or
'Ades/Steedman Grammar' (Ades & Steedman 1982) or whatever

RITCHIE: I think that particular work is independent of the
syntax: I don't think the categorial thing imposes strongly
that that is the kind of parser ...

THOMPSON: Then in the same breath let one mention the
existence of let's call it 'Combinator Grammar' - although
I'm not sure what Mark [Steedman] is calling it now - which
is an attempt to run (putting it simplistically) the type-
derived semantic composition rules backwards, and say if you
have the types you don't need the syntax, because the
combinators that you need to do the semantics will do just
as well for the syntax. The categories you need are the
categories that you can induce from the combinators. There
is a certain amount of type-raising that goes on,
surprisingly, to get what little you need of non-left-

branching structures, but you are biased in favour of left-branching structures as much as possible, which tend to cut across traditional constituent structures. For those interested see Steedman (1985) or a couple of less easily accessible papers [Steedman (1983, 1987)].

Bob MOORE: There are a lot of complications that make incremental semantic interpretation a bit more difficult than it might seem. One is that in sorting out a very great many intensional ambiguities, you can't really ask the right question until you get to the top level, because ultimately the questionthat matters is, which interpretation of the sentence makes the most sense, given the entire context? If you're trying to do it incrementally and you're analyzing a little bit of a phrase, if that phrase happens to be embedded inside a context like It is impossible that ..., then the whole thing can flip on you. Fortunately for your point of view, there are certain things that seem to be insensitive to that. Word-sense selection is obviously insensitive to that: if you say something like

(13) It's impossible for a jack to hold up a car.

I take it that that sentence doesn't make too much sense to most of you?

PULMAN: It makes sense - it's just not true.

MOORE: Right. Now if you really follow the strategy of finding a reading of the individual word-senses that makes the whole sentence most plausible, you might for instance be forced to select the reading for jack of 'a playing card'. So at least in word-sense selection of that kind, these local strategies do seem to work.

PULMAN: And you've also got to distinguish between different kinds of ambiguity. The case where I would claim the computation of the various syntactic alternatives is entirely redundant is where the only difference between the two things is in terms of the trees above them, and the lexical categories down at the bottom are the same. Prepositional-phrase modification is a classic case of that, because the only thing that is going to be able to decide between them then is going to be things about what's given, what's new, what's contextually unique. So it's not going to be things about word-sense, by definition. So let me back-pedal and say that for those kinds of ambiguity, complete computation of syntactic possibilities is always going to be redundant.

KAPLAN: It may well be true that people, when they're processing sentences, take into account all levels of constraints about semantics, interleaved or on-line, but it's not obvious when you're building a particular natural language processing system for a particular purpose that that's what you want to do, even if you could. There's one question which is 'Can you do it, given some sort of specification of syntax, and some database with a semantic theory or whatever? Can you actually get the computations to mutually constrain each other on-line?' But even if you could, you might not want to, because you're basically trading off resolution of ambiguities at the semantic level against resolution of ambiguities by subsequent syntactic constraints. Depending on the role of the complexity of your syntactic versus semantic computations - suppose for example that whenever you ask a question of your semantic component, you take a page fault. Well there's a lot of syntactic processing you could do that perhaps would rule out the whole path anyway. So it's not a given that the most efficient system will be one in which you do this kind of interleaved computation, because it could be funny properties of your semantics versus your syntax ...

PULMAN: To put it in syntactic terms, you'd actually be finding more 'garden paths' than there really are, simply because you're not looking ahead far enough.

KAPLAN: That's right. There are local ambiguities that are resolved syntactically by subsequent syntactic context, perhaps a long ways away, perhaps we could say a buffer's distance or whatever, but nonetheless there, and you can't predict whether or not they're there, and when you're building your practical system, and what you want is good performance, there are a lot of other issues to be taken into account.

Stu SHIEBER: It's this question of where to do it. What you're saying is you may not want to do it all the time, but maybe just at a couple of key points.

KAPLAN: That's right. I don't know how you want to control it, but it's not obvious that you want to do it all the

time. It's not uniformly true that resolving ambiguities on
the basis of semantic constraints, and eliminating syntactic
processing, is better than letting the syntactic processing
go all the way through way into the string, without ever
having to ask about the semantic end of things.

SHIEBER: I assumed the point here was that there are
certain cases where there is just no way to tell the
context, and that's when you have to do this kind of thing.
Like [examples (11) and (12)], both of them are grammatical.

Mitch MARCUS: The framework that I am working in would say
that you'd have to try and find the solution syntactically
rather than semantically. If you're doing a purely non-
deterministic search, simulating everything (this is in fact
just what happens with LUNAR (Woods 1973)), then you're
considering enough very spurious paths that are going to die
soon enough, and furthermore you can't tell when you want
something to be put aside till later when you can afford to
do semantics, because in fact they may all turn out to be
silly. But that's the cost you pay for the non-determinism.
This is why I raised the ante on this with you, because I
want to go one step further.

But first note that in fact one has to determine these
things as soon as possible for practical systems. If I've
got a system that's doing speech recognition, and I'm going
to go on for 30 seconds, or I'm sitting there typing a long
sentence, and after I'm done it sits there and says 'Sorry,
I didn't understand the second word of the sentence', I'm
going to be very annoyed. There's a nice and extremely
useful property of people, that when they're confused they
know they're confused very immediately, and they let you
know.

The other thing that I think is interesting is that,
thinking about quantifier scope ambiguities in particular,
when you need to know what the quantifier scope is - and you
don't compute it if you don't need it - but when you do,
then the information's there to make the decisions with.
And if you don't need to know, in fact it would be rather
hard to make the decision anyway. So for example if you say

(14) I couldn't make the phone-call because someone
     was in every phone-booth.

the natural reading of that, modulo the pragmatics, is that
it's a different person in each phone-booth. Then you have
(15):

(15)   ∃x person(x) ∀y phone-booth(y) in(x,y)

But of course you don't notice that. One could say that
that's a problem for this account of ours, because we're
going to have to compute, and exactly the thing that pushes
me to the other reading is the fact that this one is
bizarre. What is interesting though is that if you assume
that you're not just pushing the stuff through the system,
that there's something pragmatically pulling the stuff
through as it needs it, my guess is that you'd just never
compute the scope on that because it doesn't matter.

PULMAN: That's my suspicion too, or hope perhaps.

KAPLAN: That's sort of the intuition that Halvorsen (1983)
had in doing this LFG interpretation, which is that you
don't want to enumerate all the possibilities that there
are. You might as well have a description of the fact that
there are those possibilities, and defer actual enumeration
until somebody cares. You can take that same idea and push
it all over the place. Push it back to the syntactic level,
as Ken Church says, where we can have descriptions of
alternatives. And that was all for the case of the syntactic
ambiguity of the prepositional phrases. He said that what
we'll have is a representation that says, here's the set of
prepositional phrases and they have arbitrary attachment
possibilities, syntactically. There are no syntactic
constraints here, so we won't bother even trying to
enumerate all those possibilities, we'll just defer it until
there's some information or somebody cares.

MARCUS: I think there's a difference between the two cases
though. I don't have any example sentences to hand, but
again I think there are cases where if you don't have the
referent to a noun phrase, you try the thing as finished and
you go on to something else, my guess is that in most
contexts you would immediately stop the person who's talking
and ask them to help you. You'd be aware that there's a
problem. And Kurt van Lehn put out the fact that you think
you understand sentences, especially examples with
quantifier scope, when you have no idea what the quantifier
scope was. The most compelling example of Kurt's is (16):

(16) A simple pharmacological test showed each of the
     drugs to be psycho-active.

You understand the sentence just fine, then I ask 'Is it the
same test for each drug or a different test?' Now you all
think about it for five seconds, and hope for intuition.
But the crucial thing is that you had to think for five more
seconds. Whereas if I'd asked you 'Do you want to feed the
drugs to your dog?', this is instinct, and then the answer's
maybe yes or no depending on what you think of your dog.
But you understood that much of the sentence, and somehow
there's clearly a different kind of understanding. It's not
clear that you need to know, say, the referent of a noun-
phrase immediately, if you didn't have the intuition to spot
it immediately. There's a difference. Chris (Mellish 1981)
is playing the same kind of game that I'm playing (or vice
versa), and in fact it's not clear to me if this is the
right game to be playing here. It isn't that we want
representation that is vague between the two choices: it may
be that we just don't have any representation of that choice
at all.

THOMPSON: But it's actually the pragmatic content of the
sentence that determines that fact about quantifier scope.
One of the nice things in Chris Mellish's thesis is he shows
how in the case of sentences like

(17) A tree stands in each corner of a
     triangular field.

you do know how many trees there are instantaneously. But
that sentence is exactly parallel to (16), where you don't
care, so you don't figure it out.

MOORE: I think these cases aren't problems for the
universal/existential approach, because they have some
properties which aren't shared by other syntactic
ambiguitites, namely that one is strictly weaker than the
other and the stronger one would be viewed as adding a very
particular piece of information. If you think of it in
terms of Skolem functions, it's adding the extra information
that Skolem functions are constant functions, and if you
don't care whether the Skolem function in question is a
constant function or not, you just don't have any motivation
for continuing the analysis. Whereas for many other kinds
of ambiguities, if you have to carry along the ambiguity,

you have to carry it along in terms of two quite different descriptions. So I think it's misleading to concentrate on this case.

SPARCK JONES: You were saying that the incremental approach gives more problems than might have been suggested by Steve [Pulman]. Do you think that it's a fundamentally mistaken enterprise?

MOORE: No, but I think you have to look very carefully and only apply it to those parts of semantic analysis where it's apt. For example I don't think it's applicable to scope analysis. I think getting scope analysis right really depends on globally speaking what's the most plausible thing to be saying in this situation. I think the example Henry [Thompson] gave from Chris Mellish's thesis [(17)] is a good one, where you have to bring in this outside knowledge of geometry.

PULMAN: But that doesn't affect the scope, that simply gives you more information.

SPARCK JONES: Wouldn't that in fact be the use of context that Steve had in his intermediate step? He had logical form first and then with some context you can get your final logical forms.

RITCHIE: The example you want is Mitch's one of the guys in the telephone booth (14), where you need real world knowledge to know that there's not one guy running between the phone booths. That's a better example.

SHIEBER: Well depending on how you construe that, you're right, but in that case one obvious thing is that you can't make this decision on the fly, you have to wait till you get to the end of the sentence, so to speak, and take the whole pre-logical form and add context to it. So you can't do it incrementally.

MOORE: If I can elaborate Mitch's example (14), this is a case where my 'impossible' test - It is impossible that ... [cf. (13)] - works. If you say that it is impossible for one person to be occupying every phone-booth, then you get it. But if you use Mitch's original case

(18) I couldn't use the telephone because there was one person in every phone-booth.

then you get the other scope. It's only when you take the whole sentence in context and say which reading is plausible for the whole sentence that you can decide on the scope of the quantifiers in the embedded clause.

PULMAN: I suppose that there's an assumption behind what I was saying that this shares too, which is that by and large in real discourses, people are co-operative, and that you've actually got the information more or less at the time you need it. So for the cases that you just talked about, the information when you've got impossible to resolve, you can actually do it right away there.

MOORE: I'm not sure what it means to have the information ...

PULMAN: Mechanics problems are not a natural piece of discourse.

THOMPSON: Nonetheless I find those utterances unexceptional.

SPARCK JONES: You don't think you go into a special frame of mind which says 'Here is some nasty thing being posed to me and it's a mechanics problem so I've got to think about it in a certain sort of way'.

THOMPSON: What if I said (19)?

(19) I walked into the room and there was a policeman sitting at both ends of the table.

That seems to me a perfectly reasonable utterance that I interpret without difficulty and arrive at a hypothesis that there were two policemen in the room. It has nothing to do with mechanics problems.

SHIEBER: I convinced myself at one time - though I suppose I'm willing to be convinced otherwise - that ambiguities of pronoun reference are local, in the sense that they can be resolved by just looking at the local plausibility rather than the global plausibility. Though it's sort of touchy. In other words you can come up with a sentence with a pronoun in it which has an obvious referent, because of context, to previous discourse, then take the same thing and put it inside one of these It's impossible that ... contexts or something like that, but you still get the same referent, even though it should be the other referent, because the thing that was ridiculous was the other.

MARCUS: This may be irrelevant, but take (20), which I think has he being Bob, whereas in (21) with [stress on Herbert] sort of intonation, I think he is John on the first reading.

> (20) John insulted Bob and then he insulted him.
> (21) John insulted Bob and then he insulted **Herbert**.

I can't be sure, but my guess is that the intonation is roughly the same until you have the second analysis. I don't know if that counts as counter-evidence against this.

MOORE: You've got a contrastive stress. There's a kind of default in the use of pronouns not to shift the focus; but this default is overridden in the other case by the contrastive stress. I'm not sure what that gives us.

SPARCK JONES: There was one thing I was not too sure about, because you went through the examples rather quickly. You were saying that you want to have a two-stage production of the ultimate logical form, and then you also said before you sat down that you could think of some aspects of logical form as instructions to build other bits. Now is that tied in any particularly complex or straightforward or intimate way with doing it in two stages? That's what I wasn't quite clear about.

PULMAN: In that particular example (11)-(12) it was, in that there's a representation that you get from the grammar and the lexicon, and that's not actually going to contain any information about the context in which the sentence is uttered. Now the suggestion was that at least part of that information, and in fact you hypothesize that it's in a sense the 'given' part of that information, in the linguistic sense, is actually used to marry the rest of it up with stuff in the context. The particular example there was locating the actual discourse referent that the definite article was pointing to.

SPARCK JONES: But it's used in a particular way, and is it
then thrown away or is it also carried forward?

PULMAN: I was just tossing out as a possibility that you
might throw it away, since in some sense it's done what it
was there for, it's got you to pointing to the actual thing
out there in the world, or the representation of it, that
the speaker was referring to.   Though I've no doubt that you
could find various linguistic examples where you needed it
to do something later on.

MOORE: Your comment "SHRDLU revisited" was well taken, and
I think what was wrong with the way it was done in SHRDLU
(Winograd 1972) was that that was the **only** mechanism
provided to handle definite noun phrases.   In fact there are
times when you seem to want to do something like that, and
there are times when you seem to want to have something like
the sort of standard logical representation.   But I think
that Barwise & Perry's distinction (1983:150) between the
'value-loaded' and 'value-free' interpretations of sentences
is a nice way of classifying that.   For example, we might be
reading headlines in the paper about the deplorable state of
international affairs and world economy and one of us might
say to the other

> (22) The next American president is going to have an
>   awful time straightening out the mess left by his
>   predecessor.

There's a case where, in the context, it's pretty obvious
that what we have in mind is the value-free interpretation,
that is the descriptive interpretation, and given the
pragmatics of the situation, if you did that sort of
evaluation, all that you'd get out of it is a Skolem
function that gives you absolutely no information anyway.
The important thing there is that you have the alternative.
I think there are cases where you have to do what you said
because if you don't you would have to pack in all the
current textual information into the definite description.
There are relatively few definite descriptions that get used
in ordinary discourse that have enough actual descriptive
content in them that they can be extracted from their
context of utterance and still give you anything worthwhile
at all.   So I think in many if not most cases that's
probably exactly what you do in processing them.

PULMAN: But you're right in that distinction. Is this the same distinction as 'attributive' and 'referential'?

MOORE: I think of attributive and referential as a pragmatic distinction and value-loaded and value-free as the analogous semantic distinction.

PULMAN: That's too deep for me!

MOORE: Kripke (1977) in a very nice paper made the distinction between 'speaker's references' and 'semantic references'. Attributive and referential are speaker's references, what the speaker is attempting to do with the language. Whereas semantic references are what the rules of the language say the reference ought to be. Value-loaded and value-free are more on the side of the rules of the language, whereas attributive and referential are more on the side of what the speaker is doing.

Doug ARNOLD: I think an outsider listening to the conversation would be quite surprised that the topics that have been discussed are actually only pronoun reference and quantifier scope. I think that reflects the state of the field, or at least what I know about the field. So the question is: what is there to say about the interaction of syntax and other kinds of semantics, in particular lexical semantics? Syntax has got to interface with semantics, both structural semantics which is what we've talked about, and the kind of thing that happens when you have quick swimmer and clever swimmer. They have different sorts of semantic representations, those two things. So what do people think about how these things can be done, relating both lexical and structural semantics in such a way that you can get meanings out?

PULMAN: Well in the kinds of approach that I've been talking about, either that problem is just not noticed or is swept aside, or it's assumed that you're going to be able to force that kind of information within the framework, by way of meaning postulates or something like that.

SPARCK JONES: Is there meant to be an assumption that in the same way that you want to do some of this structural stuff by reference to context in two stages, you might also need to use context in the same two-stage way to help you to sort out some of the rest of the things?

PULMAN: Oh yes.   It's just that I haven't a clue how to set about that!

SPARCK JONES: But you would say that you might need to do the two-stage stuff there too?

PULMAN: In that case there's no alternative to computing enough structure to get the two possibilities up and running, and then consulting the context to see which was the favoured one.   But the kind of examples that Bob [Moore] had (22) showed that that's probably not the sort of thing that's going to get you much mileage doing it incrementally because some of the information may not be there yet.

MOORE: As far as these lexical problems go, the problem is everybody these days is afraid of trying to say anything about lexical structure, which it seems you'd have to say something about to deal with that kind of problem in a non-ad hoc way.   In structural semantics what everybody is leaning heavily on is using syntactic structure in order to constrain the way you assign semantic structure.   But with lexical problems of that kind there don't seem to be any guideposts, and as a result many - one might even hazard to say most - of the proposals that have been made in lexical semantics have just seemed totally ad hoc, and it's just very hard to get a grip on and know how one could go about attacking the problem in a principled way.   So that's why everybody works on structural semantics.

PULMAN: As far as things like the prepositional-phrase attachment problem, you can get a lot of mileage in terms of ruling out things where it couldn't possibly be modifying this noun phrase, by simply in effect doing a parse on semantic attributes of the things involved in the kind of way that Bran [Boguraev] did in his thesis (Boguraev 1980). So that you know that inanimate things can't be described by such-and-such a modifier and so on.   You can actually get quite a long way with that.   But there's always the tricky cases that McCawley and people used to float, where that's just not going to work, and Bob's impossible-type cases [cf. (13)], which were in fact among those.

SPARCK JONES: I think in some ways that's probably a comment on the people doing the computational work, namely that in many tasks that one tries to build systems for, you really assume that the reference domain is so limited that you get rid of a lot of lexical ambiguity problems. You know, there they were with LUNAR (Woods 1973) with these samples and these rocks and so on. But what's actually more interesting is that you fudge all the laws with the prepositions, because the relations are given by the domain as well. You may say that prepositions in principle ought to be ambiguous everywhere all over life, but somehow if the domain is small enough even prepositional interpretation becomes less of a problem.

KAPLAN: But that wasn't done by looking at data bits of the rocks. It was actually done by having explicit markers which were limited for that domain.

SPARCK JONES: You did it by a sort of economical method.

KAPLAN: It was basically a marker theory.

SPARCK JONES: Because the domain was restricted you could put it into the semantics.

PULMAN: The thing is that people don't say anything much about lexical structure because there actually isn't very much to say about lexical structure, and as soon as you go beyond that you're just into the big problem about representing factual knowledge in a way that's amenable to doing inference in a controlled way, and that's somebody else's problem. We've got enough of our own!

ARNOLD: First of all, you can't get away with that. But second, somebody could equally appropriately have had that same discussion about pronoun reference: you can do a little bit and as soon as you get beyond that you're in the whole ball-game with pragmatics. But that doesn't stop that discussion.

PULMAN: Exactly the same is true for pronoun reference: you can do it in a limited domain, and after that it's just uncontrollable.

ARNOLD: There's an important reason why it won't do: it won't do for theoretical reasons and it won't do in general just to say that about language.

KAPLAN: Why not?

ARNOLD: Because <u>fast</u> <u>swimmer</u> means 'a swimmer who swims fast', and <u>clever</u> <u>swimmer</u> means 'a swimmer who is clever'.

PULMAN: I just don't think that that's part of the grammar of English.

ARNOLD: I think I disagree. But in any case for some applications, and MT is one ...

PULMAN: Well for that example and for a lot of examples of that type I think simply you've just got to know a hell of a lot about the world to get the right answer.

MOORE: But it's generally productive in English that when you have a noun that's formed by adding -<u>er</u> to a verb such that it means 'one who (verb)-s' and if you modify that noun with an adjective that can be applied to the nominalized form of the verb that means that activity, you combine them together and you get that reading. That's a fact about English.

KAPLAN: I guess I don't quite see why lexical meaning should be treated any differently than structural meaning. I think that you have to allow for constructive processes in the lexicon. In English perhaps not so much, but in Japanese clearly. The problem is that you're thinking of the lexical semantic thing as being basically an add-on, without any really interesting combinatorial properties, or even rich structural properties, and I think that you have to think of there being morphological and even syntactic processes that operate in the lexicon. If you have a rule-to-rule semantic interpretation in the syntax, well you get rule-to-rule procedures going on in the lexicon as well.

Mary McGee WOOD: There are examples in English. There's a nice one which was debated in **Journal of Linguistics** in '78 and '79 (Watt 1978, Sampson 1979) about what were called 'covert antecedents', where you can have sentences like (23).

> (23) John is a Nixonite, but I think he was the worst
>   president ever.

That pronoun has got to refer to <u>Nixon</u> which is inside the derived word <u>Nixonite</u>, so that sub-lexical structure has got to be available to the syntax.

ARNOLD: I wasn't asking a question about linguistic
phenomena. I was asking about whether you can cope with
such things.

KAPLAN: I think that those things can be reduced to the
previously unsolved problem of knowing what the hell's going
on. What I'm trying to say is that those kinds of example
are no different in principle from the examples that you
have that involve large syntactic structures and structural
meaning. If you have any mechanisms for handling those,
formally or however, then the mistake is thinking that you
shouldn't use those inside the lexicon. Because you should.
There are other examples like compound nouns, and in
polysynthetic languages, where that's the only way to go.
Why should you think that you shouldn't do that, just
because you have English that has relatively flat sub-
lexical structures?

MARCUS: There is another question about other parts of
lexical semantic issues though, on which there is now some
work being done which looks promising, and that's this whole
class of verbs in English in the _smear_, _load_, _jam_ class,
that has a 'completive'/'non-completive' distinction. If
you say (24a) it means it's completive, but (24b) is non.

(24a) He loaded the truck with hay.
      He jammed the jar with pencils.
(24b) He loaded hay on the truck.
      He jammed the pencils into the jar.

There's a class of these things. Beth Levin at MIT, who is
part of the MIT Lexicon Project - which is one place that
actually is (as far as I know - there may be others)
attacking this stuff - has the argument that this class of
verbs is in fact not a class, because you can show that most
of the members of it are involved in other sub-classes of
other kinds. But you can begin saying things about the sub-
lexical semantics, about the internal structure of lexical
items, and about the range of them, such that you can have
these things fall out from the kinds of primitives that seem
to make sense to cover each one of these properties. Then
you play the standard game, which is that you try to take
the minimum number of differences that you need to have the
properties fall out for other kinds of things. Similarly in
English there is a limited class of verbs that can be used
causatively, e.g.

(25)   The general marched the soldiers.

Many languages have very productive systems for this, but English doesn't: the verbs that you can use this way are very limited. There are lots and lots of verb classes in English whose semantics seems rather regular, and that's attackable. It seems to me that there's no way you can attack that problem by saying you just use here the kinds of structural methods you have already developed, because there isn't any structure to attach.

MOORE: The cases you cited are rather different from the fast swimmer cases. That's basically just classifying verbs according to categories of entailment, which don't present the kind of representational problems. The problem with things like fast swimmer is that you seem to need to have access to the internal structure of that lexical item in order just to represent the difference of meaning. The suggestion that you do it by taking English morphology seriously is an interesting suggestion, and it raises the question 'Is it only in cases where you can hand the ambiguity, or the different way of attaching the modifier, to the morphological structure of lexical items that that kind of problem arises?'

THOMPSON: No, clearly not. An efficient salesman versus a handsome salesman moves you out of the -er derivation. I'm willing to wager that by tomorrow morning I can come up with an example which has no lexical verb in it by any active morphological process.

WOOD: Try something suppletive, like jewel thief, which otherwise corresponds to the paradigm which gives you wood-cutter and so on: you don't have stealer because you've got thief, but it falls in that paradigm perfectly.

ARNOLD: Large jewel thief is ambiguous between large jewel and large thief.

SPARCK JONES: The point that I was trying to make was that they work in so many different ways that they leave the kind of things that Doug [Arnold] was talking about to some larger-scale structure. If you look at some of those analyses that people have made, people working on huge samples and trying to describe what's going on in them in systematic and motivated ways, they give classes of examples which illustrate a whole lot of different processes going on, some of which are like the swimmer case, and some of which are quite different, like whole reduced elaborate syntactic structures, many different kinds of relationship.

MOORE: But I think the fast swimmer cases really present a very sharp technical problem not shared by any of these other examples that have been discussed. Take the ambiguity of beautiful dancer: if you were unwilling to say anything about the lexical structure of dancer, if you insisted on treating that atomically, you would be forced to say that the word beautiful is ambiguous because the whole phrase is ambiguous. If on the other hand you treat dancer as structurally complex, you have the alternative of applying the interpretation of beautiful in the structure of dancer, or to the representation of dance.

PULMAN: But you still have to make it ambiguous.

Nick OSTLER: It's structurally complex. Why can't you leave it structurally complete but have some semantic representation of it in its place? There's the meaning of beautiful knocking around for when you want to put together the semantic structure if you ever get round to it and similarly there's the meaning of dance and there's the meaning of -er, and then you decide whether you want to apply ...

MOORE: I wasn't trying to distinguish them. You have to have some structural complexity somewhere, associated with dancer, whether you associate it in syntax or morphology or what.

OSTLER: I think it's unfortunate if you suggest that it has to be at the traditional syntactic level.

WOOD: There are very good arguments for taking morphology seriously -

OSTLER: You might well be taking it seriously to take the different parts of the meanings seriously, without saying -

WOOD: The thing is that that stuff is there, you may as well use it.

PULMAN: But that's straightforward, beause that's a distinction that's going to have to be in your grammar anyway, so it's there to hang the semantics off. But there are other cases where there's no obvious grammatical distinction, but there is a clear logical distinction, like the difference between intensional and extensional adjectives, e.g. fake Rembrandt and red Rembrandt. I can't think of a very well motivated syntactic distinction between adjectives like fake and alleged and so on and adjectives like red and heavy and so on, but there's a clear logical difference.

THOMPSON: I like that approach for the beautiful dancer / fast swimmer argument anyway. I would rather say that fast has an adverbial reading and induces a process reading on its object and beautiful has both an adverbial reading and an adjectival reading if you will, and clever has only an adjectival reading.

MOORE: So you can say beautiful swimming but not *clever swimming. Or perhaps we can find a better example. That's a good point. Clever swimmer is not ambiguous ...

THOMPSON: And neither is fast swimmer.

PULMAN: I'm actually not so sure about that. It seems to me that for all of these things, if there's a structural possibility there for one of the pair then if you work hard enough you can find it for the other one too.

THOMPSON: Fair enough, but I think that actually contributes to the argument that it's the modifier that's driving the process.

MOORE: No, I think that's just false, I really do.

ARNOLD: It can't be to do with the lexical items, because you can get the same effect with other kinds of modifier, e.g. swimmer in the municipal baths.

PULMAN: Heavy bricks and heavy smokers.

ARNOLD: It's not just to do with the lexical items.

RITCHIE: Does the issue of productivity affect any of these views here? The fact that the minute you get a new verb you

get the same phenomenon happening for the -er version of it.
Doesn't that count as evidence on this issue?

THOMPSON: Yes, but I don't think it actually discriminates
the two proposals, at least on my account, which I admit I'm
advancing on the basis of 30 seconds' thought. An obvious
heuristic for finding an entity suitable for adjectival
modification if that's what you need and you have a
morphologically complex head, is to do the indicated
morphological decomposition. That's perfectly sensible. So
if you have either fast swimmer or handsome dancer, then you
do the sensible thing. But it's a question of who's in
charge. The other reason I think that I would like to see
the modifier in charge is my favourite wandering non-
compositional sentences:

> (26a) He smoked a quiet cigarette.
> (26b) He ate a hurried meal.

There's something that is adjectival in form but adverbial
in meaning which actually, at least conceptually speaking,
clearly modifies the process and not the object. What I'm
saying is that you're driven by the semantic type of the
modifier, which says 'I need an object suitable for being
handsome' or 'I need a process suitable for being fast', and
the morphology may give you clues as to where to find that
object or that process.

KAPLAN: If what you're saying is that in general there are
bracketings of syntactic structure that you want to ignore,
then you might as well draw the morphological bracketings
too. That falls into the general class of bracketing
paradoxes: the brackets that are there, or the groupings
that are there, for one set of reasons, are just not
supposed to be there, are in the way, for other reasons.
Then you have to say that there's another structure that
doesn't have those bracketings, but there's a
correspondence. So you get yourself out of the confusion
about what a given structure means.

MARCUS: But what do you do with an example like

> (27) I only have time for a hurried meal.

because you can't raise the hurried there anywhere at all.

MOORE: I think <u>hurried</u> <u>meal</u> and <u>quiet</u> <u>cigarette</u> are
different, because a meal is primarily an event and
secondarily the food that you eat.

PULMAN: But you can't eat events [cf. (26b)].

WOOD: That brings up something that I've had in the back of
my mind, broadening out this discussion a bit, because
there's one very fundamental issue in lexical semantics
which interacts quite directly with what you're going to do
about processing. That is the debate as to whether you go
for a very detailed explicit lexical semantics, or, to pinch
a term from Aronoff (1980:71), 'sparse semantics'. This is
going to cash out in terms of ambiguity versus
indeterminacy, and in that case I think you would want to
say that <u>meal</u> is being allowed to be indeterminate between
the event and the food, so that it can be hurried and it can
also be eaten.   I think there were other cases when we were
talking about incremental processing having trouble with
ambiguous cases, where if you go for a sparse lexical
semantics it's not ambiguous but indeterminate.   You pick up
some sort of impoverished concept, just as when you pick the
word <u>cousin</u> in English you don't actually bother to wonder
whether it's a male or a female cousin unless it's for some
reason really crucial in the context, or you're translating
into another language or something.   When you get one of
these words you process it immediately as indeterminate and
then you allow that specification to be sharpened up as you
carry through incrementally.   In other words a sparse
semantics I think is more conducive to incremental
processing, and a very detailed semantics and the ambiguity
that that entails are somewhere else in the system.   So the
two different things interact.

Eric ATWELL: Presumably this idea can also extend back to
prototypes, that in certain circumstances it would be nice
not to have to choose between the interpretations.

THOMPSON: Mitch, you're absolutely right by the way: I
wouldn't want to suggest any analysis of anything like (26)
that involved any kind of raising.

MOORE: You don't want it to turn into something like 'quick
raising' or 'cigarette raising'!

PULMAN: Well I'm getting signals from the back that people are ready for 'glass raising' ...

References

Ades, A.E. & Steedman, M.J. 1982. On the Order of Words. **Linguistics and Philosophy** 4, 517-558.

Aronoff, M. 1980. Contextuals. In Hoekstra, T., van der Hulst, H. & Moortgat, M., eds., **Lexical Grammar.** Dordrecht: Foris, 49-72.

Bach, E. 1983. On the Relationship between Word-grammar and Phrase-grammar. **Natural Language and Linguistic Theory** 1, 65-89.

Barwise, J. & Perry, J. 1983. **Situations and Attitudes.** Cambridge, Mass.: MIT Press.

Boguraev, B.K. 1980. **Automatic Resolution of Linguistic Ambiguities.** PhD dissertation, University of Cambridge. Technical Report no. 11, Cambridge University Computer Laboratory.

Bresnan, J., ed. 1982. **The Mental Representation of Grammatical Relations.** Cambridge, Mass.: MIT Press.

Chomsky, N. 1980. **Rules and Representations.** Oxford: Basil Blackwell.

Chomsky, N. 1982. **Lectures on Government and Binding.** Dordrecht: Foris.

Cooper, R. 1975. **Montague's Semantic Theory and Transformational** Syntax. PhD dissertation, University of Massachusetts at Amherst.

Cooper, R. 1983. **Quantification and Syntactic Theory.** Dordrecht: D. Reidel.

Gazdar, G., Klein, E., Pullum, G. & Sag, I. 1985. **Generalized Phrase Structure Grammar.** Oxford: Basil Blackwell.

Haddock, N. 1985. Noun Phrase Reference and the Resolution of Syntactic Ambiguity. Linguistics Association of Great Britain (Liverpool), September 1985.

Halvorsen, P.-K. 1983. Semantics for Lexical-Functional Grammar. **Linguistic Inquiry** 14, 567-615.

Kamp, J.A.W. 1981. A Theory of Truth and Semantic Representation. In Groenedijk, J.A.G., Janssen, T. & Stokhof, M., eds., **Formal Methods in the Study of Language**, Amsterdam: Mathematical Centre Tracts, 277-322.

Kaplan, R.M. & Bresnan, J. 1982. Lexical-Functional Grammar: A Formal System for Grammatical Representation. In Bresnan, ed., 173-281.

Kripke, S.A. 1977. Speaker's Reference and Semantic Reference. **Midwest Studies in Philosophy** 2, 28-41.

Mellish, C.J. 1981. **Coping with Uncertainty: Noun Phrase Interpretation and Early Semantic Analysis.** PhD dissertation, University of Edinburgh.

Montague, R. 1973. The Proper Treatment of Quantification in Ordinary English. In Hintikka, J., Moravcsik, J. & Suppes, P., eds. **Approaches to Natural Language.** Dordrecht: D. Reidel, 221-242. Reprinted in Thomason, ed., 247-270.

Russell, B. 1905. On Denoting. **Mind** 14, 479-493.

Sampson, G. 1979. The Indivisibility of Words. **Journal of Linguistics** 15, 39-47.

Shieber, S.M., Uszkoreit, H., Pereira, F.C.N., Robinson, J.J. & Tyson, M. 1983. The Formalism and Implementation of PATR-II. In **Research on Interactive Acquisition and Use of Knowledge** (SRI Project 1984 Final Report), Menlo Park, CA: SRI International, 39-79.

Steedman, M.J. 1983. A Categorial Syntax for Subject and Tensed Verb in English and some Related Languages. Ms., University of Warwick.

Steedman, M.J. 1985. Dependency and Coordination in the Grammar of Dutch and English. **Language** 61, 523-568.

Steedman, M.J. 1987. Combinatory Grammars and Parasitic Gaps. In Haddock, N., Klein, E. & Morrill, G., eds., **Edinburgh Working Papers in Cognitive Science, Volume 1: Categorial Grammar, Unification Grammar and Parsing.** Centre for Cognitive Science, University of Edinburgh.

Thomason, R.H., ed. 1974. **Formal Philosophy: Selected Papers of Richard Montague.** New Haven: Yale University Press.

Watt, W.C. 1978. Good Intensions. **Journal of Linguistics** 14, 83-88.

Winograd, T. 1972. **Understanding Natural Language.** Edinburgh: Edinburgh University Press.

Woods, W.A. 1973. Progress in Natural Language Understanding: An Application to Lunar Geology. In **AFIPS Conference Proceedings,** Montvale, NJ: AFIPS Press, 441-450.

The Lexicon

Graeme Ritchie

I do not intend to present an actual paper, but rather to make some comments which might help to stimulate and structure the subsequent discussion. I would like to consider the topic from two angles - what is needed for a lexicon for computer applications at the moment; and what do current linguistic theories have to say (or not say) about that; that is, what is the tie up between the needs of applications and a supply of ideas from the theoretical side, coming from linguistics?

I thought I'd do some ground clearing by establishing some terminology that we could use in the succeeding discussion and argument, and trying to settle what I meant by 'the dictionary' or 'the lexicon'. (I'm going to use 'dictionary' and 'lexicon' interchangeably here.)

One point I wanted to raise straight off was that, if we're talking about applications, then the considerations must focus in fairly firmly on a practically computable route through the dictionary information in whichever direction you're going. I would describe the lexicon neutrally as an **association** between **surface forms** and **linguistic information** - I'm trying to steer clear of theory-laden terms or too many assumptions, because I wanted to get on to what the nature of these things are as separate issues. That is:

1. What is the unit of information for which we need to store information in the dictionary - do we store it per morpheme, per word, or (as is often mentioned, particularly in the AI literature) on a phrasal basis?

LINGUISTIC THEORY AND COMPUTER APPLICATIONS
ISBN 0-12-747220-7

2. What is the information that we put there? This is
something that is often talked about in linguistic theory.
In fact, this is probably the issue that is most talked
about, because right through the generative grammar material
there are allusions to what you associate with a word; very
often the assumption is that 'the word' is the answer to
question 1.   Very often the answer here is 'syntax,
semantics, and phonetics'.

3. A question which is sometimes underplayed in
theoretical linguistic material is: how do you get between
surface form and the entry for that word or morpheme, and of
course the reverse mapping?   But in a computational
application that question comes much more into the
foreground than it might in purely theoretical
considerations, or has done.

Again - because I was thinking of this as a ground
clearing exercise for a discussion to follow - I decided I
would say what I meant by 'computer applications'; and I
thought of the possibilities listed in Figure 1.

Figure 1. Computer applications

        Machine translation
        Natural language front ends (input)
        Natural language front ends (output)
        -
        Speech recognition
        Speech synthesis
        Information retrieval
        Text processing
        Literary studies

I thought I'd exclude speech and text crunching and
similar applications, just in order to simplify the
discussion, and in view of what I guessed to be the
interests of many of the participants. I assume that we are
looking at what is called 'natural language processing' -
that is typed text rather than speech - and that those would
be the typical applications people would be interested in,
namely natural language front-ends and machine translation.
So as further ground clearing, let's assume we're talking
about that kind of system.

Continuing to develop the terminology or framework, I thought it was necessary to make a distinction which I sometimes find gets confused when I'm talking about this material to people informally; that is, the distinction between how the dictionary functions as a module in a natural language system and how the programmers or linguists construct the dictionary. This is particularly relevant because sometimes when you're reading material in the linguistic literature which is clearly pertinent to the lexicon and is to do with lexical structure or lexical patterns, it's not explicit which of these it's concerned with. That is, if you're going to apply the analysis that the linguist is giving in the paper to some particular system, you'd have to give quite a bit of thought to deciding which it was actually for. Discussion of, for example, lexical redundancy rules or default markings in the dictionary and so on - it's not a trivial or obvious issue whether that's something that tells you about the functionality of the dictionary module as a piece of a natural language front end in terms of how it behaves, or whether it's to do with this second issue of how a linguist can more easily and non-redundantly put material into a dictionary. I will use the terms 'dictionary use' and 'dictionary construction' to make this distinction.

Dictionary use: just to make a crude classification of how such a module might function, there is 'look-up', which is what a parser would do, going from the surface form to the linguistic information. For want of a better word I've called the other function 'selection', which is what a generator might do, going from some kind of linguistic specification of what it wants to say to a surface form that says it. Again, in the linguistic literature, if you were reading about the lexicon, they would tend not to have that distinction, because, as has been mentioned in discussions, there is this notion that linguists abstract away from tedious details like processing, and in particular they're not too worried about whether you're talking about looking something up or finding the entry to go with a particular semantic pattern. For computational application you do have to discuss which one you're talking about, look-up or selection, if you're talking about the functionality of your dictionary module.

Dictionary construction is an area where much of the material in linguistics would be relevant, because of issues

about what   shape the dictionary should be, what is the
structure of the dictionary in terms of what the fields are
in entries, what kind of lexical rules you have and so on.
Then there's the issue of the content of the entries, which
I'll come back to shortly.

Taking four questions for look-up one at a time and
trying to break them down into further issues that one might
want to discuss and have views on, there are the questions
of:

1. In looking up the surface form, how does the parser
or natural language front end break it up into units that
are pertinent to the lexical look-up? All these questions of
course tend to be tied together, so this is quite naturally
tied to how the entries are arranged in a dictionary,
whether it's per morpheme, per word, or whatever. There's a
question of: is it a simple segmentation into morphemes and
then each morpheme gets looked up, do you have to do
adjustments of the boundaries of morphemes in order to get
either orthographic adjustments (in text) or phonological
effects? And what about phrases and idioms?

2. If you've done a segmentation, how do you then glue
the bits back together? If you've analysed that the word is
made up of a certain three morphemes, what do you then do
about the lexical information for the whole word once you've
dragged out the entries for the three morphemes - what is
the system for combining the linguistic information of the
parts into linguistic information for the whole? One could
for example have some kind of grammar which defined the
internal structure of words. That's the approach that our
project, the Alvey Tools Project for morphology and lexicon
(Russell et al 1986), is experimenting with. We're trying
to look at how you can use a kind of GPSG-style (Gazdar et
al 1985) system of rules to describe the internal
morphological structure of words.

3. Now remember that what we're looking at here is
dictionary look-up, the functionality or behaviour of a
dictionary once it's constructed and it's being used. To
what extent does lexical redundancy information actually get
computed during that look-up phase? To what extent does
default information get computed during that look-up phase,
if at all? Maybe it's all already multiplied out and in the
dictionary, instead of it being done at look-up time.

4. A special case is proper names - I'm not confident that that's of great interest at the moment in this workshop, but it is important when interfacing to a database.

Again, continuing with dictionary use, what I call selection, that is the reverse look-up, going, as one might in a generator, from some kind of underlying linguistic structure to a word which expresses it. What are the questions we have to consider there?

1. What's the nature of this mapping? What is the nature of the input to selection - semantic structure, syntactic specification, or a mixture of both? What does it start from? That seems not to be something you'd get wide agreement on if you did a quick straw poll amongst computational linguists. Generation is an area that seems less well explored, certainly in the areas I'm familiar with, which is more the AI end of computational linguistics, than the look-up phase. Indeed generation is rather neglected in terms of decent systematic or principled statements about how it might or should work, so it's very hard to speculate not only on what the answers are but what the questions might be.

2. But one point that does seem pertinent, which I don't think is so much of a problem with parsing, is this notion of how the choice of one word then affects the choice of other structures. For example, the choice of verb may bind the case-roles for the noun phrases.

3. And this blends in to the timing of lexical selection: what's the processing? How is it phased in? If the system has some semantic item and is gradually constructing a grammatical structure for it, turning it into a surface form - at what point does lexical selection happen? Again that seems to be something to which in the other direction, you can have a nice simple answer, because you just look up all the words at the beginning and then you worry about ambiguity when it comes to parsing the sentence. There's simplification in the look-up direction, but for the selection direction these and other complications seem to come up.

That was dictionary use, look-up and selection. **Dictionary construction** (i.e. building your lexicon) I

subdivided into two questions. One was **form**, that is the
structure of the lexicon. What are the issues in
constructing a lexicon? Well, I've mentioned already the
question of the unit of entry - should it be morpheme,
should it be word? I also mentioned the **content** of entries,
that is, what should the linguistic information be? I
think, as I said, you often find in linguistics that they
make some assumption about what's in the lexicon which is
enough to get them by for what they are interested in,
namely the sentence level grammar. I think the GPSG position
can be found in Gazdar et al (1985), which says that there
are four fields in each lexical entry (p. 34) and that's all
we'll have to say about it for now (pp. 107, 127). (It also
says what the four fields are - phonology, semantics,
irregular morphology and syntax.)

This is probably one of the more interesting areas
where there is work in linguistics that could be lifted
over, because the notion of lexical redundancy rules and
lexical defaults, as one can gather from the past day and a
half's discussion, is something people have thought about
and are interested in. There are possible mechanisms people
have talked about, but again, as I mentioned earlier, when
you're reading theoretical linguistics literature it's
neutral or ambiguous between whether these mechanisms are
something you want to use for dictionary construction, that
is to allow you to feed in minimal entries and have them
fleshed out at the compile-time stage, or whether it's
something that you want to use during look-up as a dynamic
computation. That may be in fact like the declarative-
procedural argument - it may be something that linguists
would deliberately want to leave vague, and don't see it as
a linguistic problem to state where that information is used
in the process.

The question of **content** in dictionary construction -
now on the assumption that we're talking about computer
applications, I'm not raising what I see as linguistic
issues, things that can be viewed purely as linguistic
problems. These are getting much nearer to the practical end
of the discussion.

1. If we're going to have dictionaries, where are we
going to get the content for them? That's actually
something that people have asked me informally - where can I
get a dictionary for my system? I usually decline to sell

them one, because we don't actually have one, and I'm not
sure who does have a large working dictionary that you can
just plug into a natural language interface, for example,
and get lots of benefits without too much difficulty
yourself.

The question of where you get the actual content of the
dictionary is not trivial. Lots of people suggest that
since the Oxford University Press has a big tape with the
Oxford dictionary on it, couldn't we use that?   Well,
possibly.   There are several problems with that.
Publishers' dictionaries tend to have in them information
which is not the kind of information that I've been talking
about, and which has been talked about for the past day and
a half. If you look in the Oxford dictionary, it tends not
to have very detailed subcategorization information.

Longman is at the useful end of the scale, as far as I
can gather talking to people about it, in that it's more
orderly and more formalized in what it does give you than
the average dictionary you buy in the local bookshop, which
would just typically give you some very crude syntactic
classification, some very crude pronunciation information,
and a string of English text about the word. And certainly
that's not what's needed for interfacing with the kind of
parsers we've been talking about here for the past day and a
half. You need a greater complexity of information.

One could envisage that you could get the raw data from
some system like that and preprocess it into a very crude
approximation. That is, you have a translation from things
like 'V.trans' into '[+V,-N,(SUBCAT 23)]', etc., and have a
preprocessor thatwould scan something like the Longman's
tape and try to do that computation.   But that would
probably only give you a first approximation, and then you'd
have to resort to going through it by hand and editing it.
Our project is working without a publisher's dictionary. For
test data we have a small-to-medium dictionary that we are
using for test purposes, and Graham Russell has written
3,500 entries by hand in feature notation.

2. If you're going to move around to other applications,
then you have the question of what you're going to do about
quickly and cleanly going from a description of the database
to what the new content words should be for your system. If
you've got lexical redundancy rules that relate not just to

things like morphology - which might be domain-independent, and could be ported across directly - that is, if you've got lexical rules that talk about the semantics of entries - then the porting involves not only getting the entries and saying that some new technical word such as <u>computer</u> refers to this particular item in the database, or that <u>carburettor</u> refers to that item in the database. If you're imposing more structure in your lexicon, somebody else has got to do that structuring for the new domain, so there's a lot of detailed work. Perhaps that might be theoretically interesting, but a lot of this is going to be highly tedious in just porting around between applications.

Then, getting even more towards a practical level, there are issues that one might want to consider in embedding a dictionary into a large system.

1. The first one is in a sense a linguistic issue in another guise, which is the question of: how much does the lexicon do and how much does the parser do? This was emerging from the discussion towards the end of this afternoon, this notion of a trade-off between what's lexical information and what's not. So interfacing of the dictionary to other parts of your model or your system is not just a practical issue, but could be discussed in theoretical terms as well.

2. User-engineering raises the question of how to make it easy for somebody actually to produce a dictionary. At the moment, for example, on our project we have two people who are computational linguists, and they, using a text editor, write all the entries. Then we bung it through a big compiler and it comes out with a final form that probably nobody could read, so there's not a lot of user-engineering involved at the moment. You really could do with some tools that work interactively and help you, and some of the systems that are around do this; for example, in Ahlswede (1985) there's discussion of allowing somebody to develop the semantic entries in an interactive way. So there's a need for various browsing tools and editing tools to make it much easier to debug a dictionary, and indeed to create one.

3. I don't know how you test a dictionary, since I'm not at all clear about what would count as testing it. Particularly if you're doing something like complex

morphology, where you've stuck in 20 morphological rules and 20 spelling rules and you're not sure if they're going to be dead right. Presumably this is the kind of area where you really just have to run it over a whole lot of data to see what happens, and then you have to read over the results.

4. There is a question of efficiency, which is linked to the next point, large-scale dictionaries. Efficiency of look-up is quite important, because if you are implementing a natural language front-end, the chances are that even if the user is prepared to wait a second for a response, you're probably going to want most of that one second to do other more interesting things at other levels of the model, not to mention perhaps accessing the back-end system that you're interfacing to. And you don't want to squander a whole lot of fractions of a second simply looking up a word. So a dictionary that is slow is not a lot of use, I would think, to most people.

5. And there's the question of managing effectively - as I said, these two points are very closely linked. A dictionary then becomes very much like a large database - you've got the issue of cross-indexing it, both for efficiency and for user engineering. If you want to allow people to browse around and look at entries and see what entries have a particular marking, then you're going to need a good set of cross indexing tables to allow the users to skip around the way they feel like and see what's there. So there's a lot of software engineering issues that come up along the line which might not be linguistically interesting, but they're far from trivial.

That concludes what I've prepared. I'm not sure how appropriate it is to try to organise a discussion round any of these questions; but it might be useful if anybody has any meta-suggestions about what they feel are the issues that need resolving, and that would be fruitful to discuss.

Stuart SHIEBER: I had a meta-suggestion, but first I wanted a little background information. Jan, in the Rosetta system, what is the approximate size of your dictionary?

Jan LANDSBERGEN: It is still an experimental system, as I said. In Rosetta1 it's 150 words, in Rosetta2 it's five or six thousand words.

SHIEBER: I was just trying to calculate what the average size of the dictionaries were in the systems built by the invited speakers. The average comes to a little over 1500, but, as I expected, if you disallow Rosetta it comes to - oh - 25, I think.

Ron KAPLAN: In the LUNAR system (Woods 1973) we had 3,000.

SHIEBER: That doesn't count.

KAPLAN: The LUNAR system counts!

SHIEBER: No. My figures were for "state of the art natural language processing systems". Although, to be fair, Ron, I know that you've done extensive work on dictionary servers, I don't believe the LFG system has ever been hooked up to one. I'm forced to admit that PATR-II (Shieber et al 1983) is no better off - ignoring the Cambridge version, which apparently has hooked up the entire Longman's dictionary though I don't know with what degree of success. This raises the question of what information the invited speakers could possibly have about the issue of connecting dictionaries to NL processing systems. So I expect most of the talking won't be by the invited speakers for a change. The situation seems pretty embarrassing for everyone except the MT people.

LANDSBERGEN: I would like to add that part of the information in our dictionaries has been put in by programs, and in some cases is wrong.

SHIEBER: Part of it has been put in by humans in our systems, and it's wrong too.

Karen SPARCK JONES: There is also the point as to whether one is talking about entries for words or stems. In a big dictionary, that's also an issue. In Rosetta, is that stems or words, full forms? There's some differences when you're doing these kind of computations. Admittedly if the size of the dictionary is small it's less important - I see one of them written here says nought. But if you've got 6,000, is that stems or full forms?

LANDSBERGEN: Stems.

SPARCK JONES: So the real size of the dictionary is

substantially larger.

LANDSBERGEN: Well, with dictionaries plus morphology ...

SHIEBER: Yes, I normalized for that.

Mary McGee WOOD: The Japanese project here at UMIST (Whitelock et al 1986) has 986.

Eric ATWELL: Another factor surely is how complex each entry is. The LOB tagger (Atwell et al 1984) has seven and a half thousand, but that's only got syntactic information of a very basic form with each entry. Presumably some of these systems which have got only fifteen entries have got very complex entries, and would be a lot more difficult to synthesise a large dictionary with.

RITCHIE: Is there anybody here on the applications side who has any comments on applications needs?

SPARCK JONES: I think in a way - I take it I can call myself at least to some extent an applications person - I think in a way you sold the pass by the cut-off you made about the type of application you were concerned with, because it's in some of the ones below your dotted line where the need for a larger lexicon cuts more clearly. If you think about interface systems, the kind that we've got any idea about how to build even modest versions of currently, a limited domain would tend to imply a limited lexicon. But for some of the text-processing things - and this is certainly a problem with information retrieval, it was the problem we had in the information retrieval project that we were doing, that you've only got to start thinking about searching scientific literature or something like that and you're really into big difficulties about the lexicon.

THOMPSON: Speech processing is the other obvious case. We already have a sort of scratch lexicon of 4,000 words for the speech input project, which is just syntactic information at the moment, because it's only being used by people at that level in the project, but we're targeting 5,000 words with syntactic, morphological, and phonemic information by the end of next year, 10,000 by the end of the project. And there's an issue which we're really worried about which I didn't think was mentioned here, which is the pressure on dictionary structure vis-a-vis look-up that comes from the need for fast updating. It's not acceptable if your dictionary is such that to add a new word requires you to re-compile the dictionary. Because if you're running an interactive speech input system and the user gives you the name of the person about whom he's writing his report, he's not going to accept it if you have to query him every time he uses that word in the rest of the letter. So you have to be able to make fast updates, and you would like to be able to do that in the same way that you do everything else. Obviously there's a cheap solution which says, well, you have a linear list of words which you've just learned and you check that first and then you have the real dictionary, but over time that's not acceptable.

ATWELL: I don't see why that is unacceptable. Graeme [Ritchie] said towards the end that the problem is like storing a large database, but really that's a bit like saying that natural language parsing can be done by an ordinary phrase-structure grammar. The point is that a dictionary of English is going to have a very much more complicated structure. You could have some short-term word-list which is augmented for each document, and at the end of every week or so, in some sort of batch system, is added to the large dictionary if required.

THOMPSON: It seems to me that that is an issue which needs to be addressed; my first-order intuitions about how it ought to be addressed probably are irrelevant. But there is a question of incremental updating - and a very closely related question, which is specialization or personalization, so you could have a dictionary, plus the site dictionary for the relevant local site, and the individual dictionary for the individual, which have the right properties in terms of what hides what.

RITCHIE: It still seems clear to me that it must be worth looking at the database field, to see the precedents there.

Mitch MARCUS: Just a couple of comments about different applications of dictionaries for speech research. Ken Church (1985) has been doing some work for about a year and a half now on stress assignment morphology, and determining national origin of names, text-to-speech systems. Much of the work is theoretical, but he's been doing it all with a 50,000 word dictionary on line on a Symbolics machine, and he has a thing working on this about ten or fifteen

different ways. It has a 40 megabyte load band that he just
starts up with, and tests these hypotheses on stress
assignment, just by programming them up and letting them
run. And he gets all the exceptions in 50,000 words of
English, in not excessively long time.

Bob MOORE: How was that dictionary constructed?

MARCUS: I think it may be the Websters Dictionary. You can
buy dictionaries which contain only words and things like
stress assignment, it has no definitions and the like.

MOORE: OK, but he was lucky that there was a previously
available product that had the information he needed in it.

MARCUS: Right, but according to some linguists both at the
labs and outside, he's done some fairly remarkable work in
stress, particularly for someone who had never seen the
stuff until six months ago. He'd literally discovered
fifteen years' worth of linguistic examples, hard-fought,
hard-won examples, inside of a month and a half by himself,
by merely doing this empirical work. I think there's a real
advantage, for theoretical work, to having large on-line
dictionaries that are accurate.

For text-to-speech we figure we need 3,000 to 5,000
words, mainly verbs, with complement structures. If you want
to do intonation phrasing, you need to know what the
complement structures are, it turns out, and that's the kind
of size that we need.

Ted BRISCOE: Can I ask are there any American equivalents,
like the Longman - dictionaries that give more detailed
information, rather than just transitive or intransitive for
verbs?

MARCUS: I don't know whether this is American or English:
the Collins Translation Dictionaries have the kind of
information that Oxford Advanced Learners has, and some of
it's in computer readable form, evidently.

BRISCOE: What are the names of those Collins dictionaries?

MARCUS: They have one for German, one for Italian, one for
French, and internally they're developing a framework for
describing semantic structure roughly the same way that the

Advanced Learners' Dictionary does for words of English. The problem with the published dictionaries is that for each language they only list those word meanings which differ between the two languages, and they just assume everything else will go through. But that looks fairly interesting.

BRISCOE: Those dictionaries contain syntactic subcategorization information about verbs?

MARCUS: It's the standard business where you have funny abbreviations for 'something', 'somebody', and the like. That essentially gives you a couple of features inside reasonable frames for that machine to set up, extremely formal. We have one American dictionary on-line that is available in computer-readable form, I forget which one it is.

Richard SHARMAN: I can support Mitch's statements about using a dictionary as a resource, by explaining some of the work we've done at Winchester. We've got Collins Larger Dictionary on line and it's got about 90,000 head words in it, but when you expand it with all the derivational forms that gives you about a quarter of a million words. We have this online on a mainframe with instantaneous access to all the fields apart from the definitions, so it has part-of-speech information, of which there are about 40 categories, the phonemic transcription, the subject matter class, like medical, and so on, and we have a simplified version of that which runs on an IBM PC (Lawrence and Kaye 1986).

RITCHIE: What do you tend to use it for?

SHARMAN: We've tended to use it mainly as a resource, for sorting out strange pronounciations, checking phonemic transcription rules, and that kind of thing, rather than as a dynamic look-up during parsing, but clearly we have that option, since it's now so fast.

SPARCK JONES: I think probably the largest dictionary that's actually been used for automatic parsing in some sense is the dictionary that was used by Klingbiel at the Department of Defense for machine-aided indexing, and I have an idea he had an absolutely enormous dictionary, it might have had about 20,000 or 70,000 words in it [in fact 26,000 - cf Klingbiel (1973)]. It was terribly crude parsing he was doing, it was selecting index terms.

SHARMAN: I think these things are becoming more possible now. Bob Borsley, who's also working with us, has done a study of the Longman classifications, with a view to automatically mapping them into some feature representation, but has found that it's probably too hard, that the Longman classifications, though interesting, don't in fact map neatly and systematically in all the cases.

BRISCOE: I'd like to dispute that. I have a system which maps into the feature system used by PATR (Shieber et al 1983), which is really very similar to the feature system used in GPSG (Gazdar et al 1985). And there's also a thesis by Michiels (1982) at the University of Liège, which gives an algorithm for deriving a generative grammar-like feature system which distinguishes raising, equi type verbs, this sort of thing, and marks subcategorization from the Longman grammar code system. So I think it is possible to do that.

RITCHIE: If there are systems like this working and being used, and have been used in the past for automatic parsing, what's the case for wheeling in some of the linguistic apparatus that I alluded to in my summary? Things like lexical redundancy rules and so on are the kind of things which are of interest to linguists both computational and theoretical. What are the benefits going to be to anybody who actually wants to build a practical system? Or is it just going to increase the elegance of it? Is it going to be a user aid for constructing a new dictionary, because there'll be less redundancy, needed in and put in? How much of the paraphernalia that is of linguistic interest actually has a pay-off practically?

BRISCOE: It seems to me, from my experience again with Longman, that the existing machine readable dictionaries are really just a fast and dirty way of getting yourself quite a long way down the road quite quickly, and there's no long-term future in playing with them unless the nature of lexicography changes so radically that they all turn into theoretical linguists overnight, and start producing totally indigestible dictionaries, which one can use more or less directly for computational implementation.

RITCHIE: What's the problem, is it the wrong sort of information?

Nick OSTLER: What sort of information do you lack in

Longman?

BRISCOE: Longman is quite good for deriving subcategorization information, and information about the semantic type of verbs, and so on. It looks as though if you play around for a lot longer you might even be able to get something out of the definitions, because you have a restricted definition vocabulary, but that really is a much harder game. It has a supposedly non-circular defining vocabulary of 2,000 words, which are supposed to be used in one core sense, to define the other 60,000 words for which there are entries in the dictionary.

Pete WHITELOCK: But it's not true that it's not circular.

Bran BOGURAEV: The senses in which the basic 2,000 words are used, if you follow them round quite closely, you find circularities.

ATWELL: And it's not 2,000 lexemes, either, or 2,000 features, because in fact a word may have several different senses.

Steve PULMAN: But what he means by semantic typing of verbs is not what you probably mean, it's a kind of an ontology of what sort of things there are, like solids and liquids and stuff, and tells you what the subject and the object are and so on.

BRISCOE: No, what I meant by semantic types of verbs was simply logical type, is it raising, equi, object equi, or whatever. One can derive from the grammar code system both subcategorization features and also, if you like, what would in GPSG be the semantic type of the verb, what used to be called equi or raising or whatever, and nowadays is part of the semantics. One can derive that very limited semantic information.

There is also the vague possibility that you might be able to do something with this definition vocabulary, although that's going to be much harder. But in any case, even if you just look at the grammar code system, what you find there is that for the verbs it's really quite good. For the nouns and the adjectives it's been done in a very half-baked way. You're very much at the mercy of the lexicographer and how he was feeling on the day when he wrote that entry. So it seems to me that, although you can get quite a long way by taking something like that and hacking for a few months, it's not in any way an approach to building dictionaries for use in NLP which has any long-term future. I think that probably the way to go is towards developing techniques for getting this kind of information out of corpora.

KAPLAN: There was a workshop about a year ago or maybe more (Calzolari 1983), and going to be another one next year, on machine-readable dictionaries, that included a bunch of lexicographers and a bunch of dictionary publishers and a bunch of people like me. It was a very interesting meeting, on the nature of machine-readable dictionaries, and how can existing dictionaries be used or be modified to be used for the kinds of theoretical purposes and practical purposes that we have in the computational linguistics community. I think we should regard ourselves perhaps as having some power to change what kinds of dictionaries the publishers are actually producing, particularly in machine-readable forms. Della Summers at Longman was very interested in understanding what kinds of dictionary entries we would like to have, and also Howard Webber at Houghton Mifflin who does the American Heritage dictionary was very interested. There were a couple of others that weren't so interested, and there was the guy at Websters in the States who wished he could get his stuff in machine-readable form just for his own purposes. But there was interest, and, to the extent that we have a coherent set of needs, it's not unreasonable that the lexicographers who get paid for doing that stuff might do it, and provide us things that are in fact more useful. Publishers are getting very interested in selling this kind of thing. They recognize it as a commercial venture, and if we can show that there's a market for having it this way rather than that way, being more careful about certain things and not other things, or in addition to other things, there can be some influence, I think, on what the available dictionaries are.

Harold SOMERS: I'm glad you brought up the commercial aspect, because another angle is something we found out a few years ago when we were looking into this, that as soon as you mentioned commercial use of your system, even very much long-term, lots of barriers came down, and the contracts that you had to sign to get hold of the stuff were just prohibitive. The question was, it seems a lot of people have got hold of big publishers' machine dictionaries -

KAPLAN: How many have them legally? Who actually either has
a licensing agreement, or paid or whatever you have to do?
[Response from Kaplan, Boguraev, Marcus, Thompson, and
Atwell] That's interesting.

SOMERS: And are you bound not to use it for commercial use?

THOMPSON: No, we're paying a very large sum of money -

KAPLAN: Which dictionary is this?

THOMPSON: I'm embarrassed to say I can't remember. It's the
speech output project at Edinburgh who in the first instance
has bought into that, and I don't actually have any formal
association with it.

KAPLAN: We have a research license for the typesetting tapes
of the American Heritage. We have a dictionary server that
can shove definitions and what not out around in the
network, so you don't have to have each workstation loaded
up with 80 megabytes of stuff most of which you'd never want
to see. You can randomly access it through the network. But
with a research license, we didn't quite get the kind of
service that one would like to get. For example, we didn't
get the last half of the G's - this is myself and Martin Kay
- they were past the end of tape mark. I think they want us
to pay more - a lot more - because since we got the license
they realized that they could really make money out of it.
But it's a research license, we can't distribute it in any
Xerox products, we can only use it for internal research
purposes. It's also kind of a disaster, we've spent years
and years and years -

THOMPSON: It took about three man-years' worth of work to
get it to the point where it was useful. About half of that
was mine and the other half was Martin [Kay] and Iris [Kay].

KAPLAN: Because it was the typesetting tapes, and the codes
in that dictionary were fairly well articulated, and even
'semantically oriented', in the sense that some code would
indicate that it was going to be pronounciations, some other
code would - you [Thompson] know more about this than I do
actually. But the problem was that if the typographical
rendition of pronounciation in terms of what font it was in

and whether it was bold or not was the same as the
typographical rendition of part of speech ... And the
proof-readers never saw the bugs in the codes. And so there
were lots of problems, and it took a long time. It was an AI
problem, that thankfully Henry and not I worked on, to try
to get useful information out.

THOMPSON: But that's really the dark ages though. Things
like Longman and Collins I think are better in that
respect, you don't have to fight your way through the
typesetting.

SPARCK JONES: There's an interesting point here for the
linguists too, that the real market is still - there may be
a growing market for the machine readable people, and we're
hypothesizing currently that the computational, natural
language processing people will want these up-market
dictionary entries that we talk about having - although it
appears not many of us have made very many of them - the
sort of stuff which is theoretically motivated which
contains this kind of information. Now of course that's not
the information that the people want who look up
dictionaries to find out what a word means. We've just been
talking about the problem of how to get what we want from
the kind of information that's in those dictionaries. What
is also a non-trivial question is, could you, if we've got
what we want, generate the kind of thing that those people
actually want to use, like simple syntax?

PULMAN: To some extent that's already true with the Longman,
because there's a lot of stuff on the tape that isn't in the
printed form of the dictionary.

SPARCK JONES: I was merely asking the question, if one makes
these tremendously 'up-market' lexical entries, of the kind
that we think we want, could you produce down-market ones
from them?

PULMAN: Well, the answer is yes.

RITCHIE: Coming out of the discussion here, I detect a
pattern of description of the way things are, that suggests
that what's wrong with these bulk dictionaries that you can
get from publishers is that the entries either have the
wrong content or the wrong form. Nobody's yet said anything
which suggests that some of the fancier linguistic

mechanisms, such as redundancy rules or defaults, are something we actually need visibly in a dictionary. We might need them as part of the dictionary construction, to make it easier, but the picture of the functionality of the dictionary in a natural language system that's emerging from this discussion, as far as I can see it, is a fully expanded dictionary where you associate information with words or morphemes, and if it's been computed from redundancy rules or default rules that's not visible, that is something that's either been compiled out or is done on the fly during lookup. People's comments when being critical of these dictionaries have been purely the nature of what the information was that was associated with the words, and that that was not suitable linguistically. The mechanism has not mattered, it's transparent to the linguistic user.

MARCUS: Two comments. We've actually been looking into buying dictionaries, and we've bought a couple. One thing that's been happening recently, and it's across the board - I think Ken Church has been looking at this, and has talked to pretty much everybody who's selling them - is that they've gotten expensive, even for a research license - and if you work for a company, by the way, research licences are iffy, because they contain clauses that might involve us in restrictions. And companies are beginning to realize that they're worth a lot. We've been talking at the labs about doing some work on building a verb dictionary of, I don't know, 3,000 to 5,000 entries, and it seems that in fact one has to have redundancy rules, because as long as we're running these systems on VAX* 750s or Lisp machines it's one thing, but if you want to put it in a PC, then you really don't want the thing to take up huge megabytes of disc. The result though, I think, is that what you have to do is to build two dictionaries, one of which is totally expanded, and the other one is your best guess at what the redundancy rules are, which you then use to reduce the other one. You actually have to do it in reverse, if you want to make sure you've got it right; you probably have to blow the whole thing out, look at that and make sure you've got it right, and then reduce it, with this compaction technique. It's rather strange, the other way round would be nice, but for large dictionaries I think that you can't trust your

---

* VAX is a trademark of Digital Equipment Corporation.

intuitions about how things work out.

THOMPSON: Right, and that's to hell with linguistics, essentially, the reduction is an information-theoretic reduction, and may or may not have anything to do with linguistic generalization.

KAPLAN: With what the child learns when he learns his language, for example.

WOOD: This term 'redundancy rule' has been used in a rather blanket, uninspected way in linguistics for a while. There are lots of different kinds of information in a dictionary that you could reduce and would want to reduce. For example, I doubt even a fully expanded dictionary would spell out all the regular plural forms with -ss on the end, would it? - and then you go to cases like an agent formation in -er, and then you go to derived nouns, at least within morphology. Or in the semantics, is your fully expanded dictionary going to say that everything which is human is also explicitly animate, so that it'll match onto a verb which requires an animate subject, or are you going to just know that if it's human it's animate, and that's OK? And the same with syntactic, say, hierarchies of 'transformational freedom', to use an old-fashioned term. There are a lot of different classes of information, a lot of different types of reduction, which you could be talking about, when you throw around this word 'redundancy rule'. Different reductions will be possible to different sizes for different purposes. I think you've got to unpack that rather loose term 'redundancy rule'.

RITCHIE: I was being deliberately loose about it, because I wanted to cover all of those in order to see which ones people wanted to vote for, as it were, bring up as necessary, and maybe pack some off to morphology and some of them elsewhere.

ATWELL: I wanted to make the point, agreeing with what you said about how to have the whole expanded dictionary, that that's what we've done on our project. And then, having the whole of the vocabulary from the million word corpus, you then work out what you can get rid of because it's redundant. And that was the only way to do it, you couldn't rely on intuitions to work out which suffixes, for example, were genuinely productive, because then you start producing all sorts of non-words.

PULMAN: But I don't understand what you mean by expanded here, because for inflexions that's feasible, but for derivation - you do a bit of arithmetic, take a couple of dozen verb stems and a few affixes, and see how many possible combinations there are, and pretty soon you get to a dictionary that's going to go all the way round the British Isles 20 times. So what do you mean by expanding a dictionary?

OSTLER: If all of those exist. You have fairly liberal intuitions about what the co-ocurrence restrictions are between these things.

PULMAN: One of the examples we had was <u>program</u>. <u>Programmable</u>, <u>reprogrammable</u>, <u>unreprogrammable</u>, <u>programm-ability</u>, <u>unprogrammability</u>, it flows up really quickly.

OSTLER: That's one example, and we don't know that that's across the board with every free class.

ATWELL: Are you trying to say that in fact the vocabulary is unrestricted, that since morphemes are joined together by some sort of grammar, you can have an infinite set of possible words, in some sense?

PULMAN: Yes. Certainly in other languages -

MOORE: There's another form of expansion that's not working out of the consequences of all these linguistic rules, that's going to massively increase the size of the dictionary, as soon as you start taking semantics seriously, and that's when you start treating as individual lexical items all the complex words and phrases that really function as individual lexical items in the language. To take our field, things like <u>mark-sweep</u> <u>garbage</u> <u>collector</u> or <u>disc controller</u> or <u>site</u> <u>licence</u> - it just goes on and on. I think that that would be a significant multiple of the number of items in the standard dictionary.

THOMPSON: Mitch [Marcus], did you actually mean morphologically exploded, or did you mean grammatical feature exploded?

MARCUS: Well first of all I have to admit to being a little

fast and loose. The level two morphology is in fact productive across the board, but it's not overly productive, and you have to decide what you're going to do about that. It seems necessary in many cases to begin by blowing things up as you put them in, and then throw them away - you do the blow-up first, and then you do the reduction if you have any chance of figuring out which ones actually never occur. Restartable's fine, restoppable's funny, rebeginnable's terrible: do you want to do anything about that, or are you just going to say, well, that just doesn't happen to occur?

PULMAN: But a lot of them sound funny. And even when you look at a big dictionary like the Oxford, I was astonished at the number of things that I thought of as derived, in the sense that you wouldn't bother to list them because they're so obviously predictable from the meanings of the parts, but they're there. But then you go off and take the front page of the newspaper, and go through and look up all the words in the dictionary, and it's astonishing how many of them aren't there. Even in a big dictionary.

RITCHIE: There's another point here, which is that you don't have to go to derivational morphology to get further multiplication. There's a sense in which the regular dictionary that you have on the shelf at home is expanded, in the sense that it'll indicate the inflexional form, maybe, of words, but it doesn't actually have them all listed, for every verb and every noun. If you're talking about full expansion even for inflexional morphology then you're going to get a multiplication there. If you just move to a slightly more interesting language than English, the factor goes up quite a lot.

KAPLAN: If you go to Spanish you get 300 forms for a verb.

BRISCOE: And in Hungarian there's something like 10,000.

THOMPSON: Finnish?

MARCUS: You've got to impose things, in fact, but the problem - say you wanted to build a system for speech recognition: it seems to me that when you get serious about not knowing what's being said at you, you really have to have some notion as to whether the words occur or not, and how you control that is very difficult. You've got to be very careful where you draw the lines, or else you start

allowing lots and lots and lots and lots of non-words into
your dictionary.

ATWELL: One thing that might be a partial solution to that,
and which you didn't mention at all in the fields for your
dictionary entries, is a frequency field. This is something
that the LOB tagger had, to some extent. That means that in
fact, although you say that the vocabulary is infinite, you
get some words which occur very frequently, and you're
always going to carry on finding one word or two words which
just occur once and that's the only time ever. So if you had
in your dictionary some count of their frequency, then it
would still be arbitrary, but you'd have a cut-off point at
a very very low frequency sort of word.

WOOD: Also these derivational processes are in fact a lot
more productive than most people normally realize, and
although you don't want a dictionary which is going to
generate a lot of neologisms, you probably do want one which
will be able to recognize them. If you're going to start
feeding in stuff like newspapers and having a parser
recognize it, you're going to want to be able to
segment, and get the -ables and the un-s.

ATWELL: Unbeginnable doesn't sound nice, but it might well
occur somewhere.

WOOD: You might well get it, and you want to be able to
handle it.

RITCHIE: It's interesting that the arguments that have been
coming forward to support rule-handled rather than listed
phenomena are ones for which so far the examples have been
mainly morphological. Does anybody want to carry a banner
for any of the other forms of lexical redundancy that are
talked about linguistically: the notions of fleshing out
entries with rules, or filling in other entries, saying that
if you've got an entry like this then you must have another
entry of that form?

KAPLAN: The 'lexical' in 'Lexical Functional Grammar'
(Kaplan & Bresnan 1982) has to do with our belief that there
are certain classes of rules that linguistically should
operate in the lexicon, and that they have certain formal
properties that are different from the kinds of things that
have been talked about today. They involve changes of

representations, not correspondences to other representations. We try to make some theoretical points that only things that have finite outputs, as opposed to recursive, infinite outputs, can be of that type. But basically, as a linguistic theory, LFG is committed to lexical rules, although we don't commit ourselves to saying when those are going to be applied in any particular processing. We think of them as redundancy rules that say, if this kind of entry exists, then this kind of entry exists, in a systematic way.

RITCHIE: Yes, but what I was trying to see if I could stimulate to the surface was some notion of what ramifications that linguistic position would have for practical implementations, and whether those could be best thought of as something to do with dictionary construction and the kind of expansion proccess that Mitch was talking about, or that has been mentioned in general, or whether you feel that it's something that would optimize the actual look-up and would be better seen as something done on the fly, perhaps because it interacts with the parsing mechanism, or for any other reason.

KAPLAN: The whole point is that it doesn't interact with the parsing mechanism. It's really a question of practical space-time trade-offs. Assuming that the rules are correct and that they apply just to the forms that they should, because of various defaults and whatever, then, whether or not you **want** to expand everything out, we know that you **can** expand everything out, because there's a finite output. Now whether you want to do that for a large lexicon, and multiply its size in some sort of arbitrary way, or not depends on the cost of your run-time interpretation of those things versus doing look-ups or the cost of storage of a large data base. It's not a theoretical question.

There is a psychological question, if you're doing psychological modelling. You might have a hypothesis that memory's cheap in the head - just feed it fish and it works, right? - that what a child does, looking at the acquisition issue, might be to use these rules -

RITCHIE: You mentioned the finiteness of output, but if you think of the arguments that were flying around a minute ago, the argument over morphology, and whether those effects should be expanded - admittedly, when we're looking at inflexion, the argument wasn't about finiteness - I think most people would concede that perhaps even Hungarian has finite inflexional morphology. But it was a question of whether this was something you would want to regard as computable in lookup, either because of the extreme variability and the unpredictablity of what you might hit in the data, or just because of the very large size of that finite output.

Gerald GAZDAR: I don't think you can assume finiteness in inflexion. In a language like Turkish the inflexional component includes things that we would call derivational in English, there's no real distinction between them. You can get iterated causatives with interspersed inflexional processes like formation of various sorts of participles and so on. I don't think there's any upper bound to the length of a Turkish word.

KAPLAN: You mean a word is sort of like a sentence.

GAZDAR: Yes, I think most of them are.

KAPLAN: But the notion of word then is sort of a morphological- phonological thing, it's contradicting the kind of analysis you'd like to give it as a syntactic or semantic structure. There's a bracketing paradox.

GAZDAR: Well you may want to say they're not words, but I don't think that that -

KAPLAN: You've still got to find them when you're looking in a dictionary.

GAZDAR: But the difference between Finnish and Turkish, where in Finnish it's all inflexion and there's 10,000 of them, and that's it, and Turkish where there's none of them -

OSTLER: In practice there is an upper limit on the length of words that you will ever encounter.

KAPLAN: But isn't that like saying that there's an upward bound on the number of words in a sentence?

OSTLER: It's not really all that interesting to say that it's 'infinite' - it's large.

GAZDAR: OK, but there's no upper bound on it, that's what I wanted to say.

SPARCK JONES: But exactly in the lexical case you don't know what you're going to want to look up in the dictionary.

KAPLAN: But there is an upward bound there,

GAZDAR: Then we can't have this discussion, because on this discussion we'll have all of English syntax in there.

MARCUS: I have two questions. (1) Is Turkish in fact utterly productive in this part of its morphology, as I would assume that it is? Anything that's guaranteed productive you clearly don't put in the dictionary, and that solves that. No-one puts English sentences in the dictionary, either, for roughly the same reason. (2) The question to Ron [Kaplan] is: given whatever large LFG grammar you guys have done, how large an explosion do you get in lexical entries for a word? How many lexical items do you get for each one?

KAPLAN: You mean how do we blow them up? You get a lot, if you start applying all these various lexical rules in various ways - perhaps about 20? - you get passive, you get dative, passive-dative, that kind of thing.

MARCUS: The question is, how many of these lexical rules do you have in a large grammar, and do you get the closure of all possibilities?

KAPLAN: You get the closure: we've been looking at around ten. It depends on what level of grain you want to have in these rules. These rules are never necessary, theoretically, and so the question is, is it worth while putting in a rule that does some fine gradation thing or not. And people have not really looked very hard at those issues.

RITCHIE: That's why I was fishing at the point about size, because I want you to try to give us a feel for it.

KAPLAN: I really don't have a good sense, because the lexical rule work has been done more at a theoretical level than actually using it in any system.

Doug ARNOLD: I think everyone has assumed that the real

problem with size was storage or access or something like that, but you can kill it off if you think about trying to construct one of these things. You haven't got time sensibly to construct a dictionary of more than 20,000 words, unless you use some sort of redundancy rules or something like that. OK, I'll up it by an order of magnitude, to 200,000. That's still not big enough to cover any natural language, except maybe Dani, or something like that.

RITCHIE: Esperanto.

SHARMAN: Can I raise another slightly different problem that we've had in dealing with large dictionaries, which is that if you look in a small dictionary, you tend to find relatively few uses for a word; so the word a is listed as a determiner in the small Collins. If you look in the large Collins it's listed as a noun, a symbol, an abbreviation, a preposition, and a verb, so that in

   (1)   A dog bit the man.

man can be a noun or a verb, and bit, and then dog, and so you get a possible parse, noun noun noun noun noun, so the whole sentence looks like a compound noun, which is probably a spurious parse.

MOORE: Can you give us a sentence where the is used as a noun? Without putting the in quotes?

KAPLAN: I want to know how a can be a verb.

SHARMAN: Be my guest and look in the dictionary. If you think of phrases like the ifs and the buts, dotting the i's and crossing the t's, and those sorts of idiomatic phrases, you can think of all sorts of examples where the word actually can be construed in those ways.

ATWELL: This is exactly a problem we had on the LOB tagger, and that's why probabilities were essential once you start dealing with a very large dictionary. Because you can say straightforwardly that, although you can't be absolutely certain, a is **almost** always an article, and therefore you just have to come up with the best analysis possible. The tagger never actually says, this is **the** analysis, but this is just the best out of the possible ones.

Rod JOHNSON: But if all you wanted was a syntactic category feature, then you wouldn't really have a big problem, would you - anyway, we wouldn't be talking about it for an hour and a half. We have to make big dictionaries, and they all have to have syntactic categories. That's not the real issue, is it? The real issue is what else goes in there, surely, and how compatible you can make that information with different kinds of manipulation. Different theories will impose different requirements on the input of the dictionary you've got.

KAPLAN: I think there's a real practical issue in the management of large dictionaries, given the current state of theory, which is that you are going to want to change the representations. One of the many reasons that we haven't invested a lot in the dictionaries is because we saw a lot of theoretical uncertainty. Not that we couldn't fix the theory at a given point and then go off and do something if we had to, but we know that there are a lot of things that we don't have right, and that we want to modify, and think of a better way of doing some day, and so forth; and that gives a disincentive to investing a lot of energy in building something. So what you'd like is a metalanguage for representing dictionary information, that can be translated out into whatever theory comes along, whichever of your theories you come up with next. And we don't have a good handle on that sort of meta-representation for lexical information that will be common to wide classes of theories.

SPARCK JONES: You certainly give a very creditable account of why one doesn't want to get down to the hard graft of mucking around with dictionaries.

KAPLAN: I've been spending a lot of time mucking with dictionaries. Really big dictionaries. We've done a lot of work on finite-state morphology, and thinking of that as a redundancy mechanism for doing morpho-graphemic and morpho-phonemic kinds of modifications. There is a practical algorithm, given a set of morpho-graphemic rules, to build a finite-state transducer that's equivalent to it - given a full-form dictionary, you can use those rules to find the minimal number of words that it takes to generate it, given the rules. So you can take out all the forms that are derivable in a systematic way, but all the irregular forms can be left in. The interesting thing is that, given a finite-state transducer, for, say, the morpho-graphemics of

Turkish, run that algorithm with an English dictionary, and you do get out an English dictionary, it's just not as compact as if you used a better set of rules. The question in my mind is, is there anything besides the information-theoretic value of these redundancies? Are there theoretical arguments you want to make about these rules, or is it just, let's find the best rules to compress the dictionary?

ATWELL: Perhaps we could take a leaf out of lexicographers' books. Lexicographers have been writing dictionaries for a long time - presumably one of their criteria is to try and pack as much as they can into a small space, and their approach is to have fully expanded forms where it's necessary, for a lot of cases, and to also include some productive affixes, and to have a whole hotch-potch of these things.

RITCHIE: The automaton that's looking it up's different, that's for human readers. I'm not sure that the arguments come out the same, if you're wanting a mechanized lookup.

THOMPSON: In particular the productivity judgment seems to be left to the reader, who after all is a native speaker and therefore should know. The problem is that you usually get a list of affixes all right, but there's no indication of to what extent you're free to combine them. And **you** know that, but it isn't explicitly represented.

KAPLAN: Surely you get something else in the dictionary - they offer a whole set of the words that take un-productively, but it's only a small sub-set, and you look at that list and say, why'd they choose **those** out from all the infinite other ones?

SPARCK JONES: This is where one wants to look at language dictionaries which are specifically designed for teaching English, or something like that, because they in principle take more care to deal with the question of not causing people to go off in the wrong productivity, if you see what I mean. At least they try to, as far as I understand from conversations at Longman.

ATWELL: The problem with Longman's defining vocabulary, 2,000 words, is that it actually includes some affixes which are used productively, so that they've actually broken their own rules in that sense in their own defining vocabulary.

SPARCK JONES: I'm saying that they do think about that particular issue, which if we're knowledgeable in a language then we may have some idea of, by analogy and generalization and so on. Longman don't necessarily get it right, it's just that they take more trouble about getting enough example or enough expansion, enough information in the entry to push them along the right direction. At least that's the aim. How far they succeed ...

KAPLAN: Does anybody here actually work in computer-assisted language teaching?

[No response.]

RITCHIE: That seems like a suitable note of ignorance on which to wind up the discussion.

References

Ahlswede, T.E. 1985. A Tool Kit for Lexicon Building. **23rd Annual Meeting of the Association for Computational Linguistics** (Chicago), Proceedings. 268-276.

Atwell, E.S., Leech, G., & Garside, R. 1984. Analysis of the LOB Corpus: Progress and Prospects. In Aarts, J. & Meijs, W., eds. **Corpus Linguistics**. Amsterdam:Rodopi, 40-52.

Bresnan, J., ed. 1982. **The Mental Representation of Grammatical Relations**. Cambridge, Mass.: MIT Press.

Calzolari, N. 1983. Machine-readable Dictionaries: Report of the Workshop held at SRI International. **ALLC Bulletin** 12, 51-53.

Church, K. 1985. Stress Assignment in Letter-to-sound Rules for Speech Synthesis. **23rd Annual Meeting of the Association for Computational Linguistics** (Chicago), Proceedings, 246-253.

Gazdar, G., Klein, E., Pullum, G. & Sag, I. 1985. **Generalized Phrase Structure Grammar**. Oxford: Basil Blackwell.

Kaplan, R.M. & Bresnan, J. 1982. Lexical-Functional Grammar:
A Formal System for Grammatical Representation. In
Bresnan, ed., 173-281.

Klingbiel, P. H. 1973. A Technique for Machine-aided
Indexing. **Information Storage and Retrieval** 9, 477-494.

Lawrence, S.G.C., and Kaye, G. 1986. Production of a
Computer Based Dictionary of Pronounciation. IBM UKSC
Report 148.

Michiels, A. 1982. **Exploiting a Large Dictionary Data Base.**
PhD dissertation, Universite de Liège.

Russell, G.J., Pulman, S.G., Ritchie, G.D. & Black, A.W.
1986. A Dictionary and Morphological Analyzer for
English. **COLING 86: 11th International Conference on
Computational Linguistics** (Bonn, West Germany),
Proceedings, 277-279.

Shieber, S.M., Uszkoreit, H., Pereira, F.C.N., Robinson,
J.J. & Tyson, M. 1983. The Formalism and Implementation
of PATR-II. In **Research on Interactive Acquisition and
Use of Knowledge** (SRI Project 1894 Final Report), Menlo
Park, CA: SRI International, 39-79.

Whitelock, P.J., Wood, M.McG., Chandler, B.J., Holden, N. &
Horsfall, H.J. 1986. Strategies for Interactive Machine
Translation: The Experience and Implications of the UMIST
Japanese Project. **COLING 86: 11th International
Conference on Computational Linguistics** (Bonn, West
Germany), Proceedings, 329-334.

Woods, W.A. 1973. Progress in Natural Language
Understanding: An Application to Lunar Geology. In **AFIPS
Conference Proceedings**, Montvale, NJ: AFIPS Press, 441-
450.

Translation

Rod Johnson

I have more or less the same preamble as Graeme [Ritchie] did yesterday. The original intention, as I understood it, was that there would be a number of 'theme sessions' about various kinds of applications. As it turns out MT is the only application left on this list of themes, which makes one feel a little bit exposed. Nonetheless I would want to maintain that under current circumstances, MT is worth spending a bit of time on, because it raises some quite interesting theoretical methodological questions which haven't really been raised up to now, or only touched upon, and in view of this I'll try to concentrate on that particular collection of issues as far as I can.

Just a few clarifications: There are all sorts of things that come under the rubric of MT systems. There are an awful lot of products on the market these days (that most of you probably know about) which are really just hyped-up word-processors or some kind of on-line dictionaries, and even some things which one might think of as MT systems proper finish up, when you examine them in some detail, looking like big sentence dictionaries. These are not what I really want to talk about. I don't think they have any particular immediate relevance to the general set of topics we're supposed to be addressing. The characteristics of the sort of MT that I think is interesting, and for which the topics we've been discussing these last few days may be of some relevance, are something like the following:

(i) I'm going to assume that MT systems are big. That doesn't here mean 'big' so much in the sense of wide coverage of language (which I'll come to in a bit), but rather 'big' in the sense that, in order to make one, you

LINGUISTIC THEORY AND COMPUTER APPLICATIONS
ISBN 0-12-747220-7

have to appeal to the knowledge of quite a large number of people and you have to do so in a fairly extensive way. The reasons for this are that MT systems - of the sort I want to talk about - involve a number of languages (cf. point (iii) below), and you're unlikely to get the sort of language expertise that you want from a single individual or even two or three individuals in one place. This fact has some consequences for the organisation of MT systems, the way you set them up and the way you design them, which I think impinge on the kind of theoretical notions you have to have before you start.

(ii)   Similarly I'm assuming that we're talking about programs which are intended to translate texts from a fairly unrestricted source, with some constraints perhaps on the text domain, but not with any artificial limitations on some set of texts of which you have prior knowledge and beyond which you're not really expecting to go.

(iii)   As I said before, things get interesting once you get beyond two languages. If you stay within two languages you can cheat in all sorts of ways without it being really apparent.

(iv)   I'm assuming that these programs don't involve human intervention. You don't have the opportunity of appealing to human intuitions about things that you can't make the program handle. This is an unrealistic assumption in general, but it's not a bad starting assumption to see where it gets you before you give in and decide that there are some things that you can't do. It's a good thing to decide a posteriori, in the light of some sensible theorizing of what you're not going to be able to do, rather than just to state beforehand and then find some way of doing the things that are left.

(v)   Lastly I would like to restrict the sorts of MT programs being talked about to ones which are in some strong sense linguistic. What I suggest by that is that it is reasonable to propose that the construction of a mapping between texts which are chunks of language is primarily organized according to linguistic principles. This is not to exclude the famous real world knowledge, which is always a bone of contention in this area, but simply to say that the driving force here is some kind of linguistic theory, or some set of linguistic beliefs. You may graft onto that some

more information which is extra-linguistic, but you don't
start off by saying, we need lots of external knowledge, and
by the way what extra bits of information do we need about
language in order to get the job done?   The assumption
being made here about MT being linguistic is quite the
converse of what some people in some areas, even people
who've claimed they're doing MT, overtly say they're doing.
And so I think it needs to be stated that that's the
assumption underlying this discussion.

Here are some pragmatic requirements that come from
outside that are likely also to have an effect on the way
that you put the things I've just mentioned together.   These
are probably not exclusive to MT by any means, but they do
turn out to be very important in view of some of the other
characteristics of MT systems.

(i) In this domain in particular, you want the systems
that you make to be easy to extend. Of all applications for
language processing, MT programs of the kind characterized
above are going to be particularly open-ended - they're
never going to be finished in any reasonable way.   The
amount you have to change them may decrease with time, but
you will never get everything right, you will never be able
to predict every single phenomenon that's going to come up
in your set of texts. Even if the only open-enededness
finishes up being in the lexicon, it will still be the case
that there are new things you have to know about. Given the
circumstances of these conditions, you are not really
allowed to suppose that if you don't have the linguistic
apparatus to treat some input text available then you throw
the text out, and if the same phenomenon occurs a couple of
weeks later then you will throw it out again.   Your
responsibility, if you get something wrong, is to try and
put it right. So it's not as if you can stay within some
restricted language. In addition to that, it's quite normal
in this area to have to add a new language: to take what
you've got and to be asked to make it handle some completely
new language in the same way as you're handling the existing
ones. And it also has been the case in the past, although
rather less successfully implemented, that people have been
asked to handle new text types using the original apparatus.

(ii) You want the system to be modular - everybody
says this, but there's a reasonable amount of truth in it
here I think - because of the size of the thing and because

of the way that you expect to put things together, quite apart from any engineering considerations about making it easy to build and to maintain. You really do want to be able to take parts of your system and plug them together in different ways. This is partly the 'more than 2 languages' question. If you're handling three or four languages, it really is very sensible, perhaps almost a priori necessary if you are going to do this thing rationally, to take something that handles, say, French and use at least some part of that intact for doing translations into German or into Italian or Arabic or whatever, and not to have to rebuild the whole thing all the way up.

(iii)   The last requirement is 'transparency', which has had a mention from time to time. The idea here is that, as for any big program in fact, if you come back and look at the system after a few weeks or a few months or if some new people come along and look at what someone else has written, you really do want to be able to understand, or you want the new people to be able to understand, what the thing is supposed to be doing. This is particularly true because these programs, if you ever get them running at all, tend not to be ephemeral. Once a system is there, and some sponsor or other has paid a lot of money for it, then they expect to use it over a long period of time, and this long period of time is such that you cannot normally anticipate that the same people will be working on it at the beginning as finish up working on it at the end when the owner actually decides to throw it away and get something else. So it becomes important, if only for engineering reasons, that you can understand the code. The thing is a 'program', with some linguists around who are its 'programmers', and they have got to know what is going on in there if the thing is to be maintained in any sensible way. You can't rely on there being one person somewhere who wrote it who understands what it does.

Perhaps these are all truisms; I think they probably are. They're the sort of statements that are made about large programs in any domain. Why I think it's still important to make these statements, even if they're very familiar to you, is that it isn't habitual that we think of language handling programs as large programs. An awful lot of them are small programs, and even set out to be small programs, and the engineering principles are perhaps different if you try to make big programs like this properly.

Now a few parenthetic remarks here: there is still a
tendency among MT people, which many of you will have
observed, to get defensive about doing MT, because there's a
feeling abroad that MT is a disreputable activity. And
especially the kind of MT that I tried to characterize
earlier on.   I'm not going to spend very long on this
particular sociological issue. I certainly don't want to
raise the standard arguments of feasibility which people in
MT these days usually raise in defence of what they're
doing. I do however, in this forum, think it's worth making
a few points about the interest of doing MT as a piece of
research, something which is very rarely said by people in
this field. Here are some reasons why it strikes me (and
also lots of other people who work in this area and who make
the same comments) why this kind of MT is worth doing in its
own right:

(i) First of all, as a piece of computational
linguistics, it is very difficult to imagine any other
computational linguistic endeavour within which you are
forced to deal with several languages at once. You don't
just deal with them because there is some interesting
phenomenon which someone tells you about so you think you'll
look at it. You have to deal with significant subsets of a
number of a different languages simultaneously. Not just
that, but you have to give an account of each of them which
is compatible with the accounts of all the others, because
in the end you're talking about some kind of similarities
between languages which you want to capture in order to get
the translation done. MT forces you to do that, and that's
very good mental hygiene in this business.

(ii) The second thing that this kind of MT makes you
do is look at rather large subsets of these languages. You
can't get away with looking at two or three phenomena and
building some program that treats them and not worrying
about the other things because they're getting in your way.
If you're going to treat the stuff at all then you've got to
treat more or less all of it, and again in a fairly
consistent way.

Now I know these things are obvious. The reason I'm
restating them is because it seems to me that, while they
may be a nuisance, and while they may make the task very

hard, they also justify the task in a very strong sense, in that it's salutary to look at language in such a way that you cannot ignore certain things, and to look at languages particularly.

(iii) Another thing that doing this makes you conscious of is the value of notation, another thing which computational linguistics has tended in the past to disregard as not being all that important, essentially because the people who have done the computation are the people who have had the linguistics in their heads. This is changing, but if you think back over the sixties and seventies then notational issues have not been considered important. Phrases like 'notational variant', or 'these systems are equivalent' spring to mind. The point here is that because of the size of the user community, because of the large number of people who have to put their ideas together and make them fit, notational issues, subjective and aesthetic as they may be, become as crucial here in whatever linguistic theory you adopt as they are in programming languages. And we all know how certain notational issues in programming languages have been quite significant over the last few years.

(iv) It also makes you think about the lexicon. Lexicons for this kind of activity have to be very large. It's very difficult to restrict them artificially, and even if you start off by restricting them you soon find that, if you want to make the thing open-ended, then it is going to grow very fast, even in restricted domains. There are a few exceptions to this. The famous one is Meteo (Chandioux 1976), which everyone cites, Meteo being the MT system that works because the people who made it very fortunately came across a domain that really suited the purpose absolutely. But there aren't many of those domains left.

(v) My last comment is a bit cryptic. I'm throwing it in at the end as a kind of after-thought because it's not had very much mention in here and it's one of those small but quite important points that perhaps deserves talking about. What you realize if you perform this exercise is that you have to have, as I said, a large description of the language. It's not clear that the description of the language that you are prepared to accept is going to be the same as the description of the language you are prepared to regurgitate at the other end. Some trivial instances of this: the one I always cite particularly is the so-called split infinitive in English. Now this is the kind of area where it may well be that someone who wants to buy an MT system off you, or someone who asks you to build it, will simply refuse to accept output texts which split infinitives. I know this is a trivial notion - I think one can find better examples with a little bit of thought. I keep it simple to make a point, the point being that if you therefore have a linguistic description which does not contain certain phenomena because you require it in order to generate your texts, you are going to get in serious trouble as soon as you try to analyze texts in that same language. I think that this particular phenomenon extends a long way beyond the split infinitive. Things like the order of certain clauses in Italian. The fact that a clause with siccome is required by some speakers of Italian who are very fussy always to come before its matrix verb, although you find lots of texts where siccome comes after it. Another example is the distribution of inanimate subjects with non-passive verbs in Japanese, which will probably come up again. I am given to understand that large numbers of Japanese speakers, and perhaps particularly those who will be managers and people requiring translations, will be very angry if they start getting texts with non-animate subjects of a certain class of action verbs, whereas I also understand reliably that these things turn up in texts quite regularly, and you can't wish them away from texts.

The idea here is that you may in the worst case need completely different descriptions of your analysis language and your synthesis language. Of course you don't want to do that. You would like some commonality between them, if possible. How do you get it? Is it possible to take a description and decompose it in such a way that you can use some parts of your English grammar twice (and not now in the 'modularity' sense, of using a description of English for translations into different languages): sometimes in analysis grammar and sometimes in synthesis grammar, substituting other parts? I don't know if anyone has asked these questions but I've never heard them talked about.

So - going back - I want to claim that some at least of these questions should be interesting even for people who think MT as an engineering practice a waste of time, and I want to claim that MT is one of the application, perhaps one of the few applications, that actually makes you think of these questions in the first place. End of apology.

Back to the real point. Here's the standard characterization of translations that we want to use: we want to see translation as an equivalence relation between classes of source language and target language texts. Jan [Landsbergen] called these equivalence classes - or these pairs of equivalence classes, perhaps - 'possible translations' of each other. That's the relation we want. Here are the standard perspectives these days on how you get it. The first two are perhaps fairly standard; the last one is fairly recent and rather less canvassed than the others, but we have a principal representative of it here, so I couldn't leave it out. The three general ideas on how you actually compute this relation are as follows:

(i) The first, perhaps the standard way, or the one you encounter most frequently, is the contrastive way. This decomposes the relation in such a way that you define abstract representations for both your source language and your target language, and you have the principle that these representations canonically represent the classes of translation-equivalent texts. Translation then comes down to mapping between those canonical representations of texts, and that's essentially contrastive.

(ii) This way of seeing the relation contrasts with the interlingual view. This view these days is particularly upheld by people from Yale (Carbonell et al 1978; Lytinen & Schank 1982) and their associates. It tends to be the way that non-linguists see translation, I think. By non-linguists I mean people who do not have good familiarity with more than one language. The idea is that there is a class of canonical representations which fully characterize all the information necessary to induce these equivalence classes of possible translations in all languages that you are dealing with. Objects within that representation theory are called 'interlingual objects' and the representation theory is called 'interlingual theory'. You can translate between source language text and this neutral representation, and you have another translation between objects in neutral representation and target language texts, and that is translation.

(iii) The third view, which is typically characterized by Jan Landsbergen (this volume), is the view that the

translation relation is captured in terms of derivational
equivalence. You have descriptions of your source language
and your target language, and instead of pairing
representations of text in source and target language, you
pair items of the descriptions. You analyse your source
language, and instead of aiming at some representation, you
keep the trace of the analysis, and the translation
equivalence between languages is captured in terms of
pairings between items in that trace. I'm not being
specific about Jan, I'm trying to characterize the general
idea. I won't pursue that now - I want to say overtly that,
as perhaps already implied, the view that I can best
characterize is the first one, the contrastive one. That's
the one which I feel I can talk about, although that need
not inhibit disussion on the others.

Here's an interesting note about all of these things.
The notion that you have an abstract representation which is
somehow canonical is taken by some to suggest that that
representation necessarily is the meaning representation,
and that the job therefore involves to some extent mapping
between texts and their meanings. I just want to point out
that, although this may in practice turn out to be so
(although you'll probably find that the grain that you want
is much finer than the grain of simple meaning
representation), in theory what you're after is translation
equivalence. Now this may be meaning equivalence; but
translation equivalence is not judged by meaning equivalence
monolingually. Translation equivalence in the end is judged
by observations about pairs of texts, and it's judged on the
basis of the **texts**. So as long as you can capture
canonically the formal essence of these classes of texts
through some apprpriate pair of representation theories, it
doesn't actually matter if the thing turns out to be a
meaning representation. In particular, even if you have to
appeal to meanings in order to perform this computation,
that doesn't necessarily require that the representations
which you translate in the contrastive view be meaning
representations. Similarly, it may well be that you have to
undo some quantifier scopes in order to get your
translations right. In order to undo these quantifier
scopes you need some kind of predicate logic representation.
But just because there is something that requires you to
make that representation in order to do some disambiguation,
say, it does not therefore follow that the basis of your
translation should be a predicate calculus representation.

This is worth saying.

Here's the real point now. With those givens, what do
we look for in a linguistic theory that will support this
kind of activity? And there's a rider on that. Some people
in MT, unfortunately - and perhaps this is one of the
reasons for its bad reputation - would rather ask the
question 'Why do we need a linguistic theory at all?' I
hope that question is not going to be raised here. I would
rather phrase it as: given that it's clear that we need a
linguistic theory to support this activity, then what should
it be like? Here are some notions which again are fairly
straightforward.

(i) I want to claim that such a theory should be
declarative, i.e. that descriptions in such a theory should
be declarative. So although MT is clearly a procedure, and
indeed you can pick out sequential components of this
procedure, I want to maintain that you would really like the
descriptions that drive that procedure to be declarative,
and this is motivated not just by aesthetics but by the sort
of engineering considerations I was trying to talk about
earlier. You want to extend the system and perhaps extend
it in a fairly massive way in the end. You don't want to
fiddle around changing pieces of program, and there are many
cases where if you did have a piece of imperative program
procedure, you would find the need from time to time not
just to add new routines, but actually to get inside this
piece of imperative programming and change bits of the
sequence of the procedure and things like that. That's
exactly what you want to avoid, with all these people
getting in there and tampering with it. I guess the typical
analogy in conventional computational linguistics is
something like an ATN managed by, say, 10 or 15 people all
contributing to it. I think you want to avoid the mess that
that's likely to give you, and I think that suggests that
you want some kind of declarative notation as your
programming language, and you want the theory to supply
that.

(ii) There's a question of 'conceptual versus
computational modularity'. We don't have time to go into
that, but some people will know what I mean: that the
decomposition of what you want to say is likely to be
different in terms of computational organization from the
way it is in terms of the organization that you have in your

head when you think of its linguistics. A declarative notation should help you to maintain that distinction and to make it not matter to the people who are dealing with each of those two cases.

(iii) You want it to be 'effective' in the technical sense that we have used a couple of times. You want to use an effective procedure, or at least you want a procedure, and if it's not effective then you would like to have some kind of grasp on the places where it isn't. This I know is obvious, but again there are some people in MT, the extremists of the linguistic MT point of view, who are almost ready to claim that this doesn't matter very much, that the linguistic description is what counts. Of course you need a meld of both things.

(iv) Because of what I was saying before about canonicity and the translation relation, I want to claim that your linguistic theory should give you a sub-theory of canonical representation of some kind. Now it may not give you all the substantive pieces of that theory, but it should at least give you the formal apparatus within which to develop it.

(v) And then the last two points - there are good engineering and conceptual considerations for wanting your theory to be restrictive. There are large numbers of people around, you want the system to be modular, so you don't want people going away and writing any kind of description and then finding you can't fit them together. So you want lots of constraints which guide the way that people actually write their descriptions down. At the same time, because of this open-endedness, you don't want to be so restrictive that, if it goes wrong, there's nothing you can do about it except go back and rebuild the whole thing, because there's no way you can capture within the constraints you've got whatever this new phenomenon is that's causing the thing to go wrong. It seems to me that there's a tension here. There are two conflicting sets of demands, and there's no real answer to this. But certainly there are some theories that give you a better compromise between those two things than others, and 'better' here is a completely aesthetic judgement, or perhaps empirical one day.

Those are the sorts of considerations involved. Now here's a short summary of the issues that people might want to talk about that seem to be interesting from various points of view. The first one says: 'Is the best way to model translation as something that passes via representations or something that passes via derivations?'

If it goes through representations - or indeed derivations, only it's a little bit harder to say then - do you want your representation, in theory, to be interlingual, that is totally universal, or do you want to be contrastive? And remember that 'totally universal' means you can't even have idiosyncratic lexical items any more. You have to decompose your lexical items so that they're language-neutral as well. That's a big enterprise, especially when you've got several hundred thousand of them. And **completely** decompose them, not just decompose some parts to help you to do some disambiguation, as Wilks (1973) does. Take them completely to pieces.

And then the question of analyzing and synthesizing: do you want the language descriptions that drive the analysis and synthesis to be the same? If not, what's the relationship between them? What do you expect from a linguistic theory to help you to capture this relationship, whatever it is? Take the notion of flexibility, which Stu [Shieber], particularly, has been advocating. He says something like: you want your theory to give you lots of escape hatches so that you don't get stuck when you're doing developmental work. And compare that to the constraints that you need if you are going to get a lot of people in a lot of different places describing a lot of different languages all saying roughly the same kinds of things, and you want to enforce that compatibility.

Then there's the issue of the incorporation of non-linguistic knowledge, which I have avoided, not because it's embarrassing (though perhaps it is), but because this gathering is primarily to talk about the linguistic applications. But if people think this is an important issue then there's certainly no reason why it shouldn't be raised. And then the last point, which I think is the crucial one: are there now linguistic theories around which are adequate to support at least some part of this MT enterprise? If they're not adequate, then can we conceive how we might extend them to do the job? If they don't exist at all, then why not? Is it that the demands of this kind of work are so different from the demands of all other computational

theoretical linguistics that there's no apparatus around? I
don't think that can be true. And there we are.

Pete WHITELOCK: I'd like to start the first discussion
point, and illustrate it with a problem that we havein our
English-Japanese system (Whitelock et al 1986). I'd like to
argue against the feasibility of doing translation by
derivation. Let me give you an example: as most of you will
know, passive constructions occur widely in many languages.
Certainly in English and Japanese there's something that
looks very similar in the sense that the active and passive
forms are inflexionally distinguished, they're often truth
conditionally equivalent (modulo quantifier scope), and they
involve demotion of something that's considered the subject
to some oblique role. Now on the surface of it that would
make it look as though English passives and Japanese
passives were going to be translation pairs but in fact (I
don't think this is crucial but just to talk about it in
some framework) there is a parameter of Universal Grammar -
I think it's called 'PRO-drop' (Chomsky, 1982:28 et passim)
- which is set in Japanese but not in English. Now because
you can have subjects in Japanese which are just not
present, what that means is that the textual distributions
of passives in English and Japanese are totally different.
Alternatively, if you're thinking of handling this sort of
thing by relating derivations, it means that the translation
rules for pairs of rules that deal with the short passive
and the long passive in English are in fact going to be
totally different. The long passive as it occurs in English
is primarily used as a mechanism for topicalization, and you
have a different mechanism for topicalization in Japanese.
So you wouldn't want to translate it as a passive. Whereas
with a short passive you might very well want to do so. So
in fact you're saying in English short passives and long
passives are syntactically very different sorts of things,
but they're not really.

Jan LANDSBERGEN: I'd like to react to that. I do not fully
understand the example, but I think that the point you want
to make is that our approach with isomorphic derivations
will have the effect that the grammar of the source language
may be influenced by the grammar of the target language. In
general that is true. What I hope and expect is that it
will not influence it too much. In addition it should be
noted that syntactic notions like passive and active are not

necessarily expressed explicitly in the derivation trees. The kind of information that is retained during translation may be a more abstract notion, for instance what the topic of the sentence is. In one language a sentence may be in the passive voice, while in the other language the corresponding main verb does not allow the passive voice, but there may be another mechanism to get an NP to the front of the sentence. That would be sufficient. So in a derivational approach one may have to translate via somewhat more abstract notions than just active and passive.

WHITELOCK: OK, but it does seem though that what you're going to end up with is a pair of linguistic descriptions that's actually a single one and there's no way that you can actually separate out very much and say this is knowledge of English, this is knowledge of Dutch or whatever. You really have to motivate the description in terms of the relation between the two languages and you have no single language information.

LANDSBERGEN: It is single language information, but its form may be influenced a bit by the other language. As I said yesterday, grammars are artefacts. There are many ways of describing a language. The particular instance we choose out of the set of possible grammars will be influenced by other languages.

Mary McGee WOOD: I wonder how far there's a tension between the different obvious practical reasons for doing this tailoring of the source language grammar to help you to get to the target language. I'm thinking of Rod's criterion that one should be able to handle more than two languages, and perhaps you ought to talk even about language families (because it's a bit of a cheat to handle, say, English and Dutch and then say 'Look, I can go easily to German', or Italian, Portuguese and then Spanish). But it's different if you have a system which does English to German and then it can go to Japanese easily as well. I think there may be a tension - in principle one wants to be able to extend, but in practice one wants to have grammars that will work together easily and keep your system working.

Henry THOMPSON: My intuition on the basis of not having heard this approach before was that it was applicable in direct proportion to the typological similarity of the languages, and that is as you move to language pairs or language triples that cut across major typological boundaries, that it seems less plausible. Now maybe that's a naive perception but I think that Peter was trying obliquely to refer to that same problem.

JOHNSON: If you believe that this is implausible - and I must say it certainly sounds it to me too - then to what extent is this a reflection of the Montague (1973) grammar that Jan claims motivates the whole approach, and to what extent does it reflect on the approach which in some way does not depend on the particular grammatical theory?

THOMPSON: I think that as an intuition coming from somebody outside the tip of the arrow on this, what I'm saying is not worth very much, but it is I think an obvious danger.

LANDSBERGEN: The question at issue here seems to be: suppose that we have a system for Dutch, English and Spanish, what happens if we want to add Japanese? I never claimed that this would be possible. I think it might be possible to add German, French, etc., because they are related to the other languages. But if we would want to translate into Japanese, we would have to take it into account right from the start. If the distance between two languages is as large as it seems to be between English and Japanese (but I do not know a word of Japanese), then it may be wise to work only on this language pair.

May I say something in favour of the derivational approach? The danger of translating via deeper levels of representation is that one does not really solve the translation problem, but splits it up into a number of translation problems that are not necessarily easier to get hold of. The deeper these levels of representation are, the more difficult it may be to understand what you are doing at these levels.

WHITELOCK: What the transfer-through-representation approach does is actually give you a place to localize the fifteen percent of hacking that you've got to do at the end. It's unavoidable. It's linguistic hacking in the sense that there's no real reason why the parameter settings for a given pair of unrelated languages should be anything other than arbitrary, so in fact what you have to do to do transfer is essentially linguistically hack.

LANDSBERGEN: If you want to hack, why don't you allow us to add a few extra rules to the English grammar to suit the Japanese?

WHITELOCK: But then your English grammar is polluted: it's no longer motivated by considerations of English only.

Doug ARNOLD: I think there are two issues being conflated in this discussion. I think in fact Pete's example, though interesting and instructive, conflates the two. One is the essentially representational issue of what the basis of the comparison or contrast between English and Japanese is - it's clearly not to do with active and passive. And the problem then is devising a representation which captures the true basis of the difference, which is this complex of focus and the free deletion of pronouns in Japanese which you're not allowed to do in English. But the other issue is this whole question of the derivational aproach to translation, and what your [Landsbergen's] question, indeed your system, requires is that these two things go together. You have a single representation, a single path of analysis, and you translate off the derivation of that analysis. Now it is quite possible to combine that with the transfer approach, where transfer goes between two derivation trees, but those derivation trees aren't the derivation trees for the surface structures of the language: they're for some other representation. For example, a representation of your own invention which described the focus and the presence of superficially absent pronouns and all that wonderful stuff.

WHITELOCK: There's no reason why you would want to map anything other than the deep representations. Why should the surface syntactic representations be relevant at all?

ARNOLD: Well normally, for simple kinds of grammar, the derivation trees and ordinary representations are identical, and the interesting case is where you have an ambiguous language. So suppose your semantic representation language is ambiguous: then the question is, do you want to have to parse that in order to work out the correct translation, or do you want to just look at it and know what the correct translation is? Well, if you just have to parse it, it looks more efficient (though this isn't the best argument) to do it off the derivation tree, which avoids the problem of having to parse the representation.

JOHNSON: Don't you choose a semantic representation language which is non-ambiguous?

ARNOLD: It's very difficult to do that, unless you're prepared to be interlingual about it, because 'ambiguity' in this case means 'ambiguous with respect to the target language'.

JOHNSON: Is anybody prepared to address the last of those points [existence of adequate linguistic theories for MT], which I think is the really important one?

KAPLAN: Let me ask a prior question. I of course believe that in order to do machine translation well, you have to have a deep theory of language, and really understand what you're doing, but that's because I'm not a banker. If I was bank-rolling this kind of activity, what I would want was something that I could go out and sell, that worked well enough.   Would I really invest in a linguistic theory at all?   What I want to know is the answer to this question, so that when people ask me this question, I'll know how to answer it. So you tell me. Why isn't machine translation like medical diagnosis?   All these expert systems now are doing medical diagnosis, and they don't understand about disease.   They use 'if...then' kinds of pattern-action rules, and it doesn't really matter how diseases get there, or how the genes go bad, or whatever. What matters is that if you see this kind of symptom you do this kind of thing. And usually that works, and if it doesn't then you try the next thing.   So why don't we use expert system technology?

THOMPSON: That's like saying 'What's the matter with sentence dictionaries?'.

KAPLAN: All I'm saying is, what's the matter with buying yourself a knowledge engineer, or a knowledge engineering work-station, and getting an expert translator, and sitting down and capturing all his rules of thumb about ...

WHITELOCK: That is the way to do it.

Jackie KNIGHT: I'd like to dispute the first point that that's the way medical expert systems work. The ones that people want to use don't work like that. That's exactly the reason why they haven't been taken up.

KAPLAN: What about oil-well logging systems, or any number of other systems?

KNIGHT: But the move is to go to the underlying knowledge, because people want that, they are able to use it.   They need explanation, they need to respect the system.   In order to do that it has to explain its own reasoning.   But that's if you have to go deeper.   So if you produced a machine translation like that, people may well not want that anyway.

Graeme RITCHIE: There's another point which is narrowness of coverage.   These expert systems work on tiny domains. I'm sure these guys round the table here could knock together a really excellent MT translation of personal pronouns between English and German without any problem.

SPARCK JONES: But Ron's point is not that we need expert systems, but what is the knowledge that's supposed to be captured within the expert system?   The guy may be a pretty good doctor, but it doesn't follow that he has a theory of healing, or a theory of the working of the human body.   He hasn't got a theory.   So the question is, what do we mean by 'theory'?   He may have a lot of knowledge, and you want to capture the deeper knowledge of the doctor, and translators may have a lot of deep knowledge - if you see the way some of these translators work, it's perfectly obvious they've got a lot of deep knowledge.   It doesn't follow that they have a theory of language.

Lieven JASPAERT: There's two things you should remember. Graeme made a good point, and that is the size of the domain.   The domain of translation is very big and many expert systems work on a much more restricted domain.   The second point is that in the case of translation, the domain is very badly understood.   We know that translation exists, we know that translators can do it.   We know they have lots of knowledge about translation.   But it's very difficult to characterize first how a human translates, and it's even more difficult to characterize how a machine should translate.   If you want to solve the MT problem, you must be able to get a grip on what translation is, and you don't do that, I think, by giving the people who work in the MT field a very liberal theory, an environment in which they can do anything they want.   It's nice for experimentation, but they will never understand where they go wrong, where they go off the tracks, because everything is possible.   I think that makes a case for a very strong linguistic theory that forces you in certain directions, maybe not the directions you want, but at least at some point you will be able to see that this is not what you want. Here is where your theory makes you do things that you don't want to do. The case for a strong theory and a notation that mirrors the strength of that theory is what is to be investigated.

THOMPSON: This is basically the software engineering argument. I think it's a good argument, but perhaps there was some suggestion, it seemed to me, in Rod's presentation that he was hoping that there was some other argument as well as the software engineering argument. Now it seems to me that the software engineering argument is a very good one. It's not clear that you need a better one, and most of the standard software engineering arguments go through more or less metaphorically - I think actually not terribly metaphorically at all, you can take them just about straight. That's I think what you were offering. It seems to me that Ron and perhaps Rod were looking for something else as well, some arguments from some different perspectives. Is that fair?

JOHNSON: I guess so.

Nick OSTLER: Is there any really authoritative statement of what constitutes an adequate translation? For example we had a dispute yesterday as to whether something should be called 'paraphrase' or 'real translation', and the force of Peter's objection was to say that your grammatical theories are talking about active and passive, but in actually assessing whether a translation is adequate or not you should be talking about focus and anaphora really. So it seems to me that what you really need in order to answer your last question 'Do adequate linguistic theories exist?' is an authoritative statement from people who do translations presumably, or people who consume translations, as to what is actually required in terms of the relation, because then you'll be able to see to what extent linguistic theories are addressing the right problems at all. It seems to me that linguists are concerned that abstract constructions present in one language should be present in the translation. Consumers of translations may be much more concerned about the overall effect of the document. Of course that is a rather ill-defined notion.

THOMPSON: The problem is that that of course varies widely
with the domain of the application. To get to the extreme
case, if you take the Finnish legal system, where the law is
written in Finnish and Swedish, then there's very clearly a
strong and strenuous definition of what constitutes an
acceptable translation, and the operating version of it is
that it shouldn't be to anybody's particular advantage to be
tried under one text as opposed to the other. And that's a
pretty serious business: one of things you go to a lawyer
for in Finland is to ask him which language you should be
tried under. That's extremely strenuous. On the other hand
the classic story is that for people who are interested in
what's happening in Russian physics and who are physicists,
almost anything counts as a translation as long as it gets
the lexical relations right about 80% of the time. That's
if you believe the publicity. I don't know if that's true
or not.

SPARCK JONES: Jonathan Slocum put it last year (Slocum
1984:558). He said it's an adequate translation if people
will pay money for it. Now that offers us no leverage on
linguistic theory at all!

OSTLER: Could we not proceed inductively then, taking these
authoritative statements, perhaps relativizing them to their
contexts, and get some general principles out of that?
Because otherwise the whole thing is so ill-defined, I don't
see how you are ever going to answer that question 'Do
adequate linguistic theories exist?'.

ARNOLD: The answer to the question would surely be a
linguistic theory of MT, or a linguistic theory of
translation, because the characterization that would come
out of whatever inductive procedure you set up will be just
a linguistic theory of MT, wouldn't it?

OSTLER: No, I feel it would be a theory of MT; it wouldn't
be a **linguistic** theory of MT unless you realized that the
things that people were really worried about were all
linguistic things.

JOHNSON: Texts are linguistic objects in an obvious sense.

OSTLER: Yes, but the aspects of them that linguists are
worried about may not be the ones that concern consumers of
translations. The active-passive one was a good concrete

example I thought. There are enough of these institutional environments where they have these requirements for translations, whether in the Finnish legal system or in the Canadian broadcasting code, or whatever. Perhaps there might be scope for an actual survey of that sort of thing. It might give some surprising results - I don't know.

JOHNSON: Perhaps. Was it Henry who just said that there were so many domains and so many text types around ...?

THOMPSON: What people are looking for when they're looking for a translation varies tremendously.

SPARCK JONES: It's not the text or the domain but the uses that people want to make of it.

OSTLER: But what are those uses? You see we don't know. We know it varies, but we don't know concretely what it is we have to worry about.

JASPAERT: Well I used to teach in a translators' school for a while, and it struck me that even those people who did translation weren't able to characterize or have a theory about how it is in human translation. Then you're asking the same question for machine translation, and I think it's impossible. You have to do it the other way round. Adequate translation is the kind of translation that, given a certain theory and a certain approach to doing machine translation, then if people are willing to pay money for it, then you have adequate translation. So I'd be a bit bottom-up about it actually.

JOHNSON: I don't know if you could get away with that.

ARNOLD: There's an assumption behind the discussion of a little earlier. It comes out clearly in Henry's remark that the software [engineering] argument is quite relevant and you don't need to look anywhere else for the motivation for looking for theoretical principles. I think that you would not have made that remark about any of the other things that have been discussed - you would not say that about morphological theory or syntactic theory. The software argument for doing it this way is enough.

THOMPSON: Au contraire! I think what Rod and Mitch [Marcus] were saying last night about morphology goes very

much along those lines. Rod was slightly apologetic by the
time he got to the most extreme version of it, but it was
still very much that version. It was saying, maybe what's
true about the relevance of morphology and lexical look-up
is that it gives you software engineering-style leverage.
Now on the syntactic front, yes I would admit to other
motivations.

ARNOLD: I wonder, are there other motivations for MT? It
seems to me there are. It seems to me that translation is a
perfectly respectable thing to be interested in. And the
most intellectually respectable way to be interested in it
in this day and age is a computational one. It surprises me
that that isn't more widely touted as a view of the
business.

KAPLAN: Well, the point that I was trying to make was that
there are different purposes and different evaluations that
you might give. You might really be interested in machine
translation as a scientific question and really want to
develop a theory of that as an important natural phenomenon.
You might want to develop a theory of it, and that has its
own justification and formulation. But there's also this
commercial aspect to it, and there might be quite different
criteria.

WHITELOCK: I don't know: your characterization of how to
achieve commercial MT actually sounds like a very good
research programme to give some data as a basis to build a
linguistic theory of translation, because I don't think
anybody knows how to start. To actually say, well you
produce some sort of representation and then an expert
translator has to understand the primitives of that
representation system, and then says 'If this and this and
this, then this is the output'.

THOMPSON: This is crazy. This is like saying that it's
perfectly sensible to start out by trying to have a theory
of the mechanics of perception involved in three-ball
cascade juggling before you have a theory about grasping.
If you want to take the task of translation as an
interesting human ability which you think it's relevant to
develop a theory of, then surely it's insane to start out
and tackle that as an undecomposed problem. There's a
greater dependency on the simpler problem of language
comprehension, for example.

WHITELOCK: I was not saying that. I was assuming that you had in the first instance some sort of off-the-shelf theory which builds you some sort of representation which abstracts away from the surface string, that was all. And I would think that the existing theories that we've got are more or less adequate in that respect.

KAPLAN: Commercially you get this translator in there and you give him a text and you say 'Here's a sentence. How would you translate that sentence and why?'. And he says 'Well, there are some big words at the beginning and some little words at the end, so I do it this way'. You know, maybe if you're doing genetic engineering experiments you need 500 [rules], but maybe for machine translation it needs 2000. You keep doing it.

Bob MOORE: The thing about translation is that the knowledge that expert translators have that's specifically knowledge about translation is based on fluent understanding of the languages that are translated. So it would not make any sense to attempt the expert systems-type approach until you'd got the technological base that gives you the equivalent of fluent understanding of both languages, and that's several lifetimes' work.

WHITELOCK: And of the relation between the two.

KAPLAN: That's what I question. Whether to get a practical useful acceptable machine translation system you really have to have all that knowledge.

WHITELOCK: Yes, I think so. There's a sort of assumption, which came through what Henry said, that all you have to do to do translation is to understand the source language and generate the target language.

THOMPSON: That's a minimal preliminary requisite, not a sufficient condition.

WHITELOCK: But that is patently insufficient.

ARNOLD: The relevant comparison with a fully automatic MT system, the kind of thing that Rod was talking about, isn't an expert system. Expert systems are semi-automatic, because the output of an expert system requires

interpretation: you have to put it together. I think you
could easily build an expert system kind of thing for doing
translation - indeed they exist. It's something like a big
lexicon, with a few bits of sentence dictionary thrown in.
What you get out at the end is a thing which is bits of
source text, and then you give people some clever editing
facilities. I think you have expert systems that do
translation, but they don't do fully-automatic translation.

SPARCK JONES: In connection with what Ron and Henry were
saying, you have different reasons for doing MT. Now a
reason we haven't talked about very much is that, supposing
you have a linguistic theory, and you're actually a person
who thinks that one of the ways to really see whether your
linguistic theory actually stands up is to make it work for
something computationally, because as somebody was saying in
one of the previous meetings, writing a program to apply a
theory is quite different from just talking about the
theory. So then you say to yourself, well what's the
program going to have to do, because of course it's got to
do some language-using task? It's not enough to have a
system which just takes some English input and prints out
some lovely diagrams in colour and different sorts of
typography that you can get nowadays with modern machines,
and you look at that and say 'Yeah, that's the deep meaning
of that sentence'. That won't do, and we know it won't do.
So you look for a task which might actually evaluate it, and
it may be the case, as Henry is suggesting, that translation
is too hard a task, because we really don't have any idea
about how to do anything. But the problem with translation
is that in some ways it is a hard task, and therefore it's a
good one, but we have this difficulty we mentioned earlier
which is how to evaluate whether the translation's actually
effective or not. So we have a problem there if our initial
motivation is to evaluate a theory by building a
computational program. The thing we want the program to do
is itself rather hard to evaluate.

WHITELOCK: It's much easier surely to evaluate the
translation than most other natural language tasks that you
can think of.

SPARCK JONES: Well is it any harder or more difficult than
paraphrasing in the same language, for example?

THOMPSON: Yes - because people regularly do it and there

are de facto standards, even if there are no analytic standards.

SPARCK JONES: Yes but we paraphrase all the time too.

THOMPSON: Not as a task that is evaluated. I think that paraphrasing (begging Bran [Boguraev]'s pardon) is an over-touted phenomenon.

KAPLAN: It also has the added pitfall that you've got to get it slightly different.

MOORE: As someone who has done no work in this area at all, I would like to hear some of the details of why being able to interpret one language and generate another is different from being able to translate. I mean I really just don't know enough about it.

JOHNSON: 'Interpret' in the non-technical sense, in the non-professional sense, you mean?

MOORE: 'Understand' if you like.

Brian CHANDLER: You can translate things you don't understand.

WHITELOCK: I think that's a red herring. If you're talking about putting together an understanding and a generating capability, then you're talking about some sort of carrier of meaning between the two. And that is presumably a static level of representation. Otherwise if it's a dynamic level, then it's being changed in some way, and you no longer have just understanding and generation. So it's a static device. You have to start talking about what should the representation in that static device be of a language value from a number system, say 'singular', where the number system is singular-plural: is that different or the same as the representation of 'singular' in a singular-dual-plural system? Or maybe there are five values for the interlingual values of features: 'singular' in a two-value system, 'singular in a three-value system, 'dual' and then 'plural' in the two systems. So what possible values can your features have in that interlingual representation? Either you say it's singular-dual-plural, and if the source language has a two-value system you just never generate 'dual', and you throw away the information about the distinction between 'plural' in a two-value and a three-value system, or you keep it, and it actually means then that just by looking at the interlingual representation, you could actually reconstruct what the source language that you came from was. Surely then what you've got isn't a language-free representation, if it's got all that information.

MOORE: I'm not sure I'm following this.

JOHNSON: Can I gloss that? In your terms, if indeed you do understand the source language, you understand it with respect to your requirements in the target language. And that's why it's different from just absorbing some text and then quite independently taking the sense of that text and regurgitating it somewhere else without any relationship whatsoever between those two linguistic systems. This I think is a generalization of Pete's point. I hope so.

MOORE: This may be very naive: let me concentrate on this number business. If you want to represent the singular-plural distinction in English in a meaning representation, presumably the language-neutral way to do that is in some formal terms to say what the truth-conditional consequences of using singular and plural in English are. Very naively in English that is that 'singular' means 'one' and 'plural' means 'more than one'. Now if you say 'Some men did x' and you translate that into a language-neutral meaning representation, you're going to have some representation of 'There exists a set of men whose cardinality is greater than or equal to 2 ...' or something like that '... who did (such-and-such)'. Now you come along and you want to express that in a language that makes the singular-dual-plural distinction ...

JOHNSON: Now you claim it's ambiguous, I guess.

MOORE: I don't know what good translators do in situations like this.

THOMPSON: But isn't that the crux of the matter, because now you are having to appeal to the question of what would translators do as opposed to what understanders of the language would do?

WHITELOCK: What they do is exploit every ounce of

contrastive knowledge they have to look around for some way of getting round the problem or finding the answer, resolving the indeterminacy, or whatever. But it's contrastive.

MOORE: I don't know what you mean by 'contrastive'.

THOMPSON: It depends on an examination of the different expressive resources of the two languages concerned.

MOORE: Let me suggest a stronger hypothesis: that at this point you can forget about the original language. You've just got abstract meaning you want to express. There's something you want to say about a set containing at least two elements and the language you want to say it in is such that it doesn't let you say that that easily.

THOMPSON: I'm sympathetic to your views because I think I would have said that our positions were the same at the beginning of this discussion. I think something that's come from the people who spend their time on this is that, if I can paraphrase what Rod said a little while ago, multilingual paraphrase is not the same as translation. What you're talking about, and what I would have said translation was as well about an hour ago, is multilingual paraphrase, i.e. you take it in, and you regurgitate it, and it happens that on the way in it came in in one language and on the way out it went out in another language. What these people are saying, and I guess I find it plausible, is that what a translator does is something more than that.

MOORE: I'm actually prepared to believe that. It's just that I would like some more convincing examples. I can't see that it makes any difference that in this case the information came in a certain language. It seems that you are in exactly the same situation in expressing a particular piece of information, taking the notion of information very abstractly, and expressing it in a language in which to express that information requires a fairly convoluted means.

KAPLAN: The problem I think is that the meaning is always under-determined by its expression in any one language. This is just generally true. There are many many things that could be said that are true of the situation that we're talking about, that are not expressed by any particular sentence. But going into another language, some of those things need to be expressed, but you don't know what they were. So you have to have some way of figuring out for the stuff that wasn't specified how you should actually fill in that information.

THOMPSON: Another good classic case is Russian to English article insertion: there are no definite or indefinite articles in Russian. People who translate from Russian to English have an extraordinarily complicated set of heuristics which are relevant to that task, which don't appear to figure in the task of understanding Russian, but do appear to figure in the task of translating Russian into English. How that could be is not clear to me, I must confess.

JOHNSON: I'm going to stop while Henry's on my side!

References

Carbonell, J., Cullingford, R.E. & Gershman, A.V. 1978. Knowledge-based Machine Translation. Research report 146. Yale University Department of Computer Science.

Chandioux, J. 1976. METEO: un système operationnel pour la traduction automatique des bulletins meteorologiques destines au grand public. **Meta** 21, 127-133.

Chomsky, N. 1982. **Lectures on Government and Binding.** Dordrecht: Foris.

Lytinen, S.L. & Schank, R.C. 1982. Representation and Translation. Research report 234. Yale University Department of Computer Science.

Montague, R. 1973. The Proper Treatment of Quantification in Ordinary English. In Hintikka, J., Moravcsik, J. & Suppes, P., eds. **Approaches to Natural Language.** Dordrecht: D. Reidel, 221-242. Reprinted in Thomason, ed., 247-270.

Slocum, J. 1984. Machine Translation: Its History, Current Status, and Future Prospects. **COLING 84: 10th International Conference on Computational Linguistics / 22nd Annual Meeting of the Association for Computational Linguistics** (Stanford, CA), Proceedings, 546-561.

Thomason, R.H., ed. 1974. **Formal Philosophy: Selected Papers of Richard Montague.** New Haven: Yale University Press.

Whitelock, P.J., Wood, M.McG., Chandler, B.J., Holden, N. & Horsfall, H.J. 1986. Strategies for Interactive Machine Translation: The Experience and Implications of the UMIST Japanese Project. **COLING 86: 11th International Conference on Computational Linguistics** (Bonn, West Germany), Proceedings. 329-334.

Wilks, Y. 1973. An Artificial Intelligence Approach to Machine Translation. In Schank, R.C. & Colby, K. M., eds. **Computer Models of Thought and Language,** San Francisco: W.H. Freeman, 114-151.

Linguistic Theory and Beyond

Karen Sparck Jones

It seems there are three different things I've got to
do in this session. The first thing is that I was just
given, like all the rest of the chairmen for sessions, a
topic to talk to. This changed its nature somewhat as
various things came to me through the post. The first
version was the heading 'Extra-linguistic Knowledge'. This
was to deal with such issues as the viability of the
linguistic/extra-linguistic distinction, the location of the
extra-linguistic material or operations in a language
processing system, how its extra-linguistic knowledge is
used to guide parsing, and how extra-linguistic elements in
the system interface with the others. So I began vaguely to
think about that and then the next thing came through the
post with a new title which was 'Linguistic Theory and
Beyond'. So now my first remit is to say something about
'Linguistic Theory and Beyond'. The second thing I was
requested to do was to try to sum up the workshop and draw
the threads together. Then the third thing is that I have
some obligations myself. Some of you may not know that I am
the so-called manager or coordinator of the Alvey 'Natural
Language' Research Theme and this workshop is, of course, at
least half Alvey funded. When Pete [Whitelock] put the idea
up to me I supported it as something we should endorse in
the Natural Language Theme. So I have some sort of
obligation to consider what the message of this workshop
might be to the Alvey Programme, i.e. what the aim of the
meeting might be in the context of the sort of things the
Alvey Programme is concerned with. For example it considers
people like Henry [Thompson]'s users: Henry was talking
about users and tools, and generally people who want to do
things. Now what I'm going to try to do is to achieve these
three aims by one common means. I don't know whether I'll

succeed in this but at least I shall try.   I should
emphasize that in what I'm going to do I'm in no way an
expert with the kind of thing that was talked about
extensively yesterday: I'm not a person who shuffles lambdas
or alphas about and argues about whether you have brackets
here or there.

   Let's focus then on thinking about building NLP
systems.   That fortunately is not just because the Alvey
Programme wants us to do that kind of thing, it's a thing
which at least some of us are actually interested in doing
ourselves for a variety of reasons.   Now of course a natural
language processing system is also a natural language
understanding system.   Any NLP system that does any half-way
serious task is going to have at least some degree of
language understanding and this involves the use of some
sort of world knowledge.   The system,   to put it
anthropomorphically, is going to have to be thinking about
some real or simulated world.   The crucial issue then is
what the relation of linguistic and non-linguistic knowledge
is, where is the boundary between linguistic and non-
linguistic in the total system?   We can see a range of
things, and it's a very long range.   Right up at one end of
this range is knowledge which we would say was pretty
unequivocally linguistic, like the fact that <u>brown</u> is an
adjective.   Then down somewhere right at the other end of
this range is stuff which we really say is pretty
unequivocally non-linguistic, like for example the fact that
my aunt typically wears brown clothes.   That, one feels, is
not anything which is within the scope of linguistic theory.
But of course this range is very long and one would like to
say, if you think about building an NLP system, where one is
going to make some sort of division: where is the cut, even
approximately, between the stuff that's in the linguistic
and the non-linguistic parts of the system?   I'm not now
talking about the architecture of the system, I'm not
concerned with the detailed architecture, say, a box up
there and another box down there and they talk like this or
they talk like that, but just in a generic way with the
system as a whole.   So if we think about what a natural
language processing system as a whole needs, what it has to
have in order to do its job, what parts deal with linguistic
knowledge and operations and so presumably (but of course
this is another point of argument) what parts fall within
the scope of a linguistic theory, what parts don't, we've
also got to think, as there is a need for both linguistic

and extra-linguistic or non-linguistic in processing, about what the connection between them is, what kind of connections linguistic theory proposes for linking its part with the other part. We might also ask what is the scope of linguistic theory in principle, and separately from that of course, what is the scope of linguistic theory as it currently exists, i.e. in practice.

As I said, my concern is thinking about the division between the linguistic and the non-linguistic, what linguistic theory offers about the linguistic, what it deems to be the scope of the linguistic part, and how it states the connections between the linguistic and the non-linguistic. First, I want to review what has been said in the workshop so far. I looked at the presentations and discussions to see what sorts of things have been said about the scope of the linguistic theory and with respect to the components or content of a language processing system, and I was rather interested because there were extremely few explicit statements on this matter. There were a few throw-away remarks and there were a certain number of tacit assumptions, but let us look at what people said on this question of the scope of linguistic theory.

Stu Shieber said absolutely nothing explicit about this at all and nothing that I could dig out that was implicit in what he said.

Gerald [Gazdar] said nothing explicit about it: it may of course be implicit in the book (Gazdar et al 1985), but he certainly didn't say anything very much about it.

Mitch [Marcus] produced a very nice example, his quick-sort example, saying that if you have to have three goes at writing a quick-sort program because somebody's asked you to, this doesn't constitute non-deterministic parsing of the request sentence: a rather extreme example of something that is not linguistic. He was also making some assumptions: in terms of the architecture of his system he kept talking about semantics and pragmatics down the line, and he mentioned at various stages various things that semantics or pragmatics individually or in some nasty sort of interaction would have to do, like dealing with thematic roles, prepositional phrase attachment, coreference, information structures. But there wasn't any detail about all this and in particular how you really divided up the stuff between the two.

Jan Landsbergen assumed a connection: he said that if you adopted a sort of intensional logic version of Montague Grammar (Montague 1973), you'd deal with your extra-linguistic aspects in the intensional logic part. (I speak rather crudely about these things.) In his approach you'd connect it with semantic derivation trees and of course he also said there might be some extra rules for dealing with things like theme which you'd have to add to the Montague Grammar apparatus.

Ron [Kaplan] said nothing about the scope of linguistic theory.

Steve Pulman was arguing that we do need a context including non-linguistic knowledge and that we need access to it. He specifically said we may have to conduct inference operations to support our interpretation, i.e. do inference on the non-linguistic knowledge. He also emphasized the fact that the form of connection between the linguistic and the non-linguistic parts was that the linguistic analyser delivers logical forms which are appropriate inputs to a reasoning engine. Also in the discussion about the syntax-semantics interface, in the arguments about examples like _fast_ _swimmer_ and _beautiful_ _dancer_ and so on, and in some references to compound nouns, there were some implications. These had a sort of resonance for the issues about linguistic and non-linguistic.

With Graeme [Ritchie] discussing the lexicon, we had quite a lot of discussion about the size of lexicon and whether we were honest guys in our field of research because we had lexicons that only had ten words in. There was very little or no discussion of what the content of lexical entries should be and how much stuff about the world you should put in your lexical entries. In that discussion I might note that there was the point made about LUNAR (Woods 1973) that if you have a very restricted domain you can, as it were, finesse the issue about extra-linguistic knowledge to a considerable extent because you can put it into your domain-specific semantic patterns. In other words you 'linguisticize' your non-linguistic knowledge. Although I think it's fair to say that while you might be able to do quite a lot of that if you have a limited domain, if you're doing a rather more demanding task than the query interpretation that LUNAR did, you might still have to have some additional domain characterization which is not embodied in semantic patterns, that you might need to do inference over. We've found that certainly in thinking about the database question-answering case.

Finally, in this morning's discussion on machine translation, we considered the question of whether one needed linguistic theory to do machine translation. Rod [Johnson] also was saying that if you think about our current situation, and anything that you hope to achieve in the nearer future in translation, we will have to focus on translation as a linguistic process and try to shovel away the extra-linguistic aspects of language understanding under the carpet in the hope that somehow the carpet you're sitting on will carry you from one language to another. Again he made the crudest of distinctions between linguistic and non-linguistic, but he didn't say anything very much about where the boundary between the two came in any detail.

So overall the workshop so far has said very little about the scope of linguistic theory. What has been said I think assumes a framework of what you might describe as parsing and composition that seems to be the dominant paradigm, at least among those here, or possibly among the most vociferous of those here. You hope to attach some goodies to this; you have a really austere approach to this like basic Montague Grammar, and you hope to attach some goodies which you jolly well need in language processing like dealing with theme, thematic relations or whatever. But the assumption seems to be that logical form is the means of connecting linguistic to world knowledge. Now assuming that logical form is the right way to connect linguistic and non-linguistic (this might of course be wrong, but let's assume it's right for the moment), then you'd finish up with a criterion for a linguistic theory that it delivers logical forms and equally a criterion for what you might describe as the non-linguistic theory, i.e. the theory of the non-linguistic parts, that it can use the kinds of logical forms that the linguistic theory delivers. Now, as I say, this might be wrong, but even if it is right we need to get much more feeling for the detail of this. This is all rather grand, and it's very noticeable that much of what's put up in transparencies has abstract symbols in it like S and VP and dots in brackets where words or meanings or things like that come. We need to get much more of an idea of exactly how this gross distinction works out in order that we can actually put something in the boxes that constitute our language processing system.

So I propose to consider a sentence and some examples of property statements about it. (This may turn out to be a bit rash.) Looking at the things which, as I suggest in the examples, are features of or are involved in understanding and so using a particular sentence in a context, where would they be dealt with? Would they be dealt with by the linguistic part of your system, and hence have to be accounted for by your linguistic theory, and if so is there a linguistic theory that does account for them? Or would they be accounted for by a non-linguistic part? I'm trying to pin down the scope of linguistic theory a bit. My examples are extremely crude: I don't make any claims to the detail. All I want to say is that I think all of these things are connected with the interpretation of the sample text at some stage or in some way. I think it's also quite interesting to think about very different views of what linguistic theories are. You can take rather radically different ones like one which I associate with a conversation I had with John Lyons about 15 years ago, that semantics is about meaning relations, not about meaning; or the thing I heard more recently which is that the theory of linguistic action is part of the theory of action. Those are very different theories. If you had theories like that what would they say about this boundary?

So take the illustrative sentence (1), and (2) - (12) as examples of things that can be said about it.

(1)   'Can you put the blue block on the table on the red block?'

(2)   'block' is a substantive
(3)   'block' is singular
(4)   'blue' modifies 'block'
(5)   'block' means cuboid
(6)   the block is coloured blue
(7)   'on the table' is a prepositional phrase
(8)   the blue block is on the table
(9)   'the' means single definite
(10) there is just one blue block
(11) 'Can you put...' is an interrogative
(12) 'Can you put...' expresses an instruction

In talking about sentence (1), I'm assuming there is a context throughout, some real world context, and there's also been some previous linguistic context. And I'm assuming that, in some way connected with the understanding or processing of this sentence in this context (and understanding it can mean using that sentence as a generator of responses and things like that) that statements (2) onwards are all true. This is an assumption, I'm not asking the question how do you get them out of (1): it's not obvious how you get them out just from that one sentence. What I'm saying is: let's assume that all these things are true, and then let's ask how many of them are linguistic things and how many of them are not, and which ones are which, to try to get some feeling of what it is we're inviting the linguistic theory to cover. I think you can make the case that you need to have all these things because of the kinds of responses that you want your system to give to this question. Of course this is mirroring an actual human case. There are also some things that may be produced during processing of the sentence rather than being actually the end product of it.

Now one might say that the fact in (2) is a pretty linguistic sort of thing; (3) is pretty linguistic; that the word <u>blue</u> modifies <u>block</u> (4) is pretty linguistic; and then we have (5), which is linguistic. Then we have (6), which is a proposition about the world, but how far does linguistic theory go with that? [Continues reading through (7)-(9)] I'm trying to use some very neutral linguistic language for these statements. We hypothesize that (10) is true in this world. (11) tells us the whole sentence is an interrogative. Let's suppose that (12) is also the case in this world.

Here are some more things about this sentence:

(13)   The speaker is addressing someone.
(14)   The speaker is being polite.
(15)   The speaker assumes the hearer is attending.
(16)   The speaker knows the blue block is on the
        table.
(17)   The speaker believes the hearer knows this too.
(18)   The speaker wants the hearer to learn about block
        stacking.
(19)   Blocks are moveable things.

Notice which of these you can extract from the sentence itself or which might be an independent piece of knowledge which is in some sense being confirmed by the sentence. Let's imagine that the following are also true:

(20) The hearer has not encountered the red block
      before.
(21) There is no red block on the table.
(22) Somebody jogged the table.
(23) Perhaps the red block fell off.

There's lots more things that you can say are all part of this, are connected in some way with sentence (1), because they could well be used to generate (24)-(26) as responses to (1):

(24) 'No I'm afraid I can't.'
(25) 'I don't see a red block.'
(26) The (robot) hearer looks under the table.

So really there are all those different kinds of things related or relevant to (1). And in some sense I'm inviting you to offer some remarks on the question of which of these things you think are part of the linguistic theory or are within the linguistic part of the system, however that system's structured in terms of actual software modules and things like that, and which things are not. In fact we can even put ticks and crosses if we want to go through them. Perhaps people would like to comment on the general point or we could consider the examples in detail.

Graeme RITCHIE: I think there's a general point about this kind of discussion which is that you've got to keep a distinction between asking which kinds of information the linguistic processing must be sensitive to or must be influenced by, and which kind of information linguists have to compile a description of. For example, notions like the current state of the world and the current state of the discourse, whether something has been mentioned before, and so on. There are a lot of things in that general area that you would expect linguistic rules to be sensitive to and to actually process. But it doesn't mean that you have to expect linguists to do a lot of description of the actual substance of that area of the universe. This is one of the fallacies of twenty years ago: the Katz & Fodor (1963) argument where they were talking about the division between world knowledge and linguistic semantics. They were saying there must be a boundary somewhere because you can't expect linguists to write down every fact about the world that is true. Winograd (1976:265) points out that this is just a fallacious argument because that's like saying the study of physics is an itemization of the state of every object in the universe. Whereas in fact physics is the study of the principles under which they interact, stating rules which for any given data about the world will tell you what's going to happen or whatever.

SPARCK JONES: I was trying to use the examples to indicate some **kinds** of things. Your remark about sensitivities is also about how the connection works the other way if there's some non-linguistic stuff going on.

RITCHIE: I wasn't knocking your examples, but saying this is a distinction we'll have to bear in mind. For some of the stuff towards the end of all this it's very pertinent.

SPARCK JONES: I was trying to get some feeling for more or less the obvious kinds of things that people talked about that you might want to take into account in a language processing system, and try to be a bit extensive about this and to have some rather borderline ones. You see I think the thing about (22) is perhaps to think about all this belief stuff. How does the language stuff connect with all that language there?

Bob MOORE: I was just thinking that in the design of an architecture of a language understanding system it may be in fact easier to say where these different bits of information go within such an architecture than it is to take that architecture and draw a line through it somewhere and say things on this side of the line are linguistic and things on that side of the line are non-linguistic. So in some sense I wonder if this question of what the limits of the linguistic theory are is to some extent an artefactual question.

Nick OSTLER: No, I think it's very important, because if you want to port your linguistic theory to a different domain or something you've got to be able to say how much you're going to put into that system to make it portable.

MOORE: That's a completely different distinction. You could do the same thing and say the portability is along multiple dimensions, and I don't think that picking out a particular one of them as being a linguistic dimension is all that important. You could port it to a different database system or a different domain or keep the same domain or the same database system and port it to a different natural language. There are just all kinds of dimensions of portability, and I think that speaks to the modularity of the system design. But returning to the question, given a modular design in a system decomposition, of which parts of the system are strictly speaking linguistic, I think the answer to that question might have to do more with the sociology of the field of linguistics.

Henry THOMPSON: There is a traditional answer which you either think is helpful or misleading which is that that part of the system which would be different if you were speaking German to it is linguistic.

MOORE: There are certainly many things that English and German have in common that wouldn't be changed.

OSTLER: You couldn't consider that as being linguistic. I mean all this stuff about the speaker being polite: that will be as relevant as input to how you formulate sentences in German as in English.

THOMPSON: But the way that you know that the speaker is being polite changes from German to English to Japanese certainly.

SPARCK JONES: The way you know that is a relevant fact to the linguistic side, and I think it's important, but I don't want to talk about parts of the system. I want to talk about what things in the system we want to look to linguists with their theories to give us some leverage for. I don't want to talk about putting things in boxes in a narrow-minded way.

THOMPSON: It's clearly within the domain to consider the notion of the encoding and the linguistic consequences (and I don't think this is a circularity) of politeness. It's clearly a matter for linguistic theory because it changes from language to language.

Mary McGee WOOD: There's a difference between language-specific and linguistic. There's a difference between the English and German form of the auxiliary verb, but there are good standard language-universal principles for how you do polite indirect questions, and there have been for several thousand years.

OSTLER: You've come on to a field where we have actual experience in the LOQUI project (Wachtel 1986). We are trying to produce a system which can be polite in both English and German and our linguist is working on that. He's got all sorts of things to say about the structure of speech acts and things which nobody else who knows about databases would have the first idea of how to address. Whereas those people **are** happy, for example, to start sketching out a schema for the knowledge used in project management and things like that where it seems that linguistic expertise isn't actually relevant. So I think your characterization of where linguistic knowledge leaves off is actually wrong for that case. Maybe we want to say there are discourse specialists who are separate from linguists.

SPARCK JONES: A more old-fashioned way of putting this thing is 'What's within pragmatics?' I didn't want to put it in that rather 'linguistics lecture' sort of style, but that's another way of putting it.

RITCHIE: Doesn't Henry [Thompson]'s criterion work one way round? It's not an 'if and only if'. Presumably if you have to change it when you change the natural language then it looks like it's linguistic.

OSTLER: You can compare it with moving from the metric system to the avoirdupois system, which might correlate with changing from one language to another.

Mitch MARCUS: One fast point on Henry's definition that what's linguistic is what changes when you change language: that has the wonderful consequence of taking all universal grammar and making it non-linguistic.

Since I started off sounding like a linguist perhaps I should continue. It seems that what falls into which of these boxes, and for that matter what the boxes are, is in fact a result. You can't tell pre-theoretically. One hopes to get some rule sets, and we have some notion of what they are - although it seems to me that the further you get back towards general cognition, the fuzzier things get. So it looks like there really are aspects of pragmatics that are sufficiently relevant, and get their own rule systems. When it comes to things like speech acts it isn't clear where you draw the line. It may well be that there are things that change from language to language but only incidentally. You could call these cultural differences. There are things that are funny in English and other things that are funny in German, and people who are bilingual have told me that some things are funny differently in German and English. So I think it's a question that is hard to tease out and is in some sense pre-theoretical. You take the best stab you can at it, but in that case one has to know what kind of rules are involved for doing what. I think it's very hard and I wouldn't have the confidence to divide it up so you can work on the pieces. But I'm afraid the pieces are really how we do it. And one reason why people have tended to stay where they have in this conference is because this is really terra firma for what we know now.

SPARCK JONES: We're all fairly happy with a lot of this stuff like (2) and (5) and those sort of things and, as you say, one may have rule sets for dealing with this speech act thing. And then the question comes, are the rules some rather informal or not very well thought out manifestation or some not very sussed out theory about speech acts or whatever it might be? Then there's a separate question: is that something that linguists think they ought to be doing something about, and similarly with all of this [the later examples]? But the thing I was really trying to do, and in some sense I think I've concealed it by putting some things [in the examples] in inverted commas, was in part I was trying to say that I think there's a very fine gradation. Is (19) something which has got something to do with the initial question (1), which actually after all has got some implications that if you're putting things somewhere you can move them? Or is it something about the world that we know independently? I was trying to have enough examples of enough different kinds that would try to make the point that it's not easy. I think we're much too crude about where we draw the boundary currently. We say this sort of stuff (2)-(3) is fine, we know where that goes. Maybe stuff about jogging the table (22) is down somewhere else and there's this huge big area in between and I don't have any guidance about how to deal with it. Maybe what you're saying is we should just try to formulate some rules about it and not worry for the moment about whether linguists can tell us anything about it.

MARCUS: No. We should turn to the linguists and club them in the head until they start working on our questions. The other thing is the business about politeness. It certainly ends up asking the question 'Is this linguistic information?' This was your point before. It goes both ways. Things come on both sides of the line. My suspicion is that the two kinds of felicity conditions for speech are much more general facts about interaction between intelligent beings. Certain kinds of facts that work themselves out linguistically work themselves out in other ways as well. You can take a lot of felicity conditions and see ways to make non-linguistic interactions violate them.

SPARCK JONES: It may be that the reason why we didn't talk about these things for much of the meeting is that we don't have any answers to them, it's all much too hard. The reason why I put stuff about believing and knowing and assuming in is that those are the kinds of things that people are getting interested in. Do you regard those kind of things as in some sense linguistic theories or are they to do with the world? Are they things that you think of as linguistic theories or non-linguistic theories?

MOORE: I don't think that matters. I have a crude idea of what the overall architecture of a language-using intelligent agent is and so I think I have crude answers about where to put some of these pieces of information, but I don't think it particularly matters whether you call the content of one of those boxes 'linguistic' or not. And the answer to whether we should expect linguists to help out in a particular area is that you have to go and look and see if the linguists know anything about it. In some cases it's pretty obvious that things that are linguistic on anybody's grounds haven't, for historical reasons, been looked at by the linguists and so they're not any help in that area anyway. I think most of the interesting work that's being done in discourse right now in a way that's compatible with formal approaches to natural language is being done by computational linguists rather than linguists full stop. There's certainly a lot of work on discourse in the traditional linguistics community, but I think it's not done in such a way that it's easy to link up with more formal approaches. The formal linguists haven't looked very much at this thing.

SPARCK JONES: Part of your reason for feeling happy is that you think of logical structures as being a kind of uniform means of connection of all these different things. That's the assumption that I said I think people were tacitly making.

MOORE: That certainly plays a large role in my feeling that I have a crude idea of what the overall architecture of a language-using agent is.

SPARCK JONES: I have the impression that most of the earlier speakers were making this assumption and I don't know whether that applies also to people who work on machine translation, who were reminding us this morning of how complicated things were. Do you think of logical form as the universal communication language in your translation system, as you might put it?

Rod JOHNSON: I think there's evidence that it's a very inappropriate medium for communicating between languages - I tried to say this this morning - though you may well appeal to logical form to do something for you with respect to a text representation for some language. But the communication medium between languages is more likely to be a text representation than something out of predicate calculus. Unless of course you've got a very wide interpretation of what logical form means. When most people say logical form they mean something model theoretic, something quantified, that kind of thing, and that kind of thing is generally acknowledged to be not very appropriate.

Jan LANDSBERGEN: In my presentation I have given my reasons for not using intensional logic in Rosetta, although it is a Montague-based system. I think that logic and model-theoretic semantics are very useful and provide a sound base, but they are not sufficient. On the other hand, if one ultimately wants to have a system with knowledge of the world and a certain deductive capacity, logic seems to be the only reliable way to incorporate this.

Doug ARNOLD: I think there are two problems with what I understand by logical form in the context of MT, and what has been said is vague between the two interpretations. One is that I think logical form in the way most people understand it gives you an explicit representation of something like quantifier scope, a few propositional connectives, maybe some tense operators, modality operators. But it is grossly impoverished when you consider what kinds of thing you have to preserve across translations. The second question is whether this thing, even if ideally enriched to an arbitrary degree, would be an appropriate thing for doing translation off. I think Rod [Johnson]'s view is that it wouldn't be even if it was completely enriched.

Steve PULMAN: If you actually take a random sample of COLING papers or something that looks as if it's using logical forms, there are two ways in which the term is used. There's the sense in which most of us have been using it, which is aspects of the meaning of a sentence which are motivated by grammatical properties and so on. There's a more general sense in which people who're actually hacking systems use it, which is that logic is just another way of representing anything so that you get things that are called logical forms. There actually are predicates in there which are to do with topic and focus and all sorts of other stuff. Presumably that's what Rod means, that even in that very extended sense it's just not a very computationally sensible representation for his particular task, though for lots of tasks it's extremely sensible, in fact the only one.

JOHNSON: It's an awful long way away from texts in its form, and whatever it is about the form of the text that you have to preserve, it's certainly true that there is something there that you have to keep. It's not at all clear that you can encapsulate this information about the form of the text into some logical form as you suggest and bring it back again. And even if you could, that would probably be an awful lot of work most of the time for nothing.

SPARCK JONES: Presumably that's the same point as Steve [Pulman]. You have to distinguish between the kinds of things that people put into logical forms currently and what logical forms on some interpretation might be capable of embodying.

PULMAN: Presumably in the limit you can put enough into it

so that if you can't represent it in logic you probably can't represent it.

JOHNSON: I guess that's true, and there's a bit of hand-waving and a few tricks here. What all the MT people are doing is relying on the fact that there are meaning equivalences in some very wide sense of 'meaning' that has to do with discourse structure and textual form and anything else, which are hidden in the structure of the text and we don't know what they are, we can't characterize them. But we can observe that when you translate between pairs of languages, things about the texts look the same. We can't abstract away enough to give names to what all these things are, but we can say if we manage texts in a particular way then these things are likely to come out. That's under the counter and it's cheating and it's almost admitting defeat, but if you can rely on that working most of the time it does mean you can concentrate your attention somewhere else on some other problems that you can characterize and to which you can find the solutions without going badly wrong in one particular area which you can't really handle, and which happens to fall out in a reasonable way.

THOMPSON: There was a way in which what Mitch [Marcus] said involved a claim about the scope of linguistic theory. A form of the scope of linguistic theory that was actually much more substantial than the one which you mention about the quick-sort because, if I understood Mitch correctly, he was also making a more detailed claim about a level of analysis at which recognizably traditionally linguistic concern was appropriate, which moved that level rather far down in some obvious hierarchy. There were a number of points at which Mitch said what would have been heretical statements even ten years ago about the point at which overtly syntactic regularities had something to say. But the largest elements that I understood Mitch to be constructing on a purely syntactic basis are rather small and I wondered if that actually constituted a claim of the sort that you are concerned with. I actually think it's a very interesting point and I think it's probably right. I think the extent to which the Radical Pragmatics people (Green & Morgan 1981) of five or ten years ago were right despite themselves has probably been under-appreciated. Mitch may not want to be interpreted in that way, but I choose to interpret him as saying the extent to which you can put things together on purely syntactic grounds is rather less than one used to think it.

SPARCK JONES: That's right in so far as linguistic theory is concerned with syntax. So we've got to look at the other parts.

MARCUS: Two comments, one of which is that the D-theory stuff I was talking about the other night is a theory of phrase structure, not of syntax. So one certainly needs to bring other things to bear if one wants to itemize things as syntactic before you know where you stop, like, say, theta roles and the like. It's nonetheless the case that even given that, I did claim (and I think I probably want to stand by the claim, although making sense of it isprobably hard, as is finding an appropriate example) that once you have to bring extra-linguistic knowledge to bear, the resulting structures are no longer in some sense purely linguistic. Now making sense of that becomes difficult, but if that's true then you can have linguistic knowledge brought to bear in a system which is not by that definition inherently linguistic.

A good example of this follows from the kind of analysis of discourse structure that Barbara Grosz and Candace Sidner (1986) are suggesting, where you essentially see what's being played out in the discourse as being the interaction of an intentional structure which is entirely cognitive and not linguistic, although a certain thing has lots of linguistic reflexes. All this has lots of linguistic reflexes, and a focus structure, where the focus structure is I think in many ways linguistic and in some ways not. Now it seems like there are things like Rachel Reichmann's (1985) 'clue' words which clearly serve some kind of use in signalling these kinds of things. They're also clearly syntactic realizations of focus. And the rules for determining this in, say, English are actually quite complicated: where you can put it and where you can't. One that is very interesting is trying to figure out what you say wa in Japanese is. This forms a large part of the literature in traditional Japanese linguistics. What this particle means and its interaction with the linguistics is in fact very funny, so one gets a sense there's linguistic knowledge that may not be used only within linguistic rule systems. My temptation is to say linguistics is the study primarily of linguistic rule systems and much less of linguistic facts.

SPARCK JONES: So if you say that having brought some extra-linguistics to bear, the resulting structures are not linguistic, that would imply for example (I speak extremely crudely) that in the compositional model you've got a sort of bag of stuff which you get from the lexicon or wherever it is to start with, and you're 'compositioning' it up. Now according, in some sense, to what kind of stuff you have in the lexicon, that might imply that your structure in this sense will not be purely linguistic because there might be all kinds of things that you'd imported and plugged in passing up the line.

MARCUS: If they were just dragged along, as it were, then that wouldn't be a problem. If an essential use was made of it, then in a certain kind of way we need to isolate it. So for example determining word sense, determining part of speech, clearly involves information about the context which is not linguistic. Once you have that, my suspicion is that you can proceed with purely linguistic information for quite a long way. So you want to delineate on both sides, in some sense, aspects of the processing of language where only linguistic rule systems are being brought to bear.

RITCHIE: Can I make a reaction to that, which I think is actually supplementary to Bob Moore's point earlier about whether it's wise to try to draw this line between linguistic and non-linguistic? It seems to me that if you do try and draw that line anywhere, you then have the problem of which rules act as a frontier across that line. What's the interface across it? And are the rules that do that interfacing linguistic or not? That seems to be one of the issues that Mitch is touching on in what he's just said. It seems to me you will always have this problem, if you feel that meta-theoretically you should draw the line, of how you're ever going to cross that line without having rules that are in some sense a hybrid. I think it's perhaps a misguided theoretical endeavour to draw the line for that reason.

WOOD: If you think in terms of cognitive psychology it makes a lot of sense to say that one has a knowledge structure and linguistic knowledge is handled that way and all kinds of other knowledge are handled that way as well. And again if I can drag in Hudson's (1984) Word Grammar, he bases that also on this idea that linguistic knowledge follows exactly the same pattern as non-linguistic knowledge and the demarcation is a non-question. There just isn't a sharp line and we shouldn't be wasting time arguing about where it is or isn't.

PULMAN: But the claim that there isn't a sharp line doesn't answer the question why it is that under certain kinds of aphasia linguistic knowledge gets zapped and the other bits of knowledge don't. If it's all one big uniform knowledge structure why does that happen?

RITCHIE: There's also the point that there's a difference between the position that I was taking, which is that it's misleading to try to draw one boundary down the middle and say even one hundred percent what's actually linguistic and non-linguistic, and the other position, which I would sympathize with, which is that drawing boundaries between different kinds of processing of different kinds of information is useful. It's the labelling of them into this great divide that I was trying to criticize, and I think if you could detect different forms of processing, and many traditional notions like syntax and semantics seem to be of this sort, then that is useful. That's substance to your theory of what's going on. But it's what Karen described as putting into boxes and labelling them, which she's ruled off the agenda.

SPARCK JONES: No, I wish to disclaim here: the title for this session was imposed on me. I had nothing to do with it. I'm carefully trying not to take a position on this. I'm extremely sympathetic to the view that having rule sets of various sorts, or having things in different boxes or these kinds of things is actually a right way of thinking about it. But I think that if one is going to put up a title like 'Linguistic Theory and Beyond', there is some presupposition there that there is something which is the proper concern of linguistic theory and something which is not.

MARCUS: I want to argue against the point briefly. Despite the fact that the rule systems we're looking at, even within linguistics, look like they are coherent, people in one position would say that there is no line between the linguistic and everything else. But then one would say there's no line between aspects of linguistic theory. I think that's just wrong. It looks to be the case that there is a rule system which one wants to call phonology. We know a bunch about particular rule systems and there is a rule system which seems to constitute, say, phrase structure. It's always been the case that there seem to be certain kinds of things that do translation between rules, which are funny. So morphology, for example, is a rule system of its own in certain kinds of ways. It's actually less neat than others, but then there's this very funny class of things which are considered morphophonemic, that fall between the phonetics and the morphology. And those rules are just evidently, by anybody's standard, barbaric and I think that that's what one could expect. You expect a rule system to work on a single representation, and I think that's what it means to be a rule system, roughly. But a rule system can map from one representation to another, and in fact the ones that we know of are somewhat pokey. Well, it may be a lack of our understanding, but it may be that that's in fact an aspect of that particular kind of stuff.

MOORE: The point was that out there in the world there is a definite distinction in the phenomena we're studying, between the phonological rules and the morphological rules and the phrase structure rules. That's what's real. What's artefactual is collecting some group of these sets of rules together and arbitrarily saying that this set of stuff is linguistics and things outside of this aren't linguistics, unless you can actually find some generalizations that fall across all those sets of rules and don't apply elsewhere.

THOMPSON: We did have a candidate. If you put a bullet through the appropriate part of your head you lose all that.

MOORE: You lose them individually. You don't lose them collectively. From time to time imperialistic linguists have made claims about there being generalizations that fall across more than one set of rules, but as far as I know none of those held up to rigorous study.

SPARCK JONES: In some sense this kind of view was partly made when Henry [Thompson] was doing his presentation, commenting on the Alvey tools projects. It's a reflection not of the views on this particular issue but in part on our general state of knowledge, that one can have a morphological tool and a parsing tool and a grammar tool. But there was no serious suggestion that we should try to have a semantic tool because there wasn't enough clarity about what that should be like. So in some sense for anybody who's going to try and build a system using the tools when they are available, even if you adopt a very strong posture about the way that the syntactic parsing drives everything else in some really rather aggressive way, what it's driving has still got to be supplied by somewhere else.

Jackie KNIGHT: Can I change the focus a little bit? A division that's been talked about a lot has been the division between theoretical linguistics and implementation, whereas there's a more 'sordid' division between implementations in research establishments and implementations which people are going to go out and use and sell. Can the fact that language processing hasn't been taken up particularly by industry be attributed to that fact that the gap is not in the linguistics - it's within the capability of current linguistics to provide systems for many applications (limited vocabulary, controlled syntax) - but that the gap is in the other areas, knowledge representation, discourse, that kind of thing?

OSTLER: Are we going to get any theories that go beyond semantic structure, or is it going to be just each person who has their own application is going to make do with it? Nobody's talked about general artificial intelligence techniques, or whether there is a methodology or some theory there which is going to be brought in which actually mediates between where intensional logic takes off or leaves off and where the constraints of running nuclear power stations begin. Because we have found that you do get what seem to be isolatable areas in this. Like if you're running an expert system, there seems to be a general body of unformulated doctrines about, and when you try to satisfy constraints you may not be able to satisfy primary constraints immediately, so you look for some secondary constraints which hold, and look for links from there. There's a certain amount of methodology which seems to be distinct from semantics. It's got to do with strategies for doing inference, say. And it's also distinct from any particular subject matter, so if we're doing that in respect of aircraft design, it's got nothing particularly to do with designing aircraft, but it's got much more to do with trying to find a design which fits certain specifications. So the question is really, are we going to get theories of these other boxes which you distinguished? Or, let's say, is linguistics, and the sort of boxes which it's managed to set in order, just the most accessible part of the discipline,

so that when we've done a bit better we can get on to more
hairy areas of knowledge representation? Or is it going to
be the case that that's as far as we're ever going to get,
and from then on we're always going to be on our own, and
experts are just going to have devise their own systems to
do these things?

MOORE: No. I think there will be theories of other areas
and an overall architecture. However, I think that for a
long time to come applications people are going to be quite
impatient with those theories, because they're striving for
generality. When you're doing a particular application, the
closer you get to the interface of the application itself,
the more apparent it is in a particular case how to do it
directly without worrying about having a general theory.
From a purely practical aspect, it's going to be so much
easier just to put together a special-purpose interface for
that particular application than to worry about how to put
the interface knowledge within some grand general framework.
I think that for quite a long time to come applications
people are not going to be very interested in the results of
theorizing about the general framework.

THOMPSON: There's no a priori reason to suppose there isn't
going to be a general purpose theory, but I perhaps am
slightly more pessimistic than Bob [Moore]. I think that the
amount of progress to date is very small, and the
expectation is that the horizon is very far away. I think
that a useful parallel is something that both Marr (1977)
and Brian Smith (1982) have commented on: we do better
approximately in proportion to how close we are to the
periphery of the human processing system. I think vision is
an obvious example: we have by now jolly good computational
theories of what goes on in the optic nerve and in the optic
cortex, but you try to get either metaphorically or
literally any further back and the theories get much less
clear. I think the same thing is true to a certain extent
in the language processing area. We're doing much better on
things that are close to the periphery than we are on things
that are further back. In some sense our phonology is a lot
closer, because the extent to which current phonological
theories are wrong is probably less than the extent to which
current syntactic theories are wrong, and current semantic
theories don't really even exist.

SPARCK JONES: They're not evaluable.

OSTLER: The analogy with vision seems to break down, because you seem to be actually moving towards a more introspectable area when you're getting higher and higher up from phonology to syntax and semantics, until you can actually ask people for a comment on how they do it, much more than you can in the case of processing their visual field and so on.

SPARCK JONES: I think this is a fallacy.

RITCHIE: I think there's another dominant issue, though I'm not sure whether it's proper to raise it here, about when you'll get this theory.   It is that these issues are really to do with the sociology and sub-cultures of the research community, and in terms of the language area there are distinct communities with sub-communities with their own methodologies which make progress in their own terms and in a limited area.   For example the generative grammar community has set up a whole set of guidelines, and it works in and makes progress within those guidelines.   Other communities you can think of are the philosophers' tradition of formal logic, and there's a lot there within its own terms.   There's possibly, one can mention, a Lisp hacking tradition in AI which also in its own terms makes some kind of progress. But these are all piecemeal, and it's not clear that there's any integrated theory of language, unless that one single community is single-mindedly working within a single methodology, which seems to be what you're asking. You're wanting something a bit less piecemeal.

OSTLER: I'm surprised you didn't mention the planning community, for example, as being a comparable sub-discipline.   The sort of considerations I was talking about don't seem to concern a particular subject matter.   They seem to concern a human activity, for example planning, which is being applied for a range of different things, even planning sentences of course.   And I've been told we'll have to wait a long time before things begin to settle down, so perhaps we'll just have to hack it.

SPARCK JONES: I think Graeme [Ritchie]'s quite right, because in fact on the first day and also yesterday some of the discussion about formalisms in parts essentially reflected the evaluative criteria of a particular community. It's not absolutely clear that their criteria are the right ones.   We're all so cowed, when doing anything in a formalism or in a formal way, and many people think that the formalists' criteria in some sense ought to be applicable to our ways of thinking. But I think this is actually false. Certainly they have criteria and the question is are they the right criteria for people who have other concerns? Of course there are global criteria we all have: don't just hack it in a totally ad hoc way because you'll get into a mess. But that's not very interesting. I don't know how far somebody like Stu [Shieber] for instance would feel that the kinds of interests or criteria that you apply are ones that are relevant or are really important for everybody who's working in computational linguistics.

It seems to me that in some way what we've emerged with is that we shouldn't fuss too much about the boundaries between the linguistic and the non-linguistic or about what linguistic theory can tell us. I think what's valuable is thinking more about the point that Mitch [Marcus] made, that we should think about what things we know we need to have rule sets for. And of course then we also have the issue of how those different things communicate with one another. I think that is where some of the issue about the means of communication is important.

Remembering that when I began I was thinking about having to link three different needs, I think we've said something about the session topic. I don't know how far that represents any kind of drawing together of the threads of the workshop. I don't quite know what message we take back to what you might describe as the people who run the Alvey Programme as to whether we're happy with the way things are going, and whether what we're doing will enable people out there to build better systems. I think there are some messages there. In fact I think the conclusion I've just produced is in a way relevant to that, because it embodies a kind of strategy about how we go about trying to build natural language processing systems, which is that we try to carve things off.

Speaking as the Theme manager, I think it's very valuable to have a workshop like this. I would particularly like to say how glad we've been in the UK to have our visitors from outside the UK. In that connection I would very much like to thank, first of all, ICL, because they have been responsible for the import of our guests from outside the UK. That was ICL and not the Alvey Directorate's part. I think also it's very much incumbent on all of us to thank the people at UMIST, Pete [Whitelock] and Paul [Bennett] in particular, first of all for having the idea of the workshop. I've certainly found it extremely interesting and I've enjoyed the presentations very much, so I have to thank them both for having the idea, and in fact also for doing all the arrangements. I find it extremely nice that the only thing that went wrong as far as I can see anywhere was one failure of the transparency projector bulb. That seems to me to be pretty good and I think we ought to thank them very much.

References

Gazdar, G., Klein, E., Pullum, G. & Sag, I. 1985. **Generalized Phrase Structure Grammar**. Oxford: Basil Blackwell.

Green, G. & Morgan, J. 1981. Pragmatics, Grammar and Discourse. In Cole, P., ed., **Radical Pragmatics**. New York: Academic Press, 167-181.

Grosz, B.J. & Sidner, C.L. 1986. Attention, Intentions and the Structure of Discourse. **Computational Linguistics** 12, 175-204.

Hudson, R.A. 1984. **Word Grammar**. Oxford: Basil Blackwell.

Katz, J. & Fodor, J. 1963. The Structure of a Semantic Theory. **Language** 39, 170-210

Marr, D. 1977. Artificial Intelligence - A Personal View. **Artificial Intelligence** 9, 37-48.

Montague, R. 1973. The Proper Treatment of Quantification in Ordinary English. In Hintikka, J., Moravcsik, J. & Suppes, P., eds. **Approaches to Natural Language**. Dordrecht: D. Reidel, 221-242. Reprinted in Thomason, ed., 247-270.

Reichmann, R. 1985. **Getting Computers to Talk Like You and Me**. Cambridge, Mass.: MIT Press.

Smith, B. C. 1982. The Seven Percent Solution. Ms.

Thomason, R.H., ed. 1974. **Formal Philosophy: Selected Papers of Richard Montague.** New Haven: Yale University Press.

Wachtel, T. 1986. Pragmatic Sensitivity in NL Interfaces, and the Structure of Conversation. **COLING 86: 11th International Conference on Computational Linguistics** (Bonn, West Germany), Proceedings, 35-45.

Winograd, T. 1976. Towards a Procedural Understanding of Semantics. **Revue Internationale de Philosophie** 3-4 (117-118), 260-303.

Woods, W.A. 1973. Progress in Natural Language Understanding: An Application to Lunar Geology. In **AFIPS Conference Proceedings,** Montvale, NJ: AFIPS Press, 441-450.

References

Ades, A.E. & Steedman, M.J. 1982. On the Order of Words. **Linguistics and Philosophy** 4, 517-558.

Ahlswede, T.E. 1985. A Tool Kit for Lexicon Building. **23rd Annual Meeting of the Association for Computational Linguistics** (Chicago), Proceedings, 268-276.

Aronoff, M. 1980. Contextuals. In Hoekstra, T., van der Hulst, H & Moortgat, M., eds., **Lexical Grammar**. Dordrecht: Foris, 49-72.

Atwell, E.S., Leech, G., & Garside, R. 1984. Analysis of the LOB Corpus: Progress and Prospects. In Aarts, J. & Meijs, W., eds. **Corpus Linguistics**. Amsterdam:Rodopi, 40-52.

Bach, E. 1983. On the Relationship between Word-grammar and Phrase-grammar. **Natural Language and Linguistic Theory** 1, 65-89.

Backus, J. 1977. Can Programming be Liberated from the von Neumann Style? **Communications of the ACM** 21, 613-641.

Barwise, J. & Perry, J. 1983. **Situations and Attitudes**. Cambridge, Mass.: MIT Press.

Bates, M. 1976. Syntax in Automatic Speech Understanding. **American Journal of Computational Linguistics** microfiche 45.

Berwick, R.C. 1985. **The Acquisition of Syntactic Knowledge**. Cambridge, Mass.: MIT Press.

Berwick, R.C. & Weinberg, A.S. 1984. **The Grammatical Basis of Linguistic Performance: Language Use and Acquisition.** Cambridge, Mass.: MIT Press.

Boguraev, B.K. 1980. **Automatic Resolution of Linguistic Ambiguities.** PhD dissertation, University of Cambridge. Technical Report no. 11, Cambridge University Computer Laboratory.

Brachman, R. 1985. 'I lied about the trees', (or Defaults and Definitions in Knowledge Representation). **AI Magazine,** 6.3.

Bresnan, J., ed. 1982. **The Mental Representation of Grammatical Relations.** Cambridge, Mass.: MIT Press.

Bresnan, J. 1982a. The Passive in Lexical Theory. In Bresnan, ed., 3-86.

Bresnan, J. 1982b. Control and Complementation. In Bresnan, ed., 282-390.

Bresnan, J. 1984. Bound Anaphora on Functional Structures. **Proceedings of the Tenth Annual Meeting of the Berkeley Linguistics Society,** University of California, Berkeley.

Bresnan, J. & Kaplan, R.M. 1982. Introduction: Grammars as Mental Representations of Language. In Bresnan, ed., xvii-lii.

Calzolari, N. 1983. Machine-readable Dictionaries: Report of the Workshop held at SRI International. **ALLC Bulletin** 12, 51-53.

Carbonell, J., Cullingford, R.E. & Gershman, A.V. 1978. Knowledge-based Machine Translation. Research report 146. Yale University Department of Computer Science.

Cardelli, L. & Wegner, P. 1985. Understanding Types, Data Abstraction and Polymorphism. Ms.

Carroll, J.A. 1983. An Island Parsing Interpreter for the Full Augmented Transition Network Formalism. **First Conference of the European Chapter of the ACL,** Proceedings, 101-105.

Chandioux, J. 1976. METEO: un système operationnel pour la traduction automatique des bulletins meteorologiques destines au grand public. **Meta** 21, 127-133.

Chomsky, N. 1957. **Syntactic Structures**. The Hague: Mouton.

Chomsky, N. 1963. Formal Properties of Grammars. In Luce, R.D., Bush, R.R. & Galanter, E., eds., **Handbook of Mathematical Psychology** Vol. II. New York: Wiley, 323-418.

Chomsky, N. 1965. **Aspects of the Theory of Syntax**. Cambridge, Mass.: MIT Press.

Chomsky, N. 1980. **Rules and Representations**. Oxford: Basil Blackwell.

Chomsky, N. 1982. **Lectures on Government and Binding**. Dordrecht: Foris.

Chomsky, N. & Halle, M. 1968. **The Sound Pattern of English**. New York: Harper and Row.

Church, K. 1985. Stress Assignment in Letter-to-sound Rules for Speech Synthesis. **23rd Annual Meeting of the Association for Computational Linguistics** (Chicago), Proceedings, 246-253.

Cooper, R. 1975. **Montague's Semantic Theory and Transformational Syntax**. PhD dissertation, University of Massachusetts at Amherst.

Cooper, R. 1983. **Quantification and Syntactic Theory**. Dordrecht: D. Reidel.

Dijkstra, E.W. 1972. The Humble Programmer. **Communications of the ACM** 15, 859-866.

Dowty, D.R., Wall, R.E., & Peters, S. 1981. **Introduction to Montague Semantics**. Dordrecht: Reidel.

Earley, J. 1970. An Efficient Context-free Parsing Algorithm. **Communications of the ACM** 13, 94-102.

Etherington, D.W. & Reiter, R. 1983. On Inheritance Hierarchies with Exceptions. **3rd National Conference on Artificial Intelligence (AAAI)** (Washington DC), Proceedings. W. Kaufmann, 104-108.

Flickinger, D., Pollard, C.J. & Wasow, T. 1985. Structure Sharing in Lexical Representation. **23rd Annual Meeting of the Association for Computational Linguistics** (Chicago), Proceedings, 262-267.

Friedman, J. & Warren, D.S. 1978. A Parsing Method for Montague Grammars. **Linguistics and Philosophy** 2, 347-372.

Gazdar, G. 1979. **Pragmatics: Implicature, Presupposition and Logical Form.** New York: Academic Press.

Gazdar, G. 1982. Phrase Structure Grammar. In Jacobson, P. & Pullum, G.K., eds., **The Nature of Syntactic Representation.** Dordrecht: D. Reidel, 131-186.

Gazdar, G., Klein, E., Pullum, G. & Sag, I. 1985. **Generalized Phrase Structure Grammar.** Oxford: Basil Blackwell.

Godden, K. 1981. **Montague Grammar and Machine Translation between Thai and English.** PhD dissertation, University of Kansas.

Goodall, G. 1983. A Three-dimensional Analysis of Coordination. **Papers from the 19th Regional Meeting of the Chicago Linguistic Society,** 146-154.

Green, G. & Morgan, J. 1981. Pragmatics, Grammar and Discourse. In Cole, P., ed., **Radical Pragmatics.** New York: Academic Press, 167-181.

Grice, H.P. 1975. Logic and Conversation. In Cole, P. & Morgan, J., eds., **Syntax and Semantics 3: Speech Acts.** New York: Academic, 41-58.

Grosz, B.J. & Sidner, C.L. 1986. Attention, Intentions and the Structure of Discourse. **Computational Linguistics** 12, 175-204.

Haddock, N. 1985. Noun Phrase Reference and the Resolution of Syntactic Ambiguity. Linguistics Association of Great Britain (Liverpool), September 1985.

Halvorsen, P-K. 1983. Semantics for Lexical-Functional Grammar. **Linguistic Inquiry** 14, 567-615.

Halvorsen, P-K. & Withgott, M. 1984. Morphological Constraints on Scandinavian Tone Accent. Technical Report CSLI-84-11, Centre for the Study of Language and Information, Stanford CA.

Hindle, D. 1983. Deterministic Parsing of Syntactic Non-fluencies. **21st Annual Meeting of the Association for Computational Linguistics** (Cambridge, Mass.), Proceedings, 123-28.

Hudson, R.A. 1984. **Word Grammar.** Oxford: Basil Blackwell.

Jackendoff, R. 1977. **X Syntax: A Study of Phrase Structure.** Cambridge, Mass.: MIT Press.

Janssen, T.M.V. 1986. **Foundations and Applications of Montague Grammar, Part I.** CWI Tract 19. Amsterdam: Centre for Mathematics and Computer Science.

Kamp, J.A.W. 1981. A Theory of Truth and Semantic Representation. In Groenedijk, J.A.G., Janssen, T.M.V. & Stokhof, M., eds., **Formal Methods in the Study of Language.** Amsterdam: Mathematical Centre Tracts, 277-322.

Kaplan, R. M. 1972. Augmented Transition Networks as Psychological Models of Sentence Comprehension. **Artificial Intelligence** 3, 77-100.

Kaplan, R.M. & Bresnan, J. 1982. Lexical-Functional Grammar: A Formal System for Grammatical Representation. In Bresnan, ed., 173-281.

Katz, J. & Fodor, J. 1963. The Structure of a Semantic Theory. **Language** 39, 170-210

Kay, M. 1979. Functional Grammar. In Chiarrello, C. et al., eds. **Fifth Annual Meeting of the Berkeley Linguistics Society,** Proceedings, 142-158. Berkeley: Berkeley Linguistics Society.

Kay, M. 1983. Unification Grammar. Technical Report, Xerox Palo Alto Research Center, Palo Alto CA.

Klingbiel, P.H. 1973. A Technique for Machine-aided Indexing. **Information Storage and Retrieval** 9, 477-494.

Kripke, S.A. 1977. Speaker's Reference and Semantic Reference. **Midwest Studies in Philosophy** 2, 28-41.

Labov, W. 1978. **Sociolinguistic Patterns**. Oxford: Basil Blackwell.

Landsbergen, S.P.J. 1976. Syntax and Formal Semantics of English in PHLIQA1. In Steels, L., ed., **Advances in Natural Language Processing**. Antwerp: University of Antwerp.

Landsbergen, S.P.J. 1981. Adaptation of Montague Grammar to the Requirements of Parsing. In Groenendijk, J.A.G., Janssen, T.M.V. & Stokhof, M.B.J. **Formal Methods in the Study of Language, Part 2**. MC Tract 136, Mathematical Centre, Amsterdam, 399-420.

Landsbergen, S.P.J. 1985. Isomorphic Grammars and their Use in the Rosetta Translation System. In King, M., ed., **Machine Translation Today**. Edinburgh: Edinburgh University Press.

Lawrence, S.G.C., & Kaye, G. 1986. Production of a Computer Based Dictionary of Pronounciation. IBM UKSC Report 148.

Lytinen, S.L. & Schank, R.C. 1982. Representation and Translation. Research Report 234. Yale University Department of Computer Science.

Marantz, A.P. 1984. **On the Nature of Grammatical Relations**. Cambridge, Mass.: MIT Press.

Marcus, M. 1980. **A Theory of Syntactic Recognition for Natural Language**. Cambridge, Mass.: MIT Press.

Marcus, M., Hindle, D. and Fleck, M. 1983. D-theory: Talking about Talking about Trees. **21st Annual Meeting of the Association for Computational Linguistics** (Cambridge, Mass.), Proceedings. 129-136.

Marr, D. 1977. Artificial Intelligence - A Personal View. **Artificial Intelligence** 9, 37-48.

McDermott, D.V. & Doyle, J. 1980. Non-monotonic Logics. **Artificial Intelligence** 13, 401-72.

Mellish, C.J. 1981. **Coping with Uncertainty: Noun Phrase Interpretation and Early Semantic Analysis.** PhD dissertation, University of Edinburgh.

Mercer, R.E. & Reiter, R. 1982. The Representation of Presuppositions using Defaults. **4th National Conference of the Canadian Society for Computational Studies in Intelligence** (Saskatoon), Proceedings, 103-107.

Michiels, A. 1982. **Exploiting a Large Dictionary Data Base.** PhD dissertation, Universite de Liège.

Montague, R. 1970a. Universal Grammar. **Theoria** 36, 373-398. Reprinted in Thomason, ed., 222-246.

Montague, R. 1970b. English as a Formal Language. In Visentini, B. et al, eds., **Linguaggi nella società e nella technica.** Milan: Edizioni di Comunità, 189-224. Reprinted in Thomason, ed., 108-221.

Montague, R. 1973. The Proper Treatment of Quantification in Ordinary English. In Hintikka, J., Moravcsik, J. & Suppes, P., eds. **Approaches to Natural Language.** Dordrecht: D. Reidel, 221-242. Reprinted in Thomason, ed., 247-270.

Moore, R.C. 1985. Semantical Considerations on Non-monotonic Logic. **Artificial Intelligence** 25.1, 75-94.

Nishida, T. & Doshita, S. 1982. An English-Japanese Machine Translation System based on Formal Semantics of Natural Language. In J. Horecky, ed., **COLING 82: Proceedings of the Ninth International Conference on Computational Linguistics.** Amsterdam: North-Holland, 277-282.

Partee, B.H. 1976. Some Transformational Extensions of Montague Grammar. In Partee, B.H., ed., **Montague Grammar.** New York: Academic Press, 51-76.

Partee, B.H. 1982. Compositionality. In Landman, F.& Veltman, F., eds., **Varieties of Formal Semantics** (Proceedings of the 4th Amsterdam Colloquium). Dordrecht: Foris, 281-312.

Pereira, F.C.N. & Warren, D.H.D. 1983. Parsing as Deduction. **21st Annual Meeting of the Association for Computational Linguistics** (Cambridge, Mass.), Proceedings, 137-144.

Pollard, C.J. 1984. **Generalized Phrase Structure Grammars, Head Grammars, and Natural Languages.** PhD dissertation, Stanford University.

Reichmann, R. 1985. **Getting Computers to Talk Like You and Me.** Cambridge, Mass.: MIT Press.

Reiter, R. 1978. On Reasoning by Default. **Theoretical Issues in Natural Language Processing (TINLAP)**, 210-218.

Roach, K. 1985. The Mathematics of LFG. Ms., Xerox Palo Alto Research Center, Palo Alto CA.

Russell, B. 1905. On Denoting. **Mind** 14, 479-493.

Russell, G.J., Pulman, S.G., Ritchie, G.D. & Black, A.W. 1986. A Dictionary and Morphological Analyzer for English. **COLING 86: 11th International Conference on Computational Linguistics** (Bonn, West Germany), Proceedings, 277-279.

Sampson, G. 1979. The Indivisibility of Words. **Journal of Linguistics** 15, 39-47.

Scott, D. 1982. Domains for Denotational Semantics. **ICALP 82**, Heidelberg: Springer-Verlag.

Shieber, S.M. 1984. The Design of a Computer Language for Linguistic Information. **COLING 84: 10th International Conference on Computational Linguistics / 22nd Annual Meeting of the Association for Computational Linguistics** (Stanford, CA), Proceedings, 362-366.

Shieber, S.M. 1986. A Simple Reconstruction of GPSG. **COLING 86: 11th International Conference on Computational Linguistics** (Bonn, West Germany), Proceedings, 362-366.

Shieber, S.M., Uszkoreit, H., Pereira, F.C.N, Robinson, J.J. & Tyson, M. 1983. The Formalism and Implementation of PATR-II. In **Research on Interactive Acquisition and Use of Knowledge** (SRI Project 1894 Final Report), Menlo Park CA: SRI International, 39-79.

Simon, H. 1981. **The Sciences of the Artificial.** Cambridge, Mass.: MIT Press.

Simpson, J. 1983. **Aspects of Warlpiri Morphology and Syntax.** PhD dissertation, Massachusetts Institute of Technology.

Slocum, J. 1984. Machine Translation: Its History, Current Status, and Future Prospects. **COLING 84: 10th International Conference on Computational Linguistics / 22nd Annual Meeting of the Association for Computational Linguistics** (Stanford, CA), Proceedings, 546-561.

de Smedt, K. 1984. Using Object-Oriented Knowledge-Representation Techniques in Morphology and Syntax Programming. In O'Shea, T., ed., **ECAI-84: Proceedings of the Sixth European Conference on Artificial Intelligence** (Pisa). Amsterdam: Elsevier, 181-184.

Smith, B.C. 1982. The Seven Percent Solution. Ms.

Soames, S. 1979. A Projection Problem for Speaker Presupposition. **Linguistic Inquiry** 10, 623-666.

Steedman, M.J. 1983. A Categorial Syntax for Subject and Tensed Verb in English and some Related Languages. Ms., University of Warwick.

Steedman, M.J. 1985. Dependency and Coordination in the Grammar of Dutch and English. **Language** 61, 523-568.

Steedman, M.J. 1987. Combinatory Grammars and Parasitic Gaps. In Haddock, N., Klein, E., & Morrill, G., eds. **Edinburgh Working Papers in Cognitive Science, Volume 1: Categorial Grammar, Unification Grammar and Parsing.** Centre for Cognitive Science, University of Edinburgh.

Thomason, R.H., ed. 1974. **Formal Philosophy: Selected Papers of Richard Montague.** New Haven: Yale University Press.

Touretsky, D.F. 1984. **The Mathematics of Inheritance Systems.** PhD dissertation, Computer Science, Carnegie-Mellon University. Published by Morgan Kaufman, Los Altos, 1986.

Wachtel, T. 1986. Pragmatic Sensitivity in NL Interfaces, and the Structure of Conversation. COLING **86: 11th International Conference on Computational Linguistics** (Bonn, West Germany), Proceedings, 35-45.

Watt, W.C. 1978. Good Intensions. **Journal of Linguistics** 14, 83-88.

Whitelock, P.J., Wood, M.McG., Chandler, B.J., Holden, N. & Horsfall, H.J. 1986. Strategies for Interactive Machine Translation: The Experience and Implications of the UMIST Japanese Project. **11th International Conference on Computational Linguistics** (Bonn, West Germany), Proceedings, 329-334.

Wilks, Y. 1973. An Artificial Intelligence Approach to Machine Translation. In Schank, R.C. & Colby, K.M., eds., **Computer Models of Thought and Language.** San Francisco: W.H. Freeman, 114-151.

Winograd, T. 1972. **Understanding Natural Language.** Edinburgh: Edinburgh University Press.

Winograd, T. 1976. Towards a Procedural Understanding of Semantics. **Revue Internationale de Philosophie** 3-4 (117-118), 260-303.

Wood, M.McG. 1985. Language Without the Lexicon: A Computational Model. CCL/UMIST Report 85/2.

Woods, W.A. 1970. Transition Network Grammars for Natural Language Analysis. **Communications of the ACM** 13, 591-606.

Woods, W.A. 1973. Progress in Natural Language Understanding: An Application to Lunar Geology. **AFIPS Conference Proceedings,** Montvale NJ: AFIPS Press, 441-450.

Woods, W.A. 1980. Cascaded ATN Grammars. **American Journal of Computational Linguistics** 8, 1-12.

Woods, W.A., Kaplan, R.M., & Nash-Webber, B. 1972. The Lunar Sciences Natural Language Information System: Final Report. Cambridge: Bolt Beranek and Newman, Inc. Report No. 2378.

Younger, D.H. 1967. Recognition and Parsing of Context-free Languages in Time n^3. **Information and Control** 10, 189-208.

Index